Exploring the Thames Rivers and Streams

50 favourite riverside walks

RICHARD MAYON-WHITE
AND WENDY YORKE

Exploring the Thames Rivers and Streams

50 favourite riverside walks

RICHARD MAYON-WHITE
AND WENDY YORKE

Conway
LONDON · OXFORD · NEW YORK · NEW DELHI · SYDNEY

CONWAY
Bloomsbury Publishing Plc
50 Bedford Square, London, WC1B 3DP, UK
Bloomsbury Publishing Ireland Limited,
29 Earlsfort Terrace, Dublin 2, Ireland

BLOOMSBURY, CONWAY and the Conway logo are trademarks of Bloomsbury Publishing Plc

First published in Great Britain 2025

Copyright © Richard-Mayon White and Wendy Yorke

Richard-Mayon White and Wendy Yorke have asserted their right under the Copyright, Designs and Patents Act, 1988, to be identified as Authors of this work

This book is a guide for when you spend time outdoors. Undertaking any activity outdoors carries with it some risks that cannot be entirely eliminated. For example, you might get lost on a route or caught in bad weather. Before you spend time outdoors, we therefore advise that you always take the necessary precautions, such as checking weather forecasts and ensuring that you have all the equipment you need. Any walking routes that are described in this book should not be relied upon as a sole means of navigation, so we recommend that you refer to an Ordnance Survey map or authoritative equivalent.

This book may also reference businesses and venues. Whilst every effort is made by the author and the publisher to ensure the accuracy of the business and venue information contained in our books before they go to print, changes to such information can occur during the production and lifetime of a publication. Therefore, we also advise that you check with businesses or venues for the latest information before setting out.

All internet addresses given in this book were correct at the time of going to press. Bloomsbury Publishing Plc does not have any control over, or responsibility for, any third-party websites referred to or in this book. The author and the publisher regret any inconvenience caused if some facts have changed or sites have ceased to exist, but can accept no responsibility for any such changes.

All rights reserved. No part of this publication may be: i) reproduced or transmitted in any form, electronic or mechanical, including photocopying, recording or by means of any information storage or retrieval system without prior permission in writing from the publishers; or ii) used or reproduced in any way for the training, development or operation of artificial intelligence (AI) technologies, including generative AI technologies. The rights holders expressly reserve this publication from the text and data mining exception as per Article 4(3) of the Digital Single Market Directive (EU) 2019/790

Bloomsbury Publishing Plc does not have any control over, or responsibility for, any third-party websites referred to or in this book. All internet addresses given in this book were correct at the time of going to press. The author and publisher regret any inconvenience caused if addresses have changed or sites have ceased to exist, but can accept no responsibility for any such changes

A catalogue record for this book is available from the British Library

ISBN: PB: 978-1-8448-6671-7; ePub: 978-1-8448-6669-4; ePDF: 978-1-8448-6670-0

2 4 6 8 10 9 7 5 3 1

Designed by Nicola Liddiard at Big Orange Door
Maps by John Plumer, JP Map Graphics Ltd
Printed and bound in India by Replika Press Pvt Ltd
The photograph on page 232 is credited to Timothy Budd / Alamy

To find out more about our authors and books visit *www.bloomsbury.com* and sign up for our newsletters
For product safety related questions contact *productsafety@bloomsbury.com*

Contents

INTRODUCTION **13**

PART 1 The rivers entering the Thames in Gloucestershire and Wiltshire **16**

CHAPTER 1 SWILL BROOK **18**
Walk 1 Lower Mill Farm and Swillbrook Nature Reserve; 4.5 miles (7.2km) **21**

CHAPTER 2 RIVER CHURN **24**
Walk 2 Around the Seven Springs; 5.8 miles (9.3km) **25**
Walk 3 Cirencester to Baunton; 5 miles (8km) **28**

CHAPTER 3 RIVER KEY **34**

CHAPTER 4 AMPNEY BROOK **37**
Walk 4 Cricklade and Down Ampney; 5.5 miles (8.9km) **40**

CHAPTER 5 RIVER RAY **42**
Walk 5 Shaw Forest to Purton Wood and back via Mouldon Park; 5 miles (8km) **46**

CHAPTER 6 RIVER COLE **48**
Walk 6 Coate Water to Chiseldon; 3 miles (4.8km) **50**

CHAPTER 7 RIVER COLN **56**
Walk 7 Chedworth Roman Villa to Fossebridge; 6.5 miles (10.5km) **58**
Walk 8 Bibury to Coln St Aldwyns; 6.5 miles (10.4km) **61**

CHAPTER 8 RIVER LEACH **64**
Walk 9 Northleach to Hampnett and Upper End; 6.5 miles (10.5km) **66**

PART 2 The rivers entering the Thames in Oxfordshire **70**

CHAPTER 9 RIVER WINDRUSH **72**
Walk 10 Sherbourne to Windrush village; 5 miles (8km) **64**
Walk 11 Minster Lovell to Crawley; 3.5 miles (5.6km) **78**

CHAPTER 10 RIVER EVENLODE **84**
Walk 12 Charlbury, Chilson and Pudlicote; 7 miles (11.3km) **87**
Walk 13 East End Roman Villa; 3.5 miles (5.6km) **89**

CHAPTER 11 RIVER CHERWELL **94**
Walk 14 Charwelton and Hellidon; 4 miles (6.4km) **95**
Walk 15 Kirtlington; 5 miles (8km) **102**

CHAPTER 12 RIVER OCK **105**
Walk 16 Letcombe Brook; 5 miles (8km) **109**

CHAPTER 13 RIVER THAME **112**
Walk 17 Dorchester to Long Wittenham; 8 miles (12.9km) **118**

PART 3 The rivers entering the Thames in Berkshire and Buckinghamshire **120**

CHAPTER 14 RIVER PANG **122**
Walk 18 Stanford Dingle to Bradfield; 5 miles (8km) **124**
Walk 19 Pangbourne to Tidmarsh and Sulham; 3 miles (5.6km) **128**

CHAPTER 15 RIVER KENNET **130**
Walk 20 Avebury to Silbury and East Kennet; 5 miles (8km) **132**
Walk 21 Speen to Donnington Castle and Bagnor; 5.3 miles (8.5km) **137**
Walk 22 Thatcham to the River Enborne and Greenham Common; 8 miles (12.9km) **140**

CHAPTER 16 RIVER LODDON **146**
Walk 23 The Basing Trail at Basingstoke; 5.7 miles (9.1km) **148**
Walk 24 Dinton Pastures to Twyford and back; 7.7 miles (12.4km) **152**
Walk 25 North Warnborough to Greywell and Odiham Castle; 4 miles (6.4km) **158**

CHAPTER 17 RIVER WYE **160**
Walk 26 West Wycombe; 3 miles (4.8km) **161**

PART 4 The Rivers entering the Thames in Surrey 166

CHAPTER 18 RIVER COLNE **168**

Walk 27 Rickmansworth to Black Jack's Lock, near Mount Pleasant; 6 miles (9.7km) **172**

Walk 28 St Albans to Childwickbury and Redbournbury; 7.5 miles (12km) **176**

Walk 29 Chess Valley at Chenies; 6.8 miles (10.9km) **180**

CHAPTER 19 RIVER BOURNE **184**

Walk 30 Chertsey Meads to Weybridge; 5 miles (8km) **184**

CHAPTER 20 RIVER WEY **192**

Walk 31 Tilford to Frensham Little Pond and Pierrepoint Farm; 5.5 miles (8.9km) **196**

Walk 32 Camelsdale to Black Down; 6 miles (9.7km) **192**

Walk 33 Godalming to Guildford; 5 miles (8km) **200**

CHAPTER 21 RIVER MOLE **204**

Walk 34 Brockham Village Circular Walk; 5 miles (8km) **206**

Walk 35 Dorking to Leatherhead, via Box Hill and the Mole Gap Trail; 5.7 miles (9.1km) **208**

Walk 36 Cobham Circular Walk; 4 miles (6.4km) **211**

PART 5 The rivers entering the Thames in West London 216

CHAPTER 22 RIVER HOGSMILL **218**

Walk 37 Riverside Walk from Ewell (source) to the Thames; 8 miles (12.9km) **220**

CHAPTER 23 RIVER CRANE **224**

Walk 38 Crane Park and Kneller Gardens; 5 miles (8km) **226**

CHAPTER 24 RIVER BRENT **229**

Walk 39 Horsenden Hill to Brent River Park; 8.3 miles (13.4km) **232**

CHAPTER 25 BEVERLEY BROOK **236**

Walk 40 Richmond Park to Putney and back to Wimbledon, using a bus from Putney to Wimbledon; 9.2 miles (14.8km) **238**

CHAPTER 26 RIVER WANDLE **242**

Walk 41 Waddon Ponds to Morden Hall; 6.5 miles (10.4km) **244**

PART 6 The rivers that meet the Thames in and near East London **244**

CHAPTER 27 RIVER RAVENSBOURNE **248**
Walk 42 Keston Common; 3 miles (4.8km) **249**

CHAPTER 28 RIVER LEA **254**
Walk 43 Hertford to Rye House; 7 miles (11.3km) **258**
Walk 44 Cheshunt, Fishers Green and Waltham Abbey; 5 miles (8km) **262**
Walk 45 Walthamstow Marshes to Hackney Marsh; 6 miles (9.7km) **265**

CHAPTER 29 RIVER RODING **269**
Walk 46 Loughton; 4 miles (6.4km) **271**

CHAPTER 30 RIVER ROM AND BEAM **276**
Walk 47 Dagenham dog bone-shaped walk; 5 miles (8km) **278**

CHAPTER 31 RIVER INGREBOURNE **280**
Walk 48 Hornchurch Country Park; 6 miles (9.7km) **282**

CHAPTER 32 RIVER DARENT **286**
Walk 49 Otford to Shoreham and Eynsford (return by train); 5.5 miles (8.9km) **288**

CHAPTER 33 THE MARDYKE **292**
Walk 50 Davy Down and North Stifford; 3.5 miles (5.6km) **294**

Amwell Nature Reserve, River Lea

This book is dedicated to
John Denman Freer-Smith,
who instilled in his only daughter
her sense of exploration and adventure,
which has helped her to discover
the sources of some of these rivers.

Introduction

Walking along a muddy track in water meadows beside the River Windrush in Gloucestershire early on a frosty November morning, you might ask: 'Why are we looking at a tributary of the Thames when we could be enjoying breakfast in a warm room?' The short answer is to see the early morning sunshine slanting through reedbeds, to explore when the wildlife is undisturbed and to have a thermos of tea at its best. This book is the longer answer.

The tributaries of the Thames are essential to the people and to the wildlife in a large part of southern England. The Thames catchment area is 6,229 square miles (16,133 square kilometres), stretching from Gloucestershire to Kent and from Northamptonshire to Hampshire. Recent campaigns on water quality have raised awareness of the urgent need to care more for the rivers and streams that flow into the Thames.

'Tributary' is a curious word derived from 'tribute', the money or goods paid by 'tribes' to their rulers. It was applied to rivers in

Windrush Mill

Introduction

Winter floods at Wheatley Bridge, River Thame

*Ekwall, E. English River Names. Oxford: Clarendon Press, 1928

the early 19th century when writers and artists pictured the Thames as a father figure or the female goddess Isis, being supplied by his or her subordinates. There are two more twists to this tale: the names of some of our tributaries are derived from the names of tribes in Celtic, Roman and Anglo-Saxon Britain; and some of the rivers were tribal boundaries. We have enjoyed reading Ekwall's *English River Names** in our attempt to understand the origins of the rivers' names.

This book is about exploring 33 of the larger tributaries. These are all the natural rivers and brooks that are at least 15ft (4.6m) wide where they join the Thames, shown on Ordnance Survey maps as a double blue line on maps instead of the single blue line used for smaller watercourses. In the spirit of 'going with the flow', the rivers are described in the order in which they enter the Thames, going from source to sea. The underground rivers in London are omitted because they are not usually accessible to the public. We have also omitted the tidal creeks in the Lower Thames and we accept the convention that the Thames ends at the Crow Stone at Southend. The explorations are by walking because this provides the best opportunity to look at the wildlife and good examples of conservation. We describe 50 of our favourite walks and include 130 more walks that are easy to find, or there are already detailed guides available for them. Some of the rivers have named trails along their valleys and others have sections of well-known long-distance paths.

Several tributaries have active conservation organisations, most of which are charitable groups. Roman villas, Saxon towns, pretty villages and stately homes show how these tributaries have been good places for people to live for many centuries. Our favourite walks connect these interesting places to the natural landscape formed by the rivers.

Several tributaries in this book are navigable, most obviously where there are canals, but we do not have reliable information about navigation rights in this book.

Trout in River Leach near Southrop

Important note

Walks in the Thames Valley are usually easy to moderate but, in wet weather, they can become difficult because of mud or impassable because of flooding. We recommend that you use maps as well as our directions, because conditions and paths may change.

PART 1

The rivers entering the Thames in Gloucestershire and Wiltshire

River Coln, Coln St Dennis

Swill Brook

LENGTH: 6 miles (9.7km)

SOURCE: Fossegate, near Crudwell

CONFLUENCE: Waterhay, near Cricklade

Swill Brook was a real discovery for us. We had seen it when visiting Lower Moor Farm and Swillbrook Lakes Nature Reserves for our first book, *Exploring the Thames Wilderness*, but we did not realise its significance as the first tributary of the Thames. Nor do many other people. Certainly not the Members of Parliament in the House of Commons in 1937, when the source of the River Thames was debated, as discussed in the next chapter.

Swill Brook illustrates four features that are part of the fun of exploring these rivers including looking for the source; puzzling about the name; finding links with the past; and enjoying the wildlife, both fauna and flora, experienced by walking beside freshwater. All four features are present in Crudwell, a village on the A433 road between Malmsbury and Cirencester. At the village green in the centre of Crudwell, there is a clear stream that flows east all year. The sources of this stream, known locally as the Brook, can be found by walking to Fossegate on the lanes to the west of Crudwell. Walk from the village green down the main road (A433) towards Malmsbury and turn right along Tetbury Lane. After ½ mile (0.8km), take the quiet lane through the small village of Chedworth and walk for nearly a mile (1.6km) to Fossegate. About halfway along this lane, you will see a pond on the left side with a stream on the opposite side flowing towards Crudwell. This is part

What's in a name?

It is not surprising that the stream in Crudwell is called simply 'the Brook' by local people. Some other Thames tributaries have names that are ancient words for 'the river or stream'. In times when few people travelled further than the next village, there was no need for rivers to have distinctive names. Tracing the Brook east, it acquires the title Swill Brook when it reaches Swillbrook Farm, presumably because the river was used for sluicing and cleaning.

The Brook at Crudwell village green

of the source of the Brook. Continue along the lane to Fossegate, which is the most westerly point of the Thames Catchment. The ditch on the eastern side of the Fosse Way develops into a stream that crosses the fields to join the stream that flows from the pond. The combined stream goes south beside Tuners Lane to the village green.

You can follow the Brook from the village green through the meadow on the opposite side of the main road. Here, the water is clear above a gravel bed with water crowfoot as a sign of health. The path ends at Eastcourt Lane, where the Brook is fed by a nearby spring – perhaps the well that gives Crudwell its name. Turn left along the lane to the church and the Potting Shed pub, and left again on the main road back to the village green. Pettifers, the hotel on the main road, has leaflets describing other local walks.

Exploring the Thames rivers, you find frequent reminders that many people have been this way before you. The Fosse Way, a Roman road from Exeter to Lincoln, is an example. At Fossegate, it is a muddy track on the boundary between Wiltshire and Gloucestershire. Further north, it is the A433 road that crosses the Thames near to its source, and later becomes the A429 that starts

1 Swill Brook

beside the River Churn in Cirencester and crosses the Rivers Coln and Leach in Gloucestershire.

Lower Moor and Lower Mill Lower Moor Farm Nature Reserve near Somerford Keynes is 3 miles (4.8km) from Crudwell. It includes Clattinger Farm, which is the only lowland farm in Britain known to have never used artificial fertilisers. As a result, its hay meadows are rich in wildflowers which have been used to seed other meadows, including those at Highgrove, the home of King Charles III when he was Prince of Wales.

The Wiltshire Wildlife Trust has built bird hides, a teaching centre and excellent information boards. The Dragonfly Café is a recent attraction, beautifully set beside a lake. In spring and summer, the meadows of Clattinger Farm on the banks of the Swill Brook are full of wildflowers, including snake's head fritillaries, orchids and meadow saffron.

Flowers at Clattinger Farm

WALK 1 Lower Mill Farm and Swillbrook Nature Reserve

4.5 miles (7.2km)

This is what we call a dog bone walk; two small, circular walks connected by one path. Take the path from the car park that passes the thatched copy of an Iron Age house and goes between Mallard and Cottage Lake, past Sandpool Farm to reach Minety Lane. Over the lane is a path in the Lower Mill Estate of holiday homes that leads to Swillbrook Nature Reserve and a walk beside the Swill Brook in the shade of poplar trees. After the nature reserve, the path reaches Flagham Lake, which has a colony of beavers.

Continue across the meadows to the eastern edge of the estate, where you can look at Pike Corner and explore the marshes at Cow Gate before you return along the same path to Lower Moor Farm. When you cross Minety Lane on the way back, take the left-hand gate, which enters Clattinger Farm. The path beside the hedge leads to the east side of Mallard Lake. Turn left to continue through the meadows near the lake to reach the hard-surfaced track that goes back to the car park.

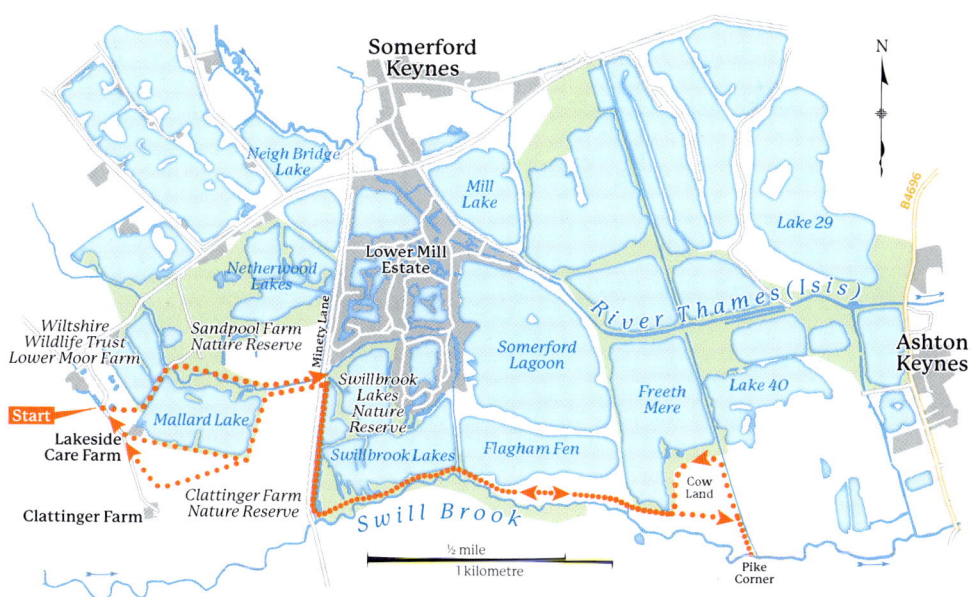

Walk 1

The junction of the Thames and Swill Brook at Waterhay

If you park at Waterhay Bridge and walk a ¼ mile (0.4km) towards Ashton Keyes, you will find a bridle path on the left. After 100 yards (91.4m) lies the Thames and its junction with the Swill Brook on the edge of the field on your left (east) side. Back at the Waterhay car park, you can go along the Thames Path to Cricklade – a lovely 3 mile (4.8km) walk in spring – with a variety of paths for the way back.

GETTING THERE

BUS SERVICE | Coachstyle no. 93 between Malmsbury and Cirencester stops at Crudwell, Oaksey and Somerford Keynes
CYCLING | Bikes can be hired in the Cotswold Water Park
OS EXPLORER MAPS | 168 Stroud, Tetbury & Malmesbury; 169 Cirencester & Swindon

RESOURCES

Lower Moor Farm: www.wiltshirewildlife.org/lower-moor-farm-including-clattinger-farm-sandpool-oaksey-moor-farm-meadow

Walks in the Cotswold Water Park: www.waterpark.org/wp-content/uploads/2017/04/2017-Walk-3.pdf

OPPOSITE *The Swill Brook in Swillbrook Nature Reserve*

ABOVE *The Swill Brook (left) and the Thames (right) meet at Waterhay*

2 River Churn

LENGTH: 29 miles (46.7km)

SOURCE: Seven Springs near Cheltenham

CONFLUENCE: Cricklade

The Churn offers a glorious mixture of landscapes from steep-sided valleys at its source, through rolling hills to the Cotswold Water Park and ending in a purple haze of fritillaries (when in flower) at North Meadow at Cricklade. In the hills to the south-east of Cheltenham, beside the A436 road, there is a pool called the Seven Springs. These are the highest constant springs in the Thames catchment area and the furthest from the sea in terms of river length. A plaque declares: *'Hic tuus o Tamesine Pater septemceminus fons'* ('Here, O Father Thames, is your sevenfold spring'). In a debate in Parliament in 1937, it was argued that this place should be called the source of the Thames. The Swill Brook at Crudwell was mentioned as an alternative source. Nevertheless, the official source of the Thames is at Thameshead, as shown on Ordnance Survey maps at Coates near Circencester.

Driving along the A435, the main road from Seven Springs to Cirencester, you see tantalising glimpses of the Churn as it flows down the valley. Walking on paths and minor roads, you can follow the course of the Churn from its source to the Thames at Cricklade. But first there is a favourite walk around the headwaters of the Churn to discover yet more springs that feed it close to the souce.

Snake's head fritillary

What's in a name?

The Churn has had its own identity since pre-Roman times, named after the local Celtic tribe, the Cornovii. The Roman town of Corinium (Cirencester) and three riverside villages, North Cerney, South Cerney and Cerney Wick, have the same derivation.

WALK 2 Around the Seven Springs

5.8 miles (9.3km)

The Seven Springs form a pool beside the A436 road to Gloucester, close to the junction with the A435 and a bus stop. There is space to park here, and the pub on the opposite side of the road has a garden beside the stream. A footpath about 200 yards (180m) west of the pub goes to Coberley, where water coming from more springs cascades down through a lovely garden. A footpath beside the garden descends to the streams and climbs up to a field. Cross this field in a south-easterly direction to a house beside the river. Staying on the west side of the Churn, the path goes over a stream (from one more spring), through a copse and over more fields to Cowley. The last paddock features dramatic animal sculptures. Walk past Cowley Manor, a hotel with a lake and parkland that you can admire as you walk along the lane to Cockleford.

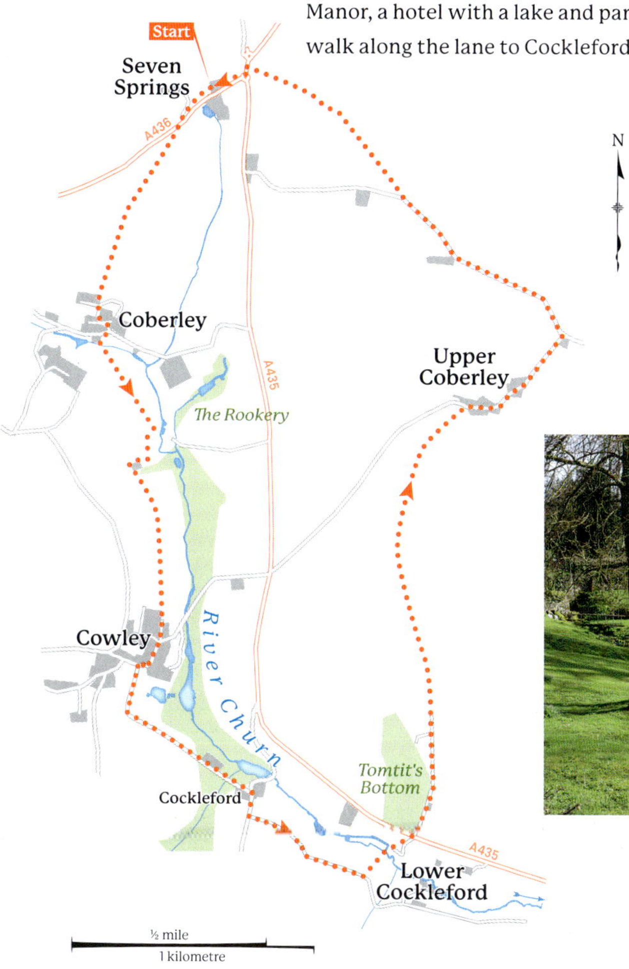

Garden at Coberley

Walk 2

When you reach the Green Dragon Inn, with a shop selling lovely tasty food, turn right and then left to the no through road signposted to Cockleford. At the house named The Cottage after ⅓ mile (0.5km), take a footpath that descends steeply to the river at Cockleford Farm. Walk up the winding driveway of the farm, and then the bridleway on the opposite side of the main road (A435). At the top of the hill there are super views of the hills around the springs that create the Churn. The track joins the lane in Upper Coberly village, where there is yet another spring forming a garden pond and a stream. It looks to us as though the River Churn has more than seven springs and that the term 'headwaters' is more appropriate than 'the source' for the starting point of some rivers.

To end the walk, continue up the lane and turn left at the T junction. After a mile (0.7km), take the bridleway on the right side of a bend in the road, to go down through a wood to the road junction close to Seven Springs.

Footbridge over the Churn near Rendcomb

The Churn beside the Bathurst Arms in North Cerney

A more ambitious walk from Seven Springs to Cirencester

If you want to walk the whole 12 miles (19.3km) from Seven Springs to Cirencester, the no. 53 bus service can return you to your starting point. There are bus stops at Colesbourne, Rendcomb and North Cerney. Start along the route of Walk 2 and instead of turning off at the Cockleford no through road at The Cottage, continue along the road to its end. There is a track that continues until you reach a lane down to the main road (the A435) in Colesbourne. Walk along the village street, past a pub (Colebourne Arms) and a garage to the road signed to Withington. After crossing the Churn, climb up the road to where it bends left. Here, you will find a bridle path going east for 1.5 miles (2.4km). Follow the bridle path where it turns south. After half a mile (1.6km) you find a lane that takes you to Rendcomb. Although this bridle path between Colesbourne and Rendcomb takes you away from the river, it gives you wonderful views of the Cotswold Hills.

From Rendcomb, take the Monarch's Way, which follows the river closely for 6 miles (9.7km) to Cirencester. The Way is based on the escape route to France that King Charles II took after losing the Battle of Worcester in 1651. The main buildings at Rendcomb are a former stately home, now an independent school, built in the Italianate style in 1865. A village shop beside the school serves coffee and tea. The pub at North Cerney – the Bathurst Arms – has a riverside garden. Although the woodland under the A417 viaduct can be muddy, the compensation is a mass of bluebells in May. When you reach Baunton, a pretty hamlet, cross the flood meadow and climb through a wood following the Monarch's Way signs to Bowling Green Lane that leads to Cirencester.

WALK 3 Cirencester to Baunton

5 miles (8km)

The long linear walk from Seven Springs to Cirencester is one to enjoy occasionally, but this circular walk at Cirencester is a favourite deserving to be repeated once a year. Starting at the beautiful St John Baptist Church in the Cirencester marketplace, walk across West Market Place to Black Jack Lane. At the far end of the lane, turn right along Park Street, passing the museum (well worth a visit) and the visitor information centre. On the opposite side of Park Street is Cecily Hill entrance to Cirencester Park, and 30 yards (27m) later, a path signposted Riverside Walk. The river is one branch of the Churn, which has divided into two streams as it enters Cirencester. Take the Riverside Path, and pass the open-air swimming pool and a former mill where the path crosses the river. The path ends at Gloucester Street, near a service station.

Walk through the service station and cross Abbey Road (A435) to a footpath in the water meadows. The path follows the line of telephone posts and reaches a group of houses on the site of Stratton Mill. Turn right along a no through road, which ends at a path across the next flood meadow, where the Churn is divided into at least three streams. It is likely that these divided streams are partly humanmade, as a means of controlling water levels and flows. The Drowner's Cottage, on the east side of the meadow, is where the people who managed the flood meadows lived.

Sign for the open-air swimming pool

At the Drowner's Cottage, turn left and you quickly reach a fork in the bridle path. Take the left fork through a rickety gate, which is almost hidden in the hedge. This is the Monarch's Way to Braunton, going across two pastures where you look down on the Churn on the left side. After walking down in a wood, you reach another flood meadow with horse jumps and then you are in Baunton. In the village, go up the street that goes straight past Meadow View. Shortly after the right bend, take the bridle path on the right side. This goes back to Cirencester, giving you good views over the Churn valley. At Drowner's Cottage again continue straight on to Bowling Green Lane to Abbey Way.

After crossing Abbey Way, you see the other branch of the Churn flowing through parkland. You can go directly back to where you started — the church tower is obvious — but it is interesting to follow the Churn downstream through the Abbey Grounds. The river expands into a lake created by a small dam at the eastern end. Close by are remains of the Roman wall that encircled the town. Cross the footbridge beside the dam to the path that returns to the marketplace.

2 River Churn

Cirencester to South Cerney

LEFT *The Churn enters South Cerney*

ABOVE *The Thames and Severn Canal*

After the Abbey Grounds, the Churn reaches City Bank, which is a group of riverside meadows managed as a nature reserve. Then it has a dreary course in a straight line between a main road and supermarkets. Enjoyable walking beside the Churn starts again at Siddington. If on foot, you can walk from City Bank Road to Watermoor Lane, through the underpass at Bristol Road, along Midlands Road, and turn left at Love Lane to a footpath beside the Royal Mail offices. This leads to Siddington and the disused Thames and Severn Canal. The canal towpath leads to the Churn. River and canal run side by side for a short distance before the canal and path cross the river. After ½ mile (0.8km) the canal enters a cutting. Take a path to the right, up a bank, across the line of a disused railway to fields looking down on the river. Two miles (3.2km) after leaving Siddington, the path reaches School Lane in South Cerney, where it runs beside the river to the Old George pub in the centre of the village.

South Cerney to Cricklade

There are two ways to walk from South Cerney to Cricklade. The shorter and more direct 4 miles (6.4km) is to use the route 45 cycle path along a disused railway track. More interesting

2 River Churn

and a longer route (5 miles/8km) starts at the Old George pub (dog and walker friendly) at the centre of South Cerney. Walk beside the Churn along Bow Wow Lane – yes, it is a dog-walking paradise – to a footbridge over the river beside a mill house. The footpath leads to Station Road, where you turn left to walk eastwards for $1/3$ mile (0.8km) to a lake. Here, the National Cycle Network Route 45 goes past a sailing club in a straight line to Cricklade. To find the Churn again, go east on Wildmoorway Lane for ½ mile (0.8km) to a footpath on the right that runs between the Churn and a lake with a watersports centre. Crossing the B4696 Spine Road, the path winds between lakes to the Thames and Severn Canal towpath, not far ($1/3$ mile/0.8km) from the Cotswold Water Park Visitor Centre.

At the canal, turn right and follow the towpath south for a mile (nearly 2km), enjoying views of the Churn on the west side, and passing Cerney Wick, where the Crown Inn has good lunches. When you reach the Basin, which was a junction of the Churn, the Thames and Severn Canal and the North Wilts Canal, turn right beside the side of a house and follow the line of the North Wilts

Bow Wow Lane in South Cerney

Thames and Severn Canal near Cerney Wick

Canal until you find a gate in North Meadow, famous for the snake's head fritillary flowers in spring. The Churn flows along the north-eastern side to the meadow before going under the road into private land, where it joins the Thames. Join the Thames Path that goes into Cricklade on the western side of the meadow. North Meadow is part of a favourite circular walk described in Chapter 4 Ampney Brook. A final thought is that the River Churn should have a properly recognised long-distance trail as an important tributary of the Thames.

GETTING THERE

BUS SERVICE | Stagecoach West no. 51 runs between Swindon, Cricklade, Cirencester and Cheltenham: *https://bustimes.org/services/51-swindon-cricklade-cirencester-cheltenham*

OS EXPLORER MAPS | 169 Cirencester & Swindon; 179 Gloucester, Cheltenham & Stroud; OL45 The Cotswolds

RESOURCES

Debate about the source of the Thames: *https://api.parliament.uk/historic-hansard/commons/1937/feb/25/ordnance-survey-maps-river-thames-source*

The Monarch's Way: A guide book is available from the Long Distance Paths Association: *https://ldwa.org.uk*

3 River Key

LENGTH: 5 miles (8km)

SOURCE: Battle Lake in Braydon Wood, near Purton

CONFLUENCE: Cricklade

The Key is the smallest of the Thames tributaries and it is the third to enter the Thames. Although the Ordnance Survey maps show it as a single blue line, the river is about 18ft (5.5m) wide at its mouth in Cricklade. Therefore, it qualifies for a chapter of its own in this book. The land through which the Key flows is flat and the clay soil is hard to cultivate. There was a local saying that it was so wet that 'it would rot a goose'. In Saxon and Norman times, the land was unpopulated, covered in marshes and woods, which were part of the large Royal Forest of Braydon, which was described as '2 leagues broad and 2 leagues long' (7 x 7 miles/11.3 x 11.3km) in the Doomsday Book. In the 13th century, the villagers of Purton on the hill that overlooks the river gained Royal permission to clear trees and drain marshes. The area around the Key is still sparsely populated, with fields used for grazing and woods belonging to the Forestry Commission. More recently a landfill waste site and acres of solar panels surrounded by high fences have not improved the landscape.

Battle Lake

Battle Lake, where the River Key rises, is in the Red Lodge Plantation to the north-west of Purton, near Swindon. A bridleway runs north-south through the plantation crossing the infant river and past the Red Lodge, a distinctive brick-built house on slightly higher ground

The Key as a woodland stream near Battle Lake

What's in a name?

We do not know the origins of the name Key, but it may come from an Anglo-Saxon name Cai, pronounced Kay. Perhaps there is a link to Sir Kay, a Knight of King Arthur's Round Table. We are equally ignorant of which battle (if any) occurred by Battle Lake in Battle Wood. What we do know is that Purton is described in the Domesday Book as having a mill, which we like to believe was on the River Key.

with a view of the lake. There is no car park close to the Red Lodge Plantation, but there is roadside parking in Purton and Stoke Purton villages.

Starting at Paven Hill in Purton, you can enjoy a walk to the Red Lodge via Ringsbury Camp, an Iron Age hill fort. It is 6 miles (9.7km) there and back. Looking north from the walls of the Camp, the panorama of the Upper Thames plain stretches before you all the way towards Cirencester. A path at the north-west corner of the Camp goes to Battle Lake Farm at the entrance to the Red Lodge Plantation. The walk through the woods is very pleasant, among ash and oak trees, with bluebells in spring. The second stream that you cross is the infant Key. When you approach Red Lodge, look back over your left shoulder to see Battle Lake. The Lodge was originally a hunting lodge in the centre of the forest. For a different way back, take the footpaths with stiles across pastures towards Purton. These paths are very wet in winter and are not well signposted. When we tried this cross-country route, we regretted not going back the way that we came via Ringwood Camp.

Purton Stoke A different approach to Red Lodge Plantation, of similar length, starts in Purton Stoke. Walk along Stoke Common Lane, once a drovers' road, from the Bell Inn. At the edge of the village, cross the Key where it has become a small river. About ½ mile (0.8km) later you pass a small stone hexagonal building set back in a grove of trees. This is the Salt's Hole, a well with salty water that became a local spa in the 19th century. Two miles (3.2km) along the lane you reach a gate across the lane. This is the entrance to Stoke Common Meadows, which is part of the Blakehill Nature Reserve owned by the Wiltshire Wildlife Trust and is managed for hay and wildflowers. Continue along the lane for ⅓ mile (0.5km) and turn left on a bridle path that takes you to Davenport Bridge over the railway. Turn right and walk on the wide track beside the railway for ½ mile (0.8km), where the track veers left and becomes a lane that passes the White Lodge. After another ½ mile, turn left on to a footpath that goes straight across a field and through Red Lodge Plantation to the Red Lodge. Once again, the easiest path back is the way you came.

3 River Key

Cricklade The river runs beside the road from Purton Stoke to Cricklade. A strip of grassland between the road and the river on the edge of Cricklade has been turned into a local nature reserve called Dance Common. It is managed by volunteers, the Friends of Dance Common, and it saves a valuable wildlife habitat in a place where new houses are being built. It is possible that the name of the common is a corruption of Danes, who might have camped here on one of their forays into Wessex. Or perhaps it is simply a memory of happier festivities. At the south end of Dance Common, there are traces of the old North Wilts Canal that linked the Berks and Wilts Canal in Swindon to the Thames and Severn Canal. At the north end, a footpath follows the line of the walls of the Saxon town of Cricklade. Here there is a good example of the ridging used in fields close to rivers partly to improve drainage but also to divide the land into strips for cultivation. The path crosses the track bed of the old Swindon and Cricklade Railway, which you encounter again when you explore the River Ray. The National Cycle Network Route 45 on this old railway is one of many paths that form short circular walks around the historic town of Cricklade.

The Millenium Stone where the Key enters The Thames

The last part of the Key and its confluence with the Thames is easily found in Fairview Fields, a recreation ground on the east side of Cricklade. Walk from the car park to the Thames, where a Millennium Stone over the mouth of the Key marks the creation of a new woodland nature reserve. The bridge here is the first to take the Thames Path over a tributary that we describe in this book.

GETTING THERE

OS EXPLORER MAP | 169 Cirencester & Swindon

RESOURCES

Friends of Dance Common: F*acebook.com/dancecommon.crickla*
Red Lodge Plantation: *https://www.woodlandtrust.org.uk/visiting-woods/woods/red-lodge-plantation/*
Salt's Hole Spa: *https://insearchofholywellsandhealingsprings.com/the-living-spring-journal-contents/wiltshire-healing-wells-and-the-strange-case-of-purton-spa/*; *https://www.geograph.org.uk/photo/1635377*

4 Ampney Brook

LENGTH: 8 miles (12.9km)

SOURCE: Ampney Crucis near Cirencester

CONFLUENCE: Easey near Cricklade

When you take the A417 road between Cirencester and Fairford (the most direct route to Oxford and London), you pass the villages of Ampney Crucis and Ampney St Peter and see signs to Down Ampney. If you stop at the Crown Inn at Ampney Cruris, you see a sparkling stream, shallow but wide, with crystal clear water. This is Ampney Brook.

Ampney Brook at Ampney Crucis

The main source is the group of springs that fill the lakes in Ampney Park on the western side of Ampney Crucis. In winter water flows in the Winterwell stream from limestone aquifers on the northern side of the Ampney estate. In the past, the flow of water was strong enough to power two mills at Ampney Crucis. The water quality of Ampney Brook is good enough for wild trout,

What's in a name?

The river's name is derived from a person's name, Amma's Brook.

St Mary's Church on the banks of Ampney Crucis

although its small size means it is susceptible to droughts. Of the villages along its banks, Ampney Crucis is the oldest. Its name comes from the stone crosses in its churchyard. Ampney St Peter was once called Eastington, a name retained by Eastington House in the village. Another village, Ampney St Mary, was originally on the river between Ampney Crucis and Ampney St Peter, but moved to higher ground at a place called Ashbrook about 1 mile (1.6km) away. Down Ampney, the lower Ampney, is about 5 miles (8km) downstream and is not so likely to be caught in the confusion of village names.

Ampney Crucis The church in Ampney Crucis has parking space and is a good place to learn about the history of the village. It is also a starting point for a short walk – 1.5 miles (2.4km) – around the village. The river is an ornamental feature of the large houses beside the church and the gardens are sometimes opened to the public for charity fundraising. To follow the river, walk back down Church Lane, passing Steppy's Mill with its beautiful water garden. Cross the bridge to the main road and go past the entrance to the Crown Inn. Continue beside the main road until you have passed another mill and its associated buildings, where there is a side road on your left, look across the main road. On the opposite side is a footpath that follows the edge of a field and through a patch of uncultivated ground to a small bridge across the river and into St Mary's Church.

St Mary's Church is the remnant of the former Ampney St Mary village. It is possible that the medieval parishioners moved away from their church because the Black Death affected the village around 1350. Or possibly because of flooding. The small church has a Norman tympanum above the north doorway and medieval wall paintings inside. Early in the 20th century it was so covered in ivy that it was called the Ivy Church. Now it receives better care and has regular services. The churchyard is a quiet place to rest beside the river.

To return to Ampney Crucis, go to the main road, where there is a small car park for St Mary's Church. Cross the main road and turn left to take the side road, which was the old London Road that followed the curve of the river. Turn right to walk up School Lane for about 200 yards (180m) to a path on the left side. Along this path, a permissive path goes off to the left around a group of young trees to the village cricket field. You have another view of the river and the Crown Inn before you arrive at Church Lane.

Ampney Peter to Down Ampney

There is a straight route from Ampney St Peter to Down Ampney along a lane and a bridleway. Apart from being near the river, this way has no great interest and there is no pub or café at either end. However, there is, nearby, a jolly place for lunch with a cheery welcome for both walkers and dogs: the Gilbertine Kitchen at the Priory Court near Poulton (GL7 5JB).

GETTING THERE

OS EXPLORER MAP | 169 Cirencester & Swindon

RESOURCES

Ampney Churches in the Cotswolds: *www.ampneychurches.info*
A survey of Ampney Brook as a habitat for fish by Vaughan Lewis, 2004: *www.wildtrout.org/assets/reports/2004AmpneyBrook.pdf*
Cotswold Flyfishers: *https://cotswoldflyfishers.com/Our-Waters.php*

WALK 4 Cricklade and Down Ampney

5.5 miles (8.9km)

This walk combines the Thames Path at Cricklade, the River Key, Ampney Brook, the Thames and Severn Canal at Eysey, Down Ampney (shops and pubs), Latton, the River Churn and North Meadow (famous for fritillaries). The start is the car park in Fairview Fields, the sports ground beside the B4040 on the east side of Cricklade. Walk north across the playing fields to the Thames and turn right to follow the Thames Path downstream. You cross the River Key beside the Millennium Stone and go under the A419. In less than 1 mile (1.6km), look for the mouth of Ampney Brook on the opposite side of the river. Cross the Thames on the footbridge at the sign to Eysey and take the path close to the Brook until you reach the place where the Thames and Severn Canal crossed the Brook. Turn right beside the canal to the entrance of Eysey Manor. Turn left to walk along the straight lane going north. At the end of the lane turn right over Gally Lease Bridge, and immediately turn left on to a footpath to Down Ampney. After passing through a copse, you come to the end of the runway of the airfield used in June and September 1944 for transporting soldiers to land by parachutes and gliders in Normandy and the Netherlands. Continue north until you reach Down Ampney Church. The church car park is an alternative place to start this walk. The church is usually open in daytime and has historical displays of the life of the composer Vaughan Williams, who was born in the vicarage in 1872, and of the airborne troops who flew from the airfield.

Clear water in Ampney Brook enters the Thames

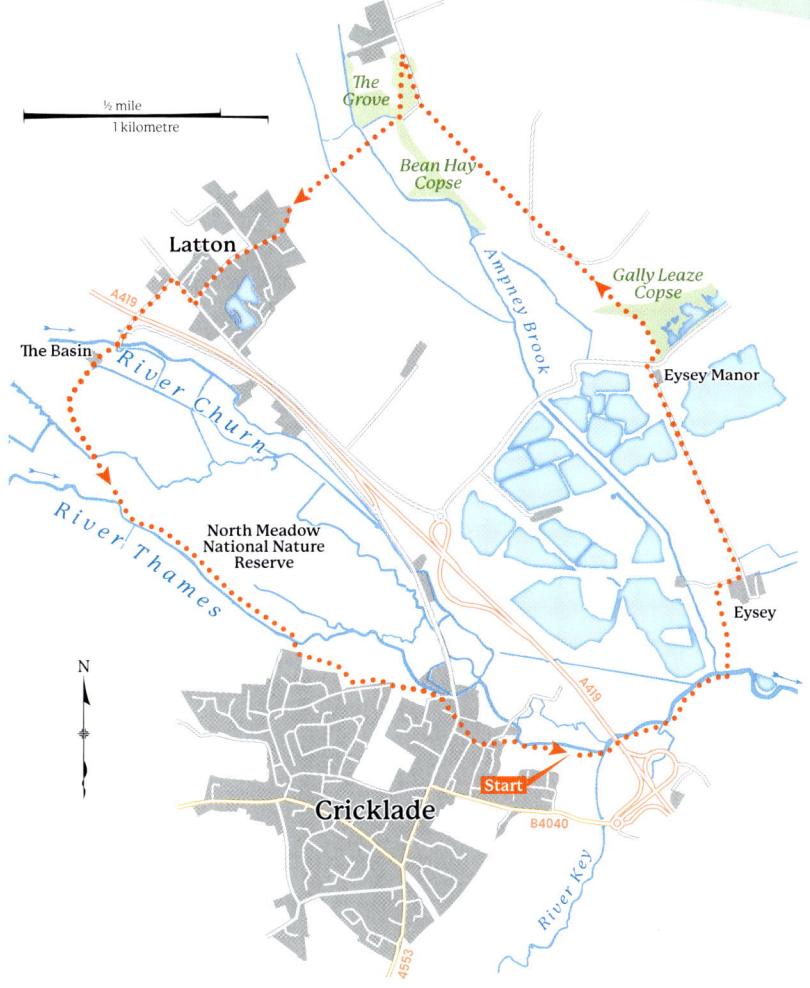

From the church, take the path beside the stone wall to cross Ampney Brook and the meadows to Latton village. In Latton, continue westward along Gosditch to the main road. Turn right and look on the other side of the road for a footpath that goes over the A491 to the junction of the Thames and Severn Canal, the River Churn and the overgrown remains of the North Wilts Canal. The old towpath of the North Wilts Canal leads to the Thames Path, where it enters North Meadow. North Meadow is a fine example of the flood meadows along the Thames and has a wonderful display of snake's head fritillaries in April and May. Take the Thames Path into Cricklade where there is a good choice of cafés and pubs. The Thames Path completes the circle to Fairview Fields.

5   River Ray

LENGTH: 13.5 miles (21.7km)

SOURCE: Wroughton near Swindon

CONFLUENCE: Water Eaton near Cricklade

Along the northern edge of the Marlborough Downs, water that has been held in the chalk meets the clay that forms the bed of the Thames Valley. The water emerges in numerous springs, to feed a network of streams running under the M4 motorway. The streams come together to make two rivers that flow around Swindon, the Ray on the west side and the Cole on the east. Old Swindon stands on a limestone hill that divides these two rivers.

The Ray makes a green corridor around the western side of Swindon, which is becoming more important as the town expands. The Borough Council appreciates this importance and has made good efforts to promote walks close to the river. Unfortunately, sewage leaking from burst drains at Haydon Wick contaminated the Ray three times in three years (2021, 2022 and 2023) killing many fish – an all-too-common problem in the Thames tributaries.

Wroughton to Rushy Platt Between the centre of Wroughton village and the M4, the Ray is little more than a ditch with a little water. The best place to start exploring is at Croft Wood Country Park in Pipers Way (A4361) where there is parking. Here are streams that have water at most times. Follow a trail with yellow signs from the car park to a triangle of woodland in the corner between Piper's Way and Croft Road. Continue on the path beside the stream, which is the infant Ray. After crossing Croft Road, walk through the rough grass

> ### What's in a name?
>
> According to Ekwall, the authority on English river names, the Ray was once called Worf, meaning 'winding', which is a good description. The name Ray is shared by a tributary of the River Cherwell (Chapter 11) and means 'to flow'.

Old Town Railway Track crosses the Wilts and Berks Canal

in the field to a bridge over the river. Climb the grassy slope to the Old Town Railway Trail. This trail is the remains of a railway line that ran from Swindon to Cricklade and Cirencester. The trail is also part of National Cycle Network Route 45 and it is a good surface for walking, pushing buggies and cycling. It offers views across the marshy valley to the Marlborough Downs in the distance and has a strong sense of local history. The trail on its viaducts draws your attention to the fact that Swindon was originally a small town on a hill surrounded by the flood plain of the Upper Thames. How much it changed into the engineering centre of the Great Western Railway! The Steam Museum caters for those people who want to know more.

After a mile (1.6km) of joining the trail, it crosses a remnant of the Wilts and Berks Canal. The local Canal Trust runs narrowboat trips in the summer. When you walk down to the canal, you find a path into Rushy Platt Nature Reserve, a small remnant of the marshes that filled the valley of the Ray. The reserve is best in the spring, when water voles are active (look for diagonal cuts on stalks, footprints and piles of droppings) and when the reed warblers are singing. When we visited in 2023, the reserve needed some work to repair the paths and to erect new information boards. There is always plenty for volunteers to do!

5 River Ray

From Rushy Platt, there are four choices to continue exploring. The simplest is to return the way you came and enjoy the views from a different angle. The second choice is to follow the canal north, leading to New Town, the part of central Swindon that grew up around the railway workshops 150 years ago. There are buses from the town centre to Croft Road (the start). The third way is to continue west along the Old Town Railway Trail and follow the signs for National Cycle Network Route 45, which will take you to Shaw Forest Park. The fourth walk is south beside the canal to the bridge at West Leaze, the site of a prehistoric settlement. This route has the attraction of a café in the nearby supermarket and a pleasant way back to Croft Wood Park. For this, walk along Mill Lane for ¼ mile (0.4km) to a footpath across a meadow on your right side. This path leads to the new housing estate, where a pavement runs between the houses and the playing fields beside the river, except where the path goes around a school. The path ends at East Wichel Way leading to Croft Road and Pipers Way.

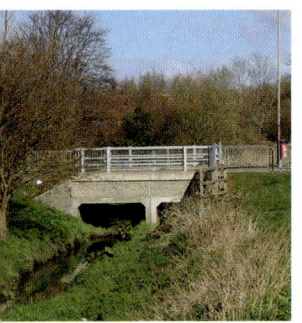

The Ray at Shaw

Mannington Recreation Ground Before we move downstream to our favourite walk beside the Ray, we want to mention Mannington Recreation Ground beside the Great Western Way (B4006). There are riverside paths on the eastern side of the park, where you can admire the work of Swindon Borough Council, the Wiltshire Wildlife Trust and the Environment Agency in restoring natural habitats beside the river.

There are no public footpaths beside the Ray north of Mouldon Hill Park. However, the Swindon and Cricklade Railway offers a different way of travelling an extra mile. Steam trains run beside the Ray from Taw Valley Halt at the north end of the park to Blunsdon station at weekends throughout the year. Before you make a return trip to Mouldon, you can enjoy a chat and refreshments in Blunsdon station café and inspect the Ray flowing under Tadpole Bridge. As it flows through the fields to the north of Blunsdon, the Ray drains a wide area of farmland. The confluence with the Thames is between Cricklade and Castle Eaton, a short distance upstream from where the Thames Path crosses the Thames on a footbridge near Water Eaton House. This tranquil spot seems many miles away from the source beside the M4 motorway.

GETTING THERE

OS EXPLORER MAP | 169 Cirencester & Swindon

RESOURCES

Mouldon Hill Park: *https://haydonwick.gov.uk/mouldon-hill-country-park/*

Purton Wood: *www.woodlandtrust.org.uk/visiting-woods/woods/purton/*

Rushy (or Rushey) Platt: *https://data.wildlifetrusts.org/reserves/rushy-platt*

Shaw Forest Park: *www.swindon.gov.uk/info/20077/parks_and_open_spaces/489/shaw_forest_park*

Steam Museum: *www.steam-museum.org.uk*

Swindon & Cricklade Railway: *https://swindon-cricklade-railway.org*

Wilts & Berks Canal Trust: *www.wbct.org.uk*

The Ray in Rushy Platt

WALK 5 Shaw Forest to Purton Wood and back via Mouldon Park

5 miles (8km)

Shaw Forest and Mouldon Park are two large green spaces established by Swindon Borough Council. They are linked by the Ray to Purton Wood, which is a relatively new reserve created by the Woodland Trust. All three places have networks of paths which invite you to explore. Shaw Forest was a landfill site, now a large nature reserve (99 acres/40ha) with wetlands to reduce flood risks. Willow and alder trees flourish in the wet soil and juniper bushes grow in the drier areas. Ponds provide homes for newts and resident ducks, and winter quarters for wildfowl. At dawn and dusk, you may see roe deer or foxes. Active volunteers play a vital part in managing this lovely community woodland.

Mouldon Lake

This walk starts at the Shaw Forest car park (SU 119 861), off Mead Way at the Hill Mead Roundabout. Go east across the grassland to a mound and continue down to the track and cycle path under the pylons. Turn left and walk north, noting the reedbeds, which help to cleanse the river, signs of an old canal and the water meadows. After a mile (1.6km), you reach the road junction at the southern end of Mouldon Hill Country Park. In the park, take the paths through meadows on the east side of Mouldon Hill to pass close to the car park. Near the car park entrance is the Tawny Owl pub at Taw Hill. From the car park, walk north to the lake, which is a good habitat for

The Ray at Mouldon Hill

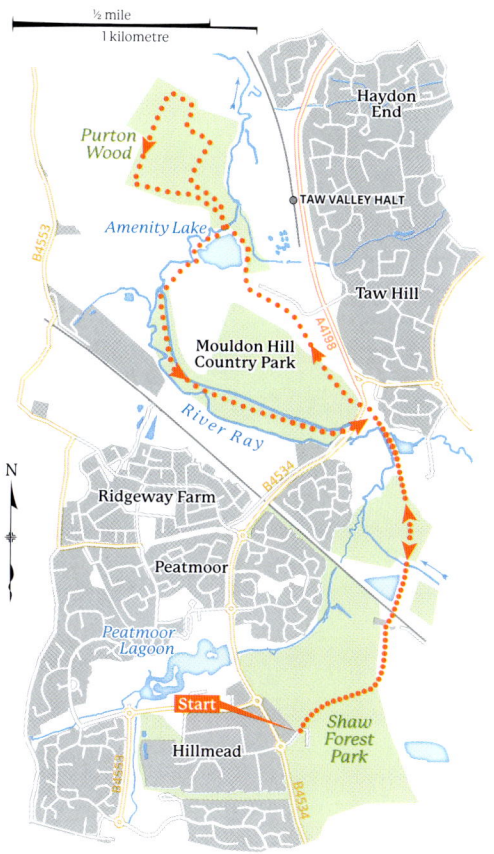

fish and birds – reeds, small islands, overhanging trees and gravel beaches. Continue north to cross the River Ray into Purton Wood.

Purton is a young wood with a lot of grass and brambles growing along the paths. As it matures, the undergrowth will diminish and the paths will become clearer. For our walk, we use a small loop in the wood, but if you had a picnic and time, there is plenty to explore. When you return to Mouldon Hill Park, go along the north side of the lake with the River Ray on your right-hand side. Cross the meadow to the far corner where you see that the river flows under a brick aqueduct which carried the old canal. Parts of the canal still have water and others are filled with reeds and rushes. Turn left to walk beside the canal back to the southern corner of Mouldon Hill Park and the cycle path to Shaw Forest. The walk finishes by retracing your steps south, with an option to explore more of the Shaw Forest using the footpaths that lead off the cycle path.

River Cole

6

LENGTH: 20 miles (32km)

SOURCE: Chiseldon

CONFLUENCE: Inglesham and St John's Bridge, Lechlade

The Cole runs from the south-east side of Swindon to the Thames near Lechlade. At its source, it is a perfect example of a chalk stream, clear water emerging out of a hillside and flowing between grassy banks close to a village green. It goes into Coate Water, a lake created to feed the Wiltshire and Berkshire Canal that opened in 1810.

What's in a name?

The river's name is said to come from an Old English word coll meaning 'hazel', which gives a suitably rural sense of its character before the Industrial Revolution.

OPPOSITE *The Cole at Chiseldon*

BELOW *Coate Water in winter*

WALK 6 Coate Water to Chiseldon

3 miles (4.8km)

Coate Water has a nature reserve, museum, car park, café and facilities for rowing, sailing and fishing. The lake is the setting for *Bevis*, the classic children's book written by Richard Jefferies, who lived nearby and whose life is displayed in the museum and information centre in the car park.

To find the source there is an easy walk along the National Cycle Network Route 45 on the east side of Coate Water to Chiseldon village. The route passes through the Coate Water Nature Reserve, where side paths to bird hides tempt you to linger. You climb a spiral ramp (like a helter-skelter) up to a bridge over the M4 motorway and walk up through peaceful woods to Chiseldon. Here, the steep-sided valley and the hazel bushes remind you of the river. The hard foundation and embankment of the path tells you that this was an old railway line (the Midland and South Western), which had a station at what is now Chiseldon village green. It is worth walking a short distance from the green to find the Washpool where the villagers have created a pretty nature reserve around the clear waters used for cleaning sheep and wool. After a picnic lunch or a snack from the village shop you are ready to return to Coate Park. At the lake, take the left-hand path on the west side of Coate Water to return to the car park.

Coate Water in summer

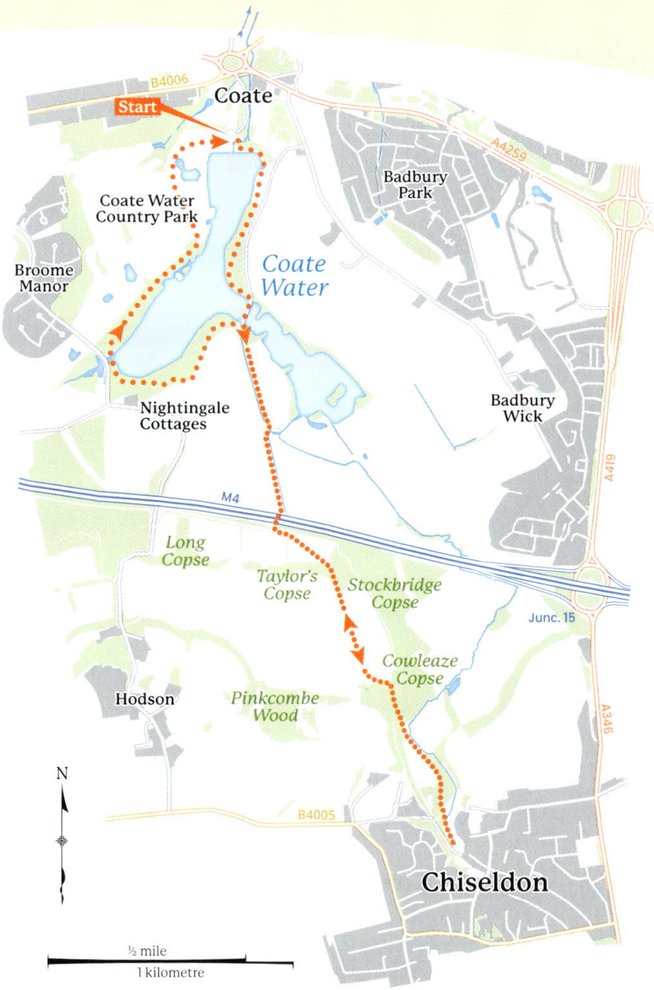
B4006
Coate
Start
A4259
Badbury
Park
Coate Water
Country Park
Broome
Manor
Coate
Water
Nightingale
Cottages
Badbury
Wick
A419
M4
Long
Copse
Taylor's
Copse
Stockbridge
Copse
Junc. 15
Cowleaze
Copse
Hodson
Pinkcombe
Wood
A346
N
B4005
Chiseldon
½ mile
1 kilometre

6 River Cole

Marshgate From Coate Water, the Cole flows underground, buried beneath houses and industrial estates until it emerges at Marshgate in Swindon. At Marshgate, the Cole is a pathetic stream spoilt by rubbish, but it gathers strength as it meanders through the clay fields between Swindon and Shrivenham. It is a big enough to be the county boundary between Wiltshire and Oxfordshire.

Coleshill Another lovely place to explore the Cole is at Coleshill. The National Trust has five circular walks around the estate. Of these, the Red Route has the best riverside walk through the water meadows, towards Strattenborough Castle. This is a farmhouse with a false front of battlements built to enhance the view from Coleshill House. This folly and the windmills (wind turbines) on the horizon evoke the spirit of Don Quixote – it is all an illusion, of course. If you leave the National Trust's route and continue along a bridle path past Strattenborough Castle, you climb up to the wind farm. Continue on to a lane and turn down the hill to find the Cole marking the county boundary at Westmill Bridge. A footpath beside West Mill Farm takes you round the spring-line of a hill to Pennyhooks Brook, 2.5 miles (4km) from Coleshill, where you can admire a stone bridge rebuilt in 2004 in a charming corner of the Vale of White Horse. Return to Coleshill for tea in the café, or at the watermill on one of their open days. When visiting Coleshill, do not miss the chance to look at the Great Coxwell Barn, ideally following a circular walk that includes Badbury Hill when the bluebells are in flower.

Inglesham and Lechlade From Coleshill to Inglesham, the Cole meanders between fields with no footpaths. This peaceful stretch has high banks and reedy corners – perfect for water voles, which are more common (less rare) here than other parts of the Thames Valley. As it nears the Thames, the Cole divides into two channels. One branch turns westward under the A361 road to join the Thames between Upper and Lower Inglesham, where there is a little church, St John the Baptist, conserved by William Morris and his friends. The other branch, which continues the county boundary, goes north for 2 miles (3.2km) to join the Thames near Lechlade at St John's Bridge, opposite the boatyard at the Trout Inn and the mouth of the River Leach. Both channels appear to be natural and are shown on John Speed's County Map of Wiltshire made in the early 17th century. Together with the Thames, they surround an island about 15–20ft (4.6–6m) high where there once stood the medieval village of Inglesham. Other tributaries (the Cherwell, the Colne and the Mole) divide into two streams before they enter the Thames, but the 3 mile (4.8km) distance between the two mouths of the Cole is unusual. The Thames Path follows the Thames riverbank between Lechlade and Upper Inglesham on a section opened in 2018 and links the two ends of the Cole. The upper reaches of the Thames are so lovely in summer that you need no other reason for a visit.

GETTING THERE

OS EXPLORER MAPS | 169 Cirencester & Swindon; 170 Abingdon, Wantage & Vale of White Horse

RESOURCES

Coate Water: *www.swindon.gov.uk/info/20077/parks_and_open_spaces/487/coate_water_park*
Richard Jefferies Society: *www.richardjefferiessociety.org*

Cole enters the Thames at St John's Lock

River Cole at Coleshill

7 River Coln

LENGTH: 20 miles (32km)

SOURCE: Brockhampton

CONFLUENCE: Lechlade

The Coln is very attractive in its upper reaches from Sevenhampton to Fairford, flowing through pretty Cotswold villages, with clear water and populated by trout and water crowfoot. Once past Fairford, the river runs through, and supplies, a collection of old gravel pits where there are few riverside paths in the eastern corner of the Cotswold Water Park.

The source of the Coln

What's in a name?

Ekwall in his book *English River-Names* has no explanation for the name of the Coln, but notes that it has the same sound as another tributary, the Colne, in Middlesex.

ABOVE *The Coln at Bibury*

BELOW *Spotted orchid at Andoversford*

There is a 2.5 mile (4km) walk in the Upper Coln Valley to the source. Sadly, one of the attractions of this walk, the Craven Arms pub in Brockhampton, closed in 2022 and has an uncertain future. The walk begins at Coln Gardens in Station Road in Andoversford, near the bus stop for services from Cheltenham, Oxford and Moreton-in-Marsh. A path crosses the A40 to a track to a water treatment plant. From here, a footpath on the right goes through a meadow, under a disused railway, and leads to Syreford, beside the first mill of the Coln. From Syreford the path goes through a wood and a meadow to Sevenhampton. Beside the ford, there is a sign to St Andrews Church. From the churchyard, which has a beautiful view across the valley, the path descends to the river and climbs to the former brewery and the Craven Arms pub in Brockhampton. Continue to the crossroads in the centre of the village, where Bakers Wood Road leads to a footpath past the field wherein lies the source.

    The river valley between Anderoversford and Yanworth is very attractive where the road follows the curves of the river between green hills. The Romans must have thought so because they built two villas with river views. One of these, Chedworth Roman Villa, belongs to the National Trust and is the starting point for our seventh favourite walk.

WALK 7 Chedworth Roman Villa to Fossebridge

6.5 miles (10.5km)

This walk follows the winding river between sheep pastures and returns in broadleaf woodland. Start at Chedworth Roman Villa. From the car park, go down to the road junction, turn right through a gateway and follow the Monarch's Way footpath at the edge of Chedworth Woods. At the far end of the wood (1 mile/1.6km) turn left along the road, crossing the Coln at Yanworth Mill to a footpath on the right. After another mile, where the path meets a road at a wooden gate, turn right off the Monarch's Way to walk through a field to a road beneath the stately house in Stowell Park.

From here, turn right to re-cross the Coln and find a footpath on the left, which goes through meadows parallel to the river until the footpath meets the road again near Fossebridge. Walk down the lane to Fossebridge, perhaps stopping at the inn which is halfway around the walk. Behind the inn is a footpath up a small valley towards Chedworth. In the hamlet of Pancake Hill, follow the lanes upwards to return to the Monarch's Way again. This leads over the hill, giving excellent views of the Coln catchment area. The Monarch's Way enters Chedworth Woods and descends to the car park where you started.

BELOW *The Cole at Yanworth*

OPPOSITE *The Arlington Row at Bibury*

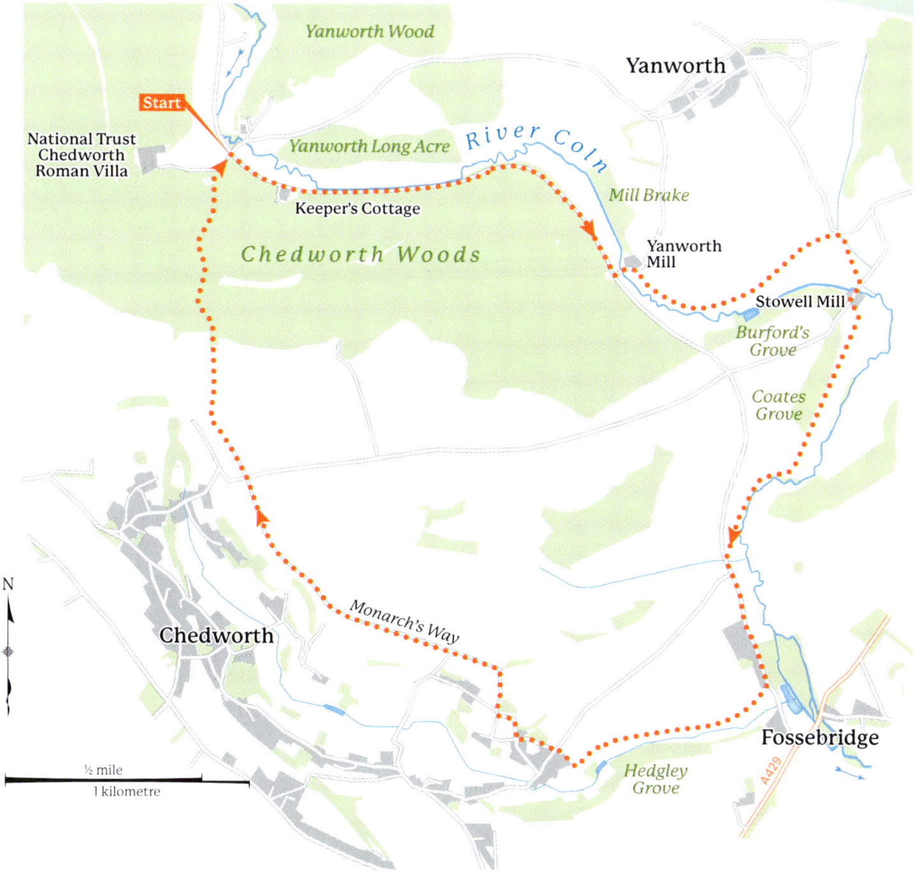
Yanworth Wood
Yanworth
Start
National Trust
Chedworth
Roman Villa
Yanworth Long Acre
River Coln
Mill Brake
Keeper's Cottage
Chedworth Woods
Yanworth
Mill
Stowell Mill
Burford's
Grove
Coates
Grove
N
Monarch's Way
Chedworth
Fossebridge
A429
Hedgley
Grove
½ mile
1 kilometre

7 River Coln

Fossebridge to Coln St Aldwyns The Coln Valley from Fossebridge to Fairford is beautiful, with gorgeous Cotswold villages beside the river. From Coln St Denys (or Dennis) to Ablington, you can find footpaths and quiet lanes to walk down one side of the river and return on the other, through Calcot, Coln Rogers and Winson.

Bibury is pretty, with a marshy island nature reserve lying between the river and a millstream. It is on a bus route between Cirencester, Northleach and Bourton-on-the-Water that links four Thames tributaries (Churn, Coln, Leach and Windrush).

Coln between Bibury and Coln St Aldwyns

WALK 8 Bibury to Coln St Aldwyns

6.5 miles (10.4km)

There is a superb riverside walk from Bibury to Coln St Aldwyns, best on a summer's evening or an autumnal afternoon when low sunlight makes the Cotswold stonework glow. Starting from the main road beside the river in Bibury, the Arlington Row of weavers' cottages at the east end of the island will catch your eye. Walk along the road to the church, which dates from Saxon times, and turn left between cottages to the main road. Turn right and right again to the road to Coln St Aldwyns. After 50 yards (45.7m), a driveway with a public right of way goes past Bibury Court Hotel to Bibury Mill, where you cross the river. The path leads you up through a field to a gateway on your left. As you go through the gate, there is a lovely view down the valley. Follow the path east as it descends gently through a wood to the riverside meadows. In these meadows, Akeman Street (the Roman road from Cirencester to St Albans) crossed the Coln beside a ford close to where a millstream leaves the main river. Continue through a wood and the parkland to the road. Turn left, cross the river and take the path on the left, which crosses the millstream and

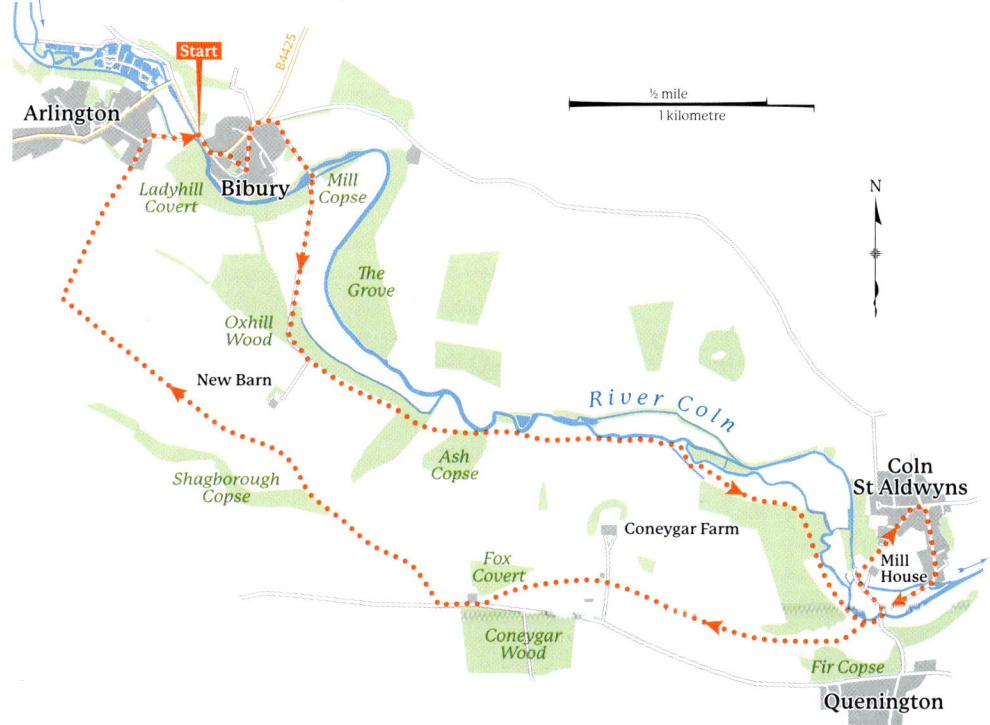

Walk 8

climbs up to a lane between the almshouses and the church. At the crossroads at the top of the lane, turn right around the village shop, which has a popular café. This is the halfway point.

Next, go down the road back to the river, passing a pub on the left side. Cross the bridge and enter the park beside Yew Tree Lodge. Fork left up the path signed as a bridleway. After about a mile (1.6km) you reach a road. Walk 150 yards (137m) to a wide track on the right. Where the track begins to go down, you cross Akeman Street again. At the bottom of the dip is a small stream. After a mile from the stream, turn right at the crossing of paths. This path goes down to Arlington to the aptly named Awkward Hill. At the foot of the hill continue past the weavers' cottages and cross the river on the footbridge to the end of the walk.

Roundhouse at the mouth of the River Coln

Coln St Aldwyns to Fairford and Lechlade

As the river passes Coln St Aldywns, it makes a northerly loop before turning south to Quenington, another attractive village with a pub and a walk in the flood meadows.

Fairford is the main town on the Coln. The car park beside the church is a useful place to start exploring the town and its riverside paths. Walk down High Street, across London Street to Back Street, and you see a sign to the Riverside Path. In 2023, this path was resurfaced to be suitable for wheelchair users as far as Snake Lane. Beyond this, the way is through rough meadows and wet woodlands to a footbridge that offers a circular walk returning by the fields and lane on the west side of the river. On the north side of St Mary's Church, the lane leads down to the Mill and Oxpens. The information at the Oxpens tells you of the Pitham Brook Path upstream to Fairford Park, 0.7 miles (1.1km). There, you can cross the river and walk up to Leafield Road to return to Fairford.

Below Fairford, the Coln becomes lost among the former gravel pits but there are several attractions. Whelford Pools Nature Reserve features short walks to bird hides and information boards. An estate of holiday homes, called The Lakes, on the south side of the A417 road between Fairford and Lechlade, provides wildflower meadows beside the Coln. Nearby, the Roundhouse Lake is a tranquil nature reserve.

Finally, the mouth of the Coln can be seen from the Thames Path by walking from Halfpenny Bridge in Lechlade to the Roundhouse at the entrance to the Thames and Severn Canal. Cross the footbridge over the Thames and you can enjoy a closer look at the last 100 yards (91.4m) of the Coln.

Riverside Park in Fairford

GETTING THERE

BUS SERVICES | Stagecoach 853 Cheltenham to Oxford via Andoversford and Burford; Pulmans Coaches 855 Cirencester to Bibury

OS EXPLORER MAPS | OL 45 The Cotswolds; 169 Cirencester & Swindon; 170 Abingdon, Wantage & the Vale of White Horse; 205 Stratford-upon-Avon & Evesham

RESOURCES

Chedworth Roman Villa: *www.nationaltrust.org.uk/visit/gloucestershire-cotswolds/chedworth-roman-villa*

Walks in Fairford: *www.fairfordtowncouncil.gov.uk/visitors/walks*

8 River Leach

LENGTH: 18 miles (29km)

SOURCE: Hampnett near Northleach

CONFLUENCE: Lechlade

The Leach is an intriguing river because it disappears and reappears along its course. Starting near Northleach, it is a clear, fast-running stream. In dry weather, it seeps underground through limestone rocks near Aldsworth and resurfaces in the meadows above Eastleach Turville. It enters the Thames downstream of Lechlade, the town named after the river.

ABOVE *Spring at Hampnett*

OPPOSITE *Hampnett: the source of the Leach, where the stream flows down the hill*

What's in a name?

According to Ekwall, the name Leach comes from an Anglo-Saxon word meaning 'a river in a bog or marsh', but there are no significant bogs or marshes along its length. Another possibility is that the name is related to the word that means 'to soak', referring to its disappearance underground.

WALK 9 Northleach to Hampnett and Upper End

6.5 miles (10.5km)

Northleach is a good place to start exploring the River Leach. There is parking and a bus stop in the market square, where our walk begins. Go along West End, across the Fosse Way (A429) at the Old Gaol (café and visitor centre), and through the fields to Hampnett (1 mile/1.6km). There you see springs on a grassy slope creating a stream that you can follow as it winds through gardens. Some people may like to turn back to return to Northleach by the lower path through the fields to the Old Gaol. The splendid church 'the cathedral of the Cotswolds' and the Mechanical Music Museum could fill the time while the rest of your party explores further.

From where the path through the gardens joins a farm track, turn right and walk along the Monarch's Way, the long-distance path already encountered by the River Churn at Cirencester. After a mile, you reach a road beside a large mound that is a water reservoir. Turn left to walk along this road that is part of an ancient Salt Way, which has come past the source of the Windrush and goes through

The young river at Northleach

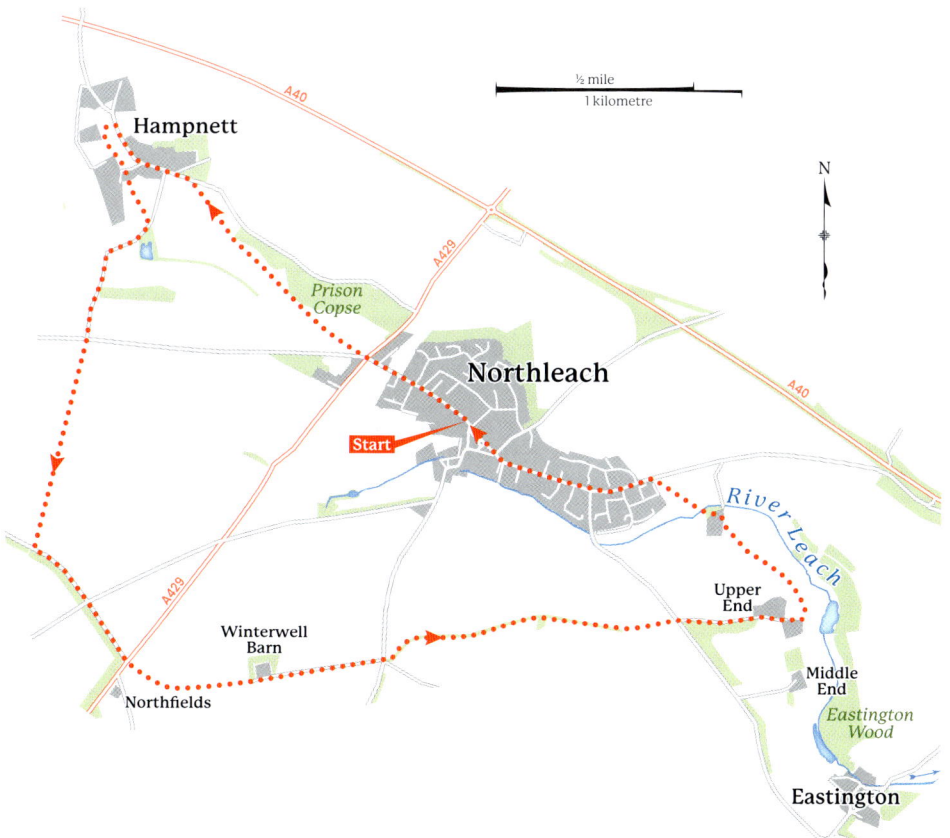

Coln St Aldwyns and on to Lechlade. In less than ½ mile (0.8km) you reach the A429, our old friend the Fosse Way. On the opposite side of the road is a bridleway that passes Winterwell Barn, crosses a minor road on National Cycle Network Route 46, and joins the Diamond Way – a modern long-distance path around the North Cotswolds designed by the Ramblers Association to celebrate the Diamond Jubilee of Queen Elizabeth II in 1995.

Cross the next road to take the lane to Upper End. After the last house, turn left on to a footpath in a field with a view of a small lake formed by the Leach. The path follows the river upstream until you reach the fence of the sewage works. Over the river, take the path that goes up diagonally across the field to the road that goes back into Northleach.

ABOVE *Keble's Bridge, Eastleach*

Lodge Park to Southrop

Lodge Park is on the banks of the Leach and can be combined with a visit to Sherborne and the Windrush (Chapter 9). This National Trust property, south of the A40 near Aldsworth, was created for the sporting gentry in the 18th century. A walk from the Lodge across the parkland has a view of the remains of an ornamental canal in the river valley.

Moving downstream to Sheep Bridge, the riverbed is often dry in summer when the water is flowing underground. Akeman Street goes over the River Leach here – an obvious choice for a crossing place. The river comes to the surface again in the meadows on the east side of the bridge to continue as a normal clear Cotswold stream down to the Eastleach villages.

Eastleach Martin and Eastleach Turville were combined as one parish in 1935 with most of the houses and the pub on the west side of the river. In 1816, John Keble, the famous Oxford clergyman, was a curate here, at the Church of St Michael and St Martin on the centre of a separate parish. A stone clapper bridge between the two villages is sometimes called Keble's Bridge. From Eastleach Turville there is a footpath through the fields on the west side of the river to Southrop, a lovely village, especially where the river runs beside the road and it has a charming pub. A 3 mile (4.8km) circular walk between the Eastleaches and Southrop is formed by returning along the lane past Coate Mill on the east side of the river.

Southrop to Lechlade

There are two routes between Southrop and Lechlade, which can be combined to make a 5 mile (8km) circular walk. If you park in a lay-by on the A361, north of the roundabout at the edge of Lechlade, you can walk up to the bridge over the Leach to find a footpath on your left hand to Southrop. This path runs close to the north-east side of the river. A different route back from Southrop can be found from the church by going through Manor Farm to a footpath that runs beside a paved drive. When you reach a lane, turn left and walk to where the road bends right. Take the footpath that is straight ahead and you can find your way through fields to the Richardson and Amey Nature Reserve. This is close to the roundabout near the lay-by where you parked your car.

Finally, at Lechlade, a popular walk starts at St Lawrence Church. The flagstone path beside the church is called Shelley's Walk after the poet who wrote *A Summer Evening Churchyard* when staying in the town. Go through the churchyard, past the school and straight on until you reach the A417 near St John's Bridge and the Trout Inn. Cross the main road to take the Kelmscott Road with a caravan park on the left side. After ¼ mile (0.4km), you find the Leach again, as it passes through a mill house and under the road. Walk a short distance further towards Kelmscott, and you find a path on your right-hand side, which leads you down to the Thames Path. Go over the footbridge to follow the Thames Path back to Lechlade, crossing the mouth of the Cole on the way.

GETTING THERE

BUS SERVICES | **Lechlade:** from Swindon (no. 64) and Cirencester (no. 877) | **Northleach:** Stagecoach no. S2 between Oxford and Cheltenham; Pulmans Coaches no. 801 between Cheltenham and Moreton-in-Marsh, and no. 853 from Cirencester via Bibury

OS EXPLORER MAP | OL45 The Cotswolds

PART 2

The rivers entering the Thames in Oxfordshire

Bourton on the Water

River Windrush

LENGTH: 40 miles (64km)

SOURCE: Taddington, Gloucestershire

CONFLUENCE: Newbridge, Oxfordshire

The Windrush offers the charm of the tourist honeypots such as Bourton-on-the-Water, an industrial history at Witney, and a more prosaic function as a source of gravel. It features two riverside trails, the Windrush Way and the Windrush Path, offering different landscapes. It has been the subject of more books than other tributaries. Eighty years ago, the author and editor Wilson MacArthur described the pleasures and difficulties of a walking holiday from source to confluence. In modern times, another author, Martin Marais, wrote about his walks beside the river in *Windrush Meander*, a title that accurately conveys the meaning 'winding through rushes'. On a less happy note, it has featured in recent news stories regarding the Windrush Against Sewage Pollution (WASP) campaign.

Upper Windrush

The Windrush starts at Taddington, a hamlet in the Cotswolds, 2 miles (3.2km) south of the picturesque village of Snowshill, which stands on the watershed between the Thames Valley and the Vale of Evesham. We found running water under a footbridge (grid reference SP 087306) that carries the Winchcombe Way south from the village of Taddington to Cutsdean. Following this path past Cutsdean Church, you reach Ford, where the Windrush is a clear stream running under the B4077 road between Stow-on-the-Wold and Tewksbury. There is a circular walk of 10 miles (16km) on the Warden's Way from Bourton-on-the-Water through Lower and Upper Slaughter to Naunton and returning on the Windrush Way,

What's in a name?

In Anglo-Saxon charters of the 10th century the river name appears as Wenris and Waenric. This has been interpreted as 'white fen', which could describe the water meadows near the village of Windrush.

Footbridge at Cutsdean, near source

which has been described by the Ordnance Survey as one of the best 100 walks in Britain.

The Windrush flows under the Fosse Way into Bourton-on-the-Water, where there is a good bus service and many attractions. Sitting beside the river in the central park where small stone bridges arch over the clear waters of the river is a great place for people watching. Alternatively, follow the river east, and you find the famous model village, a maze and Birdland. Greystones Farm Nature Reserve with a reconstruction of an Iron Age dwelling (Salmonsbury) is also on the east side of the village, at SP 176 208. This is a quiet spot, less than a mile (1.6km) from the village centre. From Greystones Farm, you can follow the River Dikker downstream by walking south along the Diamond Way to its junction with the Windrush at SP 187 179.

Sherbourne and Windrush

The next section of the Windrush to explore is at Sherbourne and Windrush villages. Sherbourne Park belongs to the National Trust and offers well-marked paths that lead from the car park (SP 143 158) down to the village, with views of the Sherbourne stream flowing to join the Windrush river near the village of Windrush.

WALK 10 Sherbourne to Windrush village

5 miles (8km)

This is a favourite walk because it is quieter than other places in the Windrush valley. It is where we were walking on the November morning mentioned at the start of this book. That day, we saw a barn owl hunting and a white hart (pale fallow deer) grazing to reward our early start.

For this walk, park at Northfield Barn (SP 176 155) where the National Trust has useful information boards and leaflets about the water meadows. Take the bridle path east through fields and marshes to the river for 1 mile (1.6km). If you have time, it is worth exploring the side paths to see more of the meadows and the network of channels used

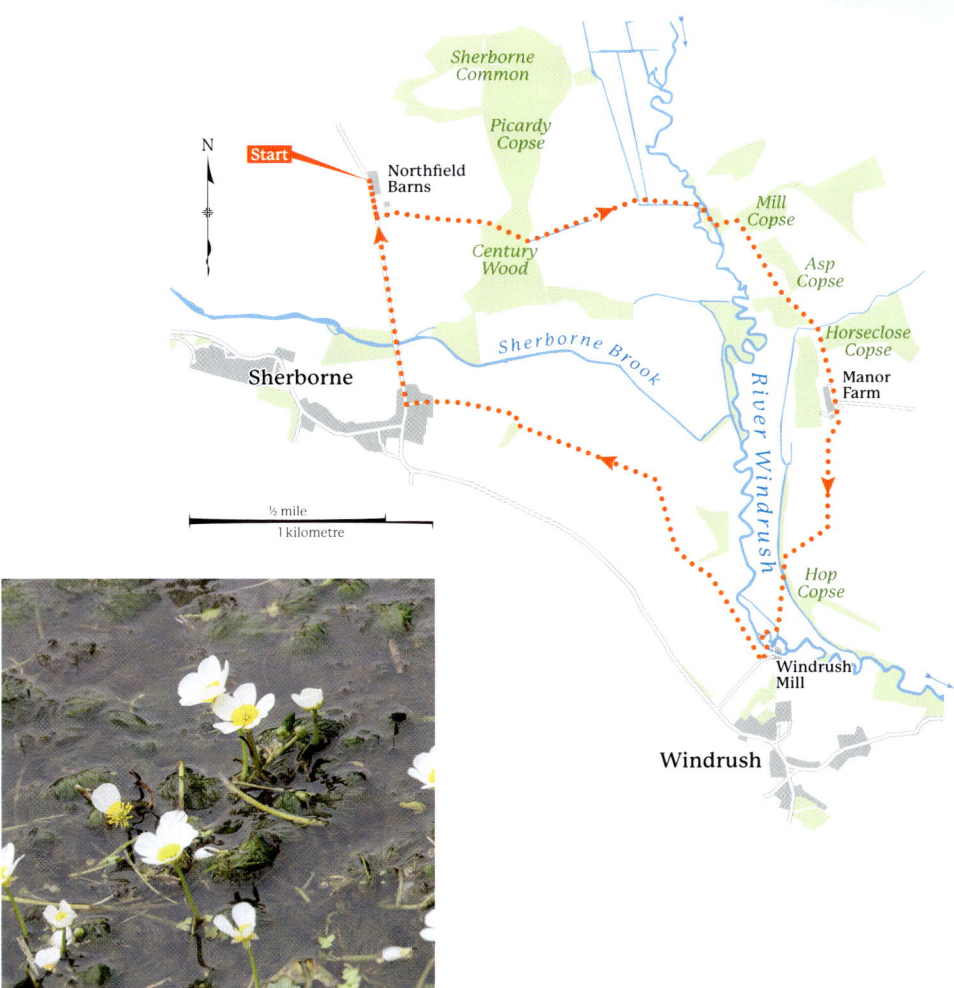

OPPOSITE *Sluice in Sherbourne Water Meadows*

ABOVE *Water Crowsfoot flowers*

to control water levels. Across the river, walk south passing Manor Farm, which features restored stone work. The stones from quarries along this part of the river were used for building the Oxford University colleges. After a second mile, you approach Windrush Mill, where you cross the river. When you reach the driveway to the mill, take the footpath on the right-hand side. Along this path, there are good views down to the river. With soft grass beneath your feet, sheep in the fields, larks in the sky, you realise why walking in the Cotswolds is much loved. The path ends between houses beside the road that leads back to the car park. If you are ready for refreshment, the village shop in Sherbourne serves teas. The nearest pub is The Fox, beside the river in Little Barrington.

9 River Windrush

Burford Burford has good shops, eating places and beautiful buildings, making it a busy tourist destination. To escape the crowds, there is a good 10 mile (16km) riverside walk from Burford to Minster Lovell and Witney. The bus service between Burford and Witney makes this linear walk easy to organise. Beginning at the bridge in Burford, go past St John's Church to Witney Road, and along this minor road to find a footpath at about ¾ mile (1.2km). Cross a stile into a field and follow the river for 1 mile (1.6km) before heading up to the road into Widford. Turn left to cross the river and find a path beside the St Oswald's Church to Swinbrook, 2.5 miles (4km).

Pause to look at the unusual Fettiplace memorials inside the church before passing through the village to find a stone stile and footpath before the Swan Inn beside the bridge. After three fields, you reach the bridge at Asthall. Cross it and maybe go into the village to find the pub, the Maytime Inn, open all day. Asthall Manor has a sculpture exhibition in its gardens in mid-summer. Akeman Street passed through the village, sadly leaving no signs of its existence. The bridle path beside Astall Farm goes to Worsham. Cross the river again to reach the path beside a cottage, which leads to Minster Lovell, nearly 7 miles (11.3km) from Burford.

BELOW *Flooded meadows near Burford*

OPPOSITE *The Old Mill at Lower Slaughter, near Bourton on the Water*

WALK 11 Minster Lovell to Crawley

3.5 miles (5.6km)

This circular walk uses the next part of the way from Burford to Witney. Start at Wash Meadow beside the river in Minster Lovell and walk round the cricket field and through the next meadow to reach the church and the ruins of Minster Lovell Hall. Go down to, and across, the river, to a path in wet woodland. The footpath climbs up the side of the valley, across a lane and drops down to give a view of Crawley New Mill. This large fulling mill was part of the blanket-making industry for which Witney was famous. For the circular walk, go down to Crawley Bridge, where you can see an old mill converted into workshops for arts and crafts. In Crawley village, Farm Lane leads to a track back to Minster Lovell. The Lamb Inn in Crawley and the Old Swan Hotel at Minster Lovell are popular lunch places.

Ruins at Minster Lovell

Crawley
½ mile
1 kilometre
N
Minster Lovell
Mill
River Windrush
Start
Maggots
Grove
Hill Grove
Farm
B4047
Minster Lovell

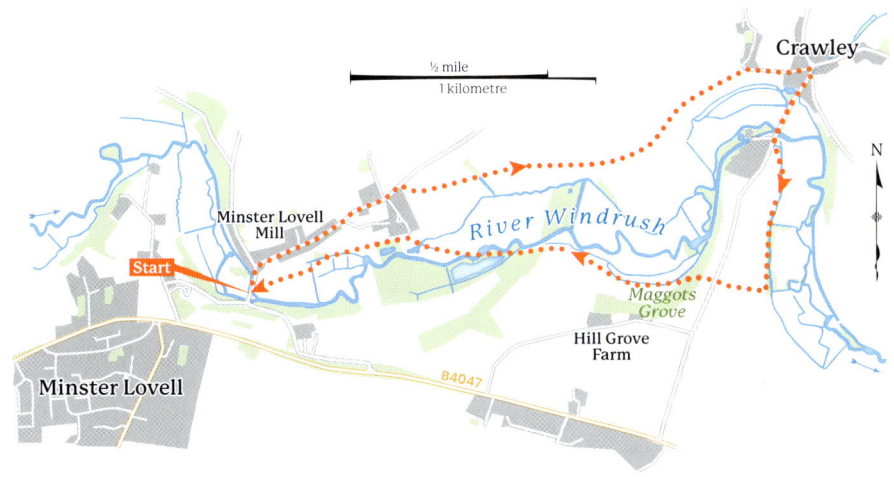

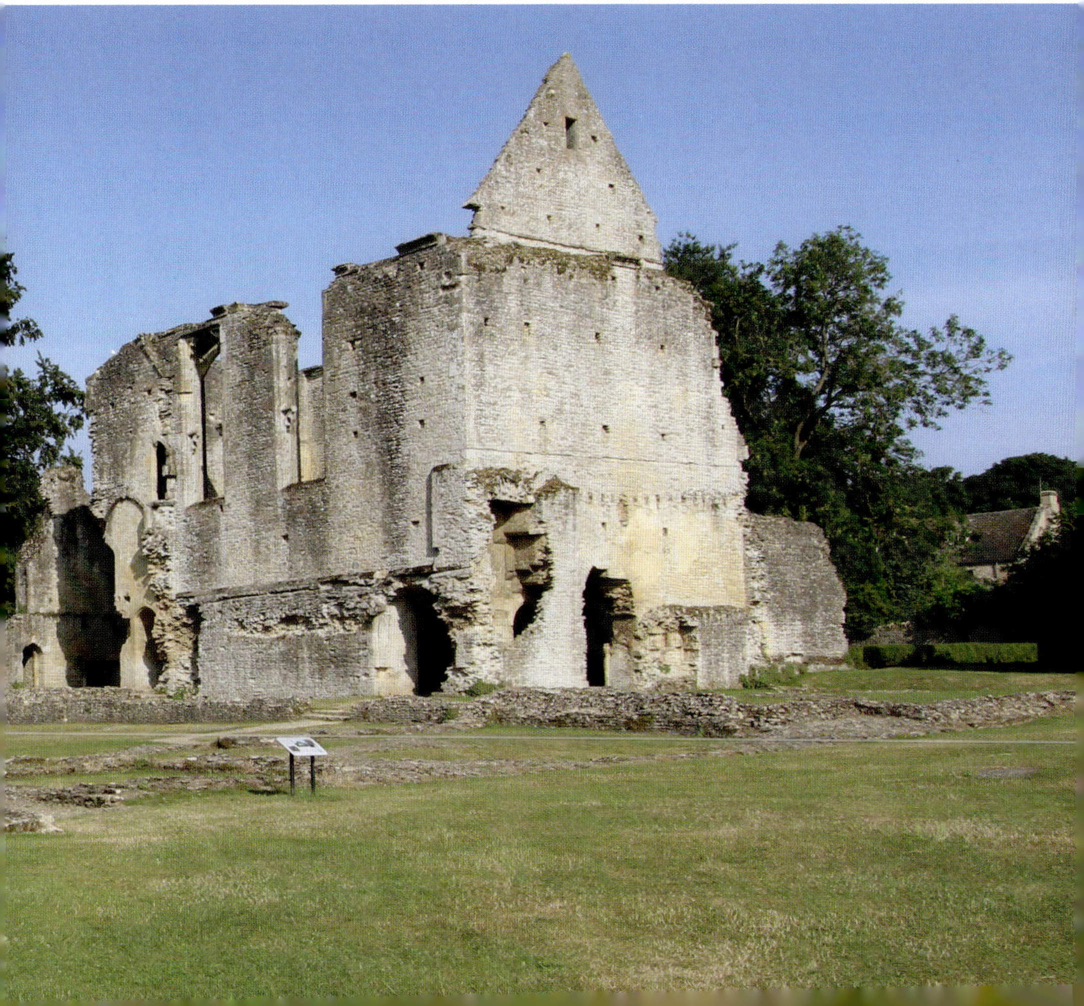

Witney to Newbridge To reach Witney, walk down to Crawley New Mill and stay on the south side of the river to follow a path through the flood meadows to the old bathing place, sadly in disrepair. Here, you enter Witney, where the old blanket mills have been converted into flats. It is a short distance along Mill Street to the central shops, cafés, pubs and bus stops.

In Witney, the Windrush divides into two streams near Cogges Manor Farm, a museum of rural life. The streams reunite 5 miles (8km) south at Standlake, enclosing a space that is occupied by gravel pits. The Lower Windrush Valley Project has developed nature reserves and walks in the area. One of the best is the Gin Mill circular walk (5 miles/8km) that explores this area, starting at Rushy Common car park (OX29 6UJ).

The final part of the river can be explored by having lunch in Rose Revived, the Maybush at Newbridge, or the Black Horse in Standlake, and taking an afternoon walk along the Windrush Path and back (3.5 miles/5.6km). Or, stand on Newbridge – actually the second oldest bridge across the Thames – and look at the Windrush flowing into the Thames.

ABOVE *Windrush near Cogges Farm, Witney*

GETTING THERE

BUS SERVICES | Pulhams Coaches no. 801 from Cheltenham and Moreton-in-Marsh; Stagecoach S1 and S2 Oxford to Witney; Swanbrook 853 Oxford to Burford

OS EXPLORER MAPS | OL 45 The Cotswolds; 180 Oxford, Witney & Woodstock

RESOURCES

Childs, Mark, *The Windrush Valley: A guide to the river, towns and villages* (Amberley Publishing, 2010)

Harris, Mollie, *Where the Windrush Flows: And will forever flow* (Alan Sutton Publishing Co., 1989)

Gin Mill circular walk: *www.oxfordshire.gov.uk/sites/default/files/file/countryside-walks-rides/GillMill_CircularWalk.pdf*

Lower Windrush Valley Project: *www.oxfordshire.gov.uk/residents/environment-and-planning/countryside/lower-windrush-valley-project/what-we-do*

MacArthur, Wilson, *The River Windrush* (Cassell, 1946)

Marais, Martin, *Windrush Meander: A walk along the River Windrush from source to the Thames* (Lulu.com and Amazon (Kindle), 2021)

Ordnance Survey, *100 Outstanding British Walks – Pathfinder Guidebook* (OS, 2018)

Windrush Against Sewage Pollution: *www.windrushwasp.org*

Witney Information Centre: Welch Way, Witney, OX28 6JH, T: 01993 775802)

Newbridge

Upsteam view of the Old Mill at Lower Slaughter

River Evenlode

LENGTH: 25 miles (40km)

SOURCE: Moreton-in-Marsh

CONFLUENCE: near Eynsham

The Evenlode rises at **Moreton-in-Marsh** in Gloucestershire and flows for 25 miles (40km) to join the Thames near Eynsham. The upper Evenlode features a broad valley and a meandering course through clay. The valley narrows between limestone hills in its middle section before the Evenlode is joined by the Glyme, its main tributary, at Bladon on to the flood plain of the Thames.

The railway from Oxford to Hereford follows the river as far as Moreton-in-Marsh and is useful for walkers exploring the river. The stations at Moreton, Kingham, Charlbury, Long Hanborough and Oxford are about 6 miles (9.7km) apart and have a regular service. Two long-distance footpaths, the Diamond and Oxfordshire Ways, give walkers a delightful route to wander between the villages along the valley, although the distances are twice as far as the crow flies (and the railway line). The National Cycle Network Route 442 between Long Hanborough and Moreton-in-Marsh is another good way of exploring the Evenlode valley along quiet roads.

Moreton-in-Marsh to Bledington

The Evenlode begins in the ditches in Blenheim Meadow on the east side of Moreton-in-Marsh railway station. The stream flows south through flat fields to Bledington, close to Kingham station. Its early course can be followed by the Diamond Way, which starts at St David's Church in the centre of Moreton-in-Marsh. It is not well signposted but is clearly shown

What's in a name?

The Evenlode was called the Bladene in the early Middle Ages, a name associated with the villages of Bladon and Bledington. The present name, meaning 'Eowla's river crossing', is taken from an Anglo-Saxon village near the source where Eowla was the headman of the village.

Bus shelter at Adlestrop

on Ordnance Survey maps. In Moreton, the route is better marked as the Moreton Eight. The Diamond Way goes south through farmland and water meadows before turning east to cross the river and the railway to reach Evenlode village. In Evenlode, leave the Diamond Way and use the minor road (National Cycle Network Route 442) directly to Adlestrop. In the village, see the station name board, which has become a memorial to the war poet, Edward Thomas, whose famous work *Adlestrop* describes a peaceful rural scene in June 1914. Past the church, take the path that goes past a chain of lakes at Adlestrop House and stay on National Cycle Network Route 442 until you reach Daylesford. The farm shop at Daylesford specialises in organic foods and has a café. From here, the Diamond Way follows the Evenlode to Bledington, where the river is big enough to power a watermill beside the B4450 road to Kingham station.

10 River Evenlode

ABOVE *The Oxfordshire Way crossing the Evenlode between Shipton and Ascott under Wychwood*

Bledington to Charlbury In Bledington, the Oxfordshire Way is well signposted and is an excellent route to Charlbury. After walking in open fields with good views of the river valley, the Way enters the wood in Foxholes Nature Reserve, where the bluebells are lovely in spring.

The Oxfordshire Way crosses the grounds of Bruern Abbey and reaches the A361 road, on the edge of Shipton-under-Wychwood. Instead of entering Shipton, the Way and the river turn east to Ascott-under-Wychwood, a pretty village with a good pub, the Swan.

The Way passes Ascott's station but there is only one train a day in each direction that stops here – the so-called Parliamentary train service. From here, the Way passes through Dean Grove (part of the Wychwood Forest) and goes along Water Lane to Charlbury. The Wychwood Forest is a huge attraction for walkers and there is a major festival in Cornbury Park every summer. There are several local circular walks designed as part of the Wychwood Project, with one close to the river in Cornbury Park on the way to Finstock.

WALK 12 Charlbury, Chilson and Pudlicote

7 miles (11.3km)

Start at Church Street (parking and bus stop in Charlbury) and walk through the churchyard to Church Lane. Turn left at Forest Road (B4437) to go downhill, over the river, past the station (an alternative starting point) and up to a no through road signed to Walcot on the right side. The entrance to the road has impressive stone pillars and there is a splendid view of the valley, railway and river. The road becomes a bridleway, which has been enhanced by planting hedgerow trees. After 2.5 miles (4km), you come to Shorthampton. Visit the exquisite tiny church with wall paintings and box pews; rated as one of the 100 best churches in Oxfordshire.

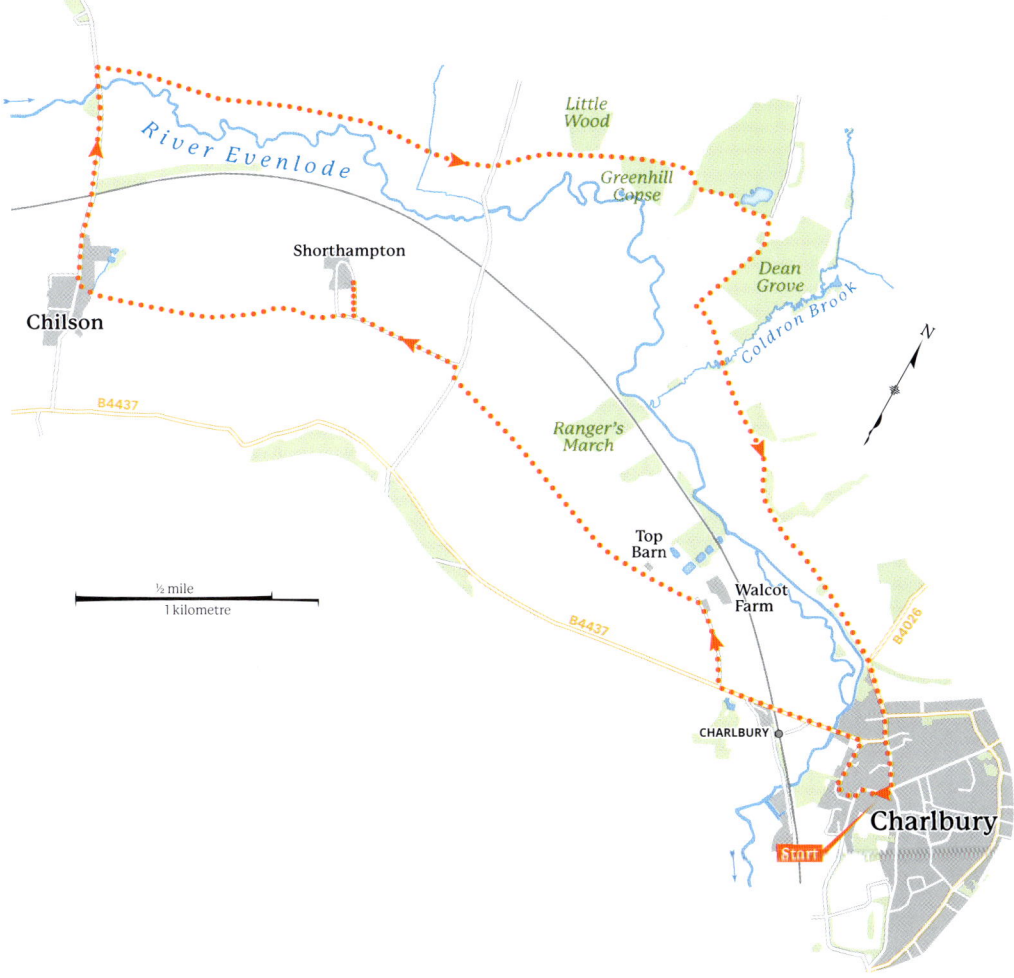

87

Walk 12

Continue on the bridleway to Chilson and turn right to go down the lane to the river at Pudlicote. The handsome Publicote House was built in 1810 on the site of a Roman villa – one of several in this valley. The Oxfordshire Way back to Charlbury follows a beautiful stretch of the Evenlode, with rows of pollarded willow trees. Further east, you walk beside a huge reedbed planted within a restoration scheme for the natural removal of pollutants from rivers. After Catsham Lane, you pass through woodland and have to climb several stiles to Water Lane, where there is a wild swimming place in the river. The walk ends by climbing up Pound Hill, where there is a great café.

This walk can be shortened by crossing the river at Catsham Bridge, or lengthened by going to Ascott-under-Wychwood (11 miles/17.7km).

Bathing place at Charlbury

Charlbury to the confluence
To the east of Charlbury, the Oxfordshire Way is less useful for exploring the River Evenlode, but there are some attractive places to visit. One of these is the Roman Villa at East End, which has been a favourite walk for many years.

WALK 13 East End Roman Villa

3.5 miles (5.6km)

From the A4095 in North Leigh, follow the signs to the villa near East End. There is space to park beside the road at the top of the bridle path (SP 396151). After walking to the villa, which is open throughout the year, find a footpath on the north side of the villa that goes down to the river beside a railway bridge. Follow the path under the railway, cross the river and turn left. Notice the outcrop of limestone, of the sort that made Stonesfield famous for roofing slates. Walking through the field, you are likely to hear ravens and to see red kites and sometimes a buzzard. They roost in the pine trees on the hill above the path. The next section of footpath, which opened in 2018, continues up the river by the quaintly named Bagg's Bottom to the footbridge and ford, where the Oxfordshire Way and Akeman Street meet. This is an ideal picnic spot.

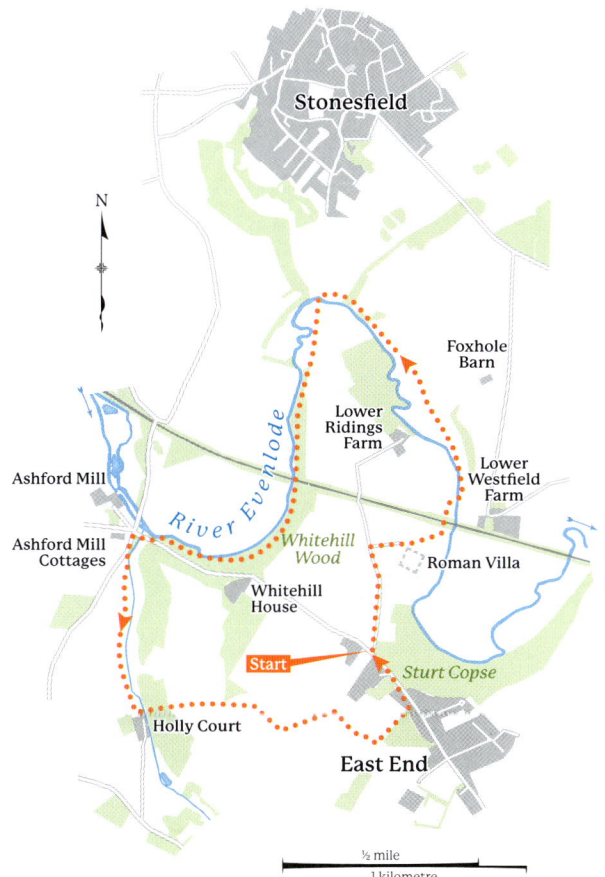

Bridge and Ford near Stonesfield

Walk 13

A short way back is along the bridle path from the ford that climbs gently up beside the villa. The longer way goes beside the river in Whitehill Wood to Ashford Bridge. At the crossroads, a bridleway goes to Holly Court Farm, where the verges are carpeted with snowdrops in February. At the farm, turn left, climbing the track beneath beech trees. The path zigzags around fields to East End. Take the path to the road in the village and turn left to return to the lay-by where you started.

Roman Villa and view of the Evenlode valley near East End

East End to the Thames Among the other local attractions is Combe Mill, the sawmill for timber at Blenheim Estate. Originally water powered and then steam driven, the mill is now an industrial museum on the banks of the Evenlode. Run by volunteers, it is open on Wednesdays and Sundays in summer, with steam engines in operation on the third Sunday of the month. It is a joy for children of all ages.

A circular walk from Eynsham village crosses the busy A40 to Mill Lane, which leads to Eynsham Mill. The mill was built in 1800 to make paper for the Clarendon Press in Oxford. What remains is a beautiful house looking south across the river and meadows, with a long rectangular pond. From here, a footpath goes downriver and across the A40 to Wharf Farm with Cassington Mill and its canal from the river. The way back to Eynsham is along a quiet lane called Cassington Road.

Chillbrook is a minor tributary that runs through Eynsham and enters the Thames 1 mile (1.6km) above the mouth of the Evenlode. Its lower part beside the Talbot Inn on the B4044 near Swinford Bridge is called the Wharf Stream. The stream is now navigable in a small boat or punt, but once held barges carrying coal for the villages of West Oxfordshire. A footpath goes beside the pub to follow the stream towards the Thames. The path crosses the stream and a field to the weir at Eynsham Lock on the Thames. From the lock, a footpath goes through a meadow directly back to the Talbot making a walk of about 1 mile (1.6km).

The Glyme The Glyme is a large tributary of the Evenlode. Its source is close to Glyme Farm near Chipping Norton and it joins the Evenlode on the southern edge of Blenheim Park at Bladon. Its name is said to mean 'bright water' and its water is indeed clearer than the Evenlode. It has cut a narrow, steep-sided valley, which is suited to the creation of ornamental lakes at Old Chalford, Cleveley, Kiddington, Glympton and most famously at Blenheim Park, designed by the landscape architect, Lancelot 'Capability' Brown.

The river can be followed using the Glyme Valley Walk for 16 miles (25.7km) from Chipping Norton to Woodstock. This walk is conveniently served by the buses along the A44 road. It can be divided into sections at Enstone (5 miles/8km, including pubs, shops and buses); at Kiddington (8 miles/12.9km, near a bus stop); and at Wootton (12 miles/19.3km, including a pub and shop). The route uses the Shakespeare Way from Chipping Norton to Cleveley, which is marked by stickers on the footpath signs. Elsewhere, the route is not well marked and a map is needed to choose the right footpaths. But the effort is rewarded with splendid views and much of interest on the way. There are grand houses and parks at Kiddington, Glympton and Woodstock, plus stone-built villages, mills and churches. Near the source, Glyme Valley Nature Reserve (SP 334 260) has south-facing sloping grassland, which provides excellent habitat for wildflowers. The path at Lipstone goes through a private woodland nature reserve climbing up from the river to fields beside the A44 road. On the south side of Wootton, the Long Meadow Nature Reserve is typical of the landscape beside the Thames tributaries that run from the Cotswolds. They feature sinuous rivers amid lush pastures grazed by cattle and sheep, overhung by copses of hawthorn, ash and oak and

The lake in Blenheim Park

Sign at the Confluence

punctuated by limestone. The Glyme Valley Walk crosses Akeman Street and the Oxfordshire Way before entering Woodstock along a track, which is part of National Cycle Network Route 5.

Blenheim Palace is a well-known tourist attraction where the public paths offer 4 miles (6.4km) of peaceful walking through lakeside pastures and woods. The lake is beautiful throughout the year, shining in a carefully designed landscape. One of the best vantage points is beside Rosamund's Well, which is a reminder that the history of this park goes back to the reign of King Henry II in the 12th century. The gates in Old Woodstock and at Combe Lodge give access to these paths, which include parts of the Wychwood, Oxfordshire and Shakespeare Ways.

GETTING THERE

BUS SERVICE | Stagecoach S3, Oxford to Charlbury and Chipping Norton

TRAIN SERVICE | Great Western Railways, Oxford to Moreton-in-the-Marsh and Hereford

OS EXPLORER MAPS | OL 45 The Cotswolds; 180 Oxford, Witney & Woodstock; 191 Banbury, Bicester & Chipping Norton

RESOURCES

Foxhole Nature Reserve: *www.oxfordshirecotswolds.org/things-to-do/attractions/foxholes-nature-reserve-p855501*

Glyme Valley Way: *www.oxfordshire.gov.uk/cms/content/glyme-valley-way*

Wychwood Circular Walks: *www.oxfordshire.gov.uk/cms/content/wychwood-circular-walks*

Wychwood Project: *www.wychwoodproject.org*

River Cherwell

LENGTH: 40 miles (64.4km)

SOURCE: Charwelton near Daventry

CONFLUENCE: Oxford

The Cherwell is the most northerly and one of the longest of the Thames tributaries. It provides a mixture of rural tranquillity, industrial and military history, water meadows and glorious views of the Oxford colleges. It can be followed by footpaths for most of its length, with public transport for return journeys. A narrow boat hired from companies in Oxford, Heyford, Twyford or Banbury can give a week of exploration along the Oxford Canal, which is close to the Cherwell between Cropredy and Thrupp.

The Jurassic Way follows the River Cherwell through Charwelton, Woodford Halse, Chipping Warden and Edgecote to Wardington (12 miles/19.3km). The Way passes the site of the Battle of Edgecote Moor (1469) and Edgecote House, where King Charles I stayed before the battle of Edgehill in 1642. The villages feature pubs, shops and a bus service (200) along the A361, and the churches and stone-built cottages are lovely. The construction of the HS2 railway building has blighted the landscape temporarily – restoration is promised.

From Wardington to Cropredy, where the Cherwell meets the Oxford Canal, the Battlefields Trail has fine views. Walk down the gentle slope to Cropredy Bridge (1.5 miles/2.4km) to where, in June 1644, King Charles I was attacked across the Cherwell as he moved his army from Banbury to Daventry.

What's in a name?

The name is often pronounced Charwell in Oxford and Cherwell in Banbury. It is obviously derived from the name of the village at its source. Ekwall suggested that Char might come from the Anglo-Saxon cear meaning 'hollow'.

WALK 14 Charwelton and Hellidon

4 miles (6.4km)

A super circular walk from **Charwelton** on the A361 road to the hilltop village of Hellidon finds the streams that create the Cherwell. Starting at the Fox and Hounds pub in the main street of Charwelton, walk towards Daventry to the Packhorse Bridge, where the infant Cherwell flows under an ancient stone footbridge. Turn left on the clearly signed Jurassic Way footpath to Hellidon (1.5 miles/2.4km). As you climb, the water in the ditches beside you flows down to begin the Cherwell, and looking south beyond the hill with a tall radio beacon lies the catchment of the Thames. Passing the top of Windmill Hill, you look down into the catchment of the River Severn. The ponds that you see on the way across the field to Hellidon are the source of the River Leam, which flows via the (Warwickshire) Avon. To the east, beyond the two humps of Arbury and Sharman's Hills, is the source of the River Nene, which runs north-east to the Wash. This feels like the centre of England!

Packhorse Bridge at Charwelton

Walk 14

Pause for refreshment at the Red Lion pub in Hellidon and walk east along the lane towards Catersby. Soon after a bend in the lane, take the bridleway on the right, close to the remains of the Great Central Railway. The most visible remains are the airshafts that look like small towers above the Catesby Tunnel. The path follows the line of the tunnel. When you are close to Charwelton, you see workshops at the entrance to the tunnel, which is now used for testing the air resistance of cars. The walk ends by following the Jurassic Way into Charwelton.

BELOW *Castle Quay at Banbury*

OPPOSITE *Airshaft at Catesby Tunnel*

Cropredy to Banbury
The towpath of the Oxford Canal between Cropredy and Thrupp is the obvious way to discover the Cherwell Valley. Cropredy is a lively place, with a major annual folk music festival held there each August, but walking from there to Banbury is disappointing. The landscape is flat, the river small, the noise of the M40 motorway unavoidable. It is better when you reach the Spiceball Country Park, a green space where you can walk beside the river in the north-east corner of Banbury. 'Spiceball' comes from the tasty meat faggots made by a local butcher, Thomas Hankinson, a mayor of Banbury who donated land for the recreation of the poor in the late 19th century.

The canal towpath at Castle Quay in central Banbury is a smart waterside area, with Toomey's Boatyard, the canal museum, shops and cafés all close to car parks, buses and the rail station.

Banbury to Thrupp
South of Banbury, the River Cherwell marks the boundary between Oxfordshire and Northamptonshire. The river valley is well defined by the ironstone hills which give a distinctive reddish colour to the buildings. Ironstone was mined at King's Sutton when the railway took the ore to smelters in the Midlands. The railway between Oxford and Banbury has stations at Tackley, Lower Heyford and King's Sutton that can be useful for walks along the canal towpath. For a walk with a return by train, try Banbury to King's Sutton (4 miles/6.4km). Start by taking the canal towpath from Banbury station to Twyford Wharf. Go a short distance on the road east to cross the river and take the footpath through the fields to King's Sutton. The magnificent church spire will guide you.

River Cherwell

The village has a rich history, from St Rumbold (born and died in AD 622) to Olga Kevelos, the champion motorcyclist (1923–2009). You can enjoy lunch in the village, admire the church and manor house, and rest on the train journey back.

From Ayhno south, the Cherwell valley is free of the M40 motorway noise and becomes more delightful to explore. Four circular walks use the canal towpath in one direction. The first starts at the small village of Clifton near Deddington. Walk down the main road to County Bridge over the Cherwell, where the river ceases to be the county boundary. On the far side of the river, a bridle path goes across fields to Wharf Farm on the canal. The fields are managed as wet grassland where lapwings and curlews have nests. As you walk, you get a good view of the railway viaduct at Aynho. At the canal, walk along the towpath to Somerton canal bridge. There is roadside parking space here, often used by fishermen. Somerton Church is ornamented with memorials to the Fermor family. From Somerton canal bridge, walk west along the

The Cherwell at Somerton Pool

Canal and railway at Lower Heyford

road, crossing several side channels of the river to the mill at North Aston. A bridle path back to Clifton starts on the right (north side) of the road, above Mill Cottage, signed as the Cherwell Valley Walk. When the Cherwell Valley Walk turns sharply left (west), nearly a mile (1.3km) past Mill Cottage, continue straight on in a copse to a bridle path crossing a small bridge (Bowman's), which leads straight back to Clifton and a well-deserved meal in the Duke of Cumberland's Head.

The Cherwell Valley Walk (14 miles/22.5km) starts at Lower Heyford where there is immediate access from the railway station, a bus service and the boat centre. The figure-of-eight walk goes north through the villages of Steeple and Middle Aston, crosses the valley to Somerton, and loops around North Aston before returning. It is described in a leaflet produced by the Bicester Local History Society (Resources). Steeple Aston is the largest village with a shop, pub and bus services.

One of the loveliest parts of the walk is the middle of the figure-of-eight along an old causeway across the valley floor from Grange Farm to the canal. The river forms a pool under an old oak and a nearby weir is evidence that Somerton Mill once stood here.

11 River Cherwell

The northern part of the walk feels more remote, but refreshment can be found at the Yurt Café in Nicholson's Garden Centre at North Aston.

The Bicester Local History Society also describes a shorter circular walk of 2 miles (3.2km) from Lower to Upper Heyford, which goes along a strip of land between the river and canal to Allen's Lock and returns to the Bell Inn in Lower Heyford. This can be extended to 4 miles (6.4km) by continuing beside the canal to Northbrook Lock. At the lock, cross the lock gate to find a stile at the top of the bank, turn left though a gate and across a field to a stile to find a bridleway that runs back to Lower Heyford. Where this path runs along the ridge above the river valley, there are splendid views across to Rousham and Steeple Aston. The fourth circular canalside walk is a favourite described on pages 102 and 3.

Thrupp to Oxford Thrupp is a popular canalside hamlet with two pubs, a tea room and a canoe hire centre. Walk beside the canal towards Shipton-on-Cherwell to see the Cherwell river below you on your right side. At Shipton, there is a path across the canal bridge that leads you over the Cherwell on a small suspension footbridge, under the

Oxford Canal at Thrupp

Cherwell Boathouse

railway and up to Hampton Gay church and ruined manor house. The railway bridge was the scene of a terrible accident on Christmas Eve 1874, in which 34 people died.

At Thrupp, the river leaves the canal to curve east around Kidlington and close to Islip, where it is joined by the River Ray. As the Cherwell approaches Oxford, it passes Water Eaton Manor, originally Tudor but restored in a Gothic style in 1890, and Cuttleslowe Park, which has a community woodland and wildlife areas, as well as playgrounds and sports pitches. Close to the A40 northern bypass is Sunnymead Park, which is a useful place to launch a canoe – a super way to explore the lower reaches of the Cherwell. For those people on foot, the cycleway beside the A40 takes you over the Cherwell to a footpath starting close to a lay-by. This path goes through fields to the Victoria Arms in Marston, a popular destination for people punting upstream from the Cherwell Boathouse in Summertown.

From the Victoria Arms, the footpath continues on the east side of the river, passing Wolfson College and the Cherwell Boathouse. Further on, after passing the Dragon School and Lady Margaret Hall, is a bridge arching above the river into University Parks, where you can continue downstream to Parson's Pleasure, a swimming place beside a weir and boat rollers to allow punts to go upstream. The Cherwell divides into three channels, and the middle one, known locally as Mesopotamia, can be followed to a former mill and a lane that goes to Marston Road beside the Islamic Studies Centre. The next short section of the Cherwell has to be viewed either from the water or from the gardens of Magdalen College. There are punts for hire at Magdalen Bridge.

The last part of the Cherwell has a fine riverside walk from the Rose Lane entrance into Christ Church Meadow down to the Thames. The river divides into two channels, creating an island with the college boathouses on the banks of the Thames. The walk continues besides the upper channel and upstream beside the Thames, where you are rewarded with a view of the Salter's Steamers opposite an avenue that leads to Christ Church. Stunning fritillaries and cowslips can be seen along the verges of the avenue. Deer and long-horned cattle graze in the marshy centre of the Meadow.

WALK 15 Kirtlington

5 miles (8km)

Our favourite of the four walks in the Cherwell Valley starts at the Green in Kirtlington. Start at the Green in Kirtlington. From the top of Mill Lane, walk along Crowcastle Lane, signed as a bridle path to Lower Heyford, which goes north along the ridge to Northbrook. At about ⅓ mile (0.5km) the lane crosses Akeman Street at a place called Peter's Cross. After 1.5 miles (2.4km) you reach a high wall that enclosed a garden, all that remains of Northbrook House, which was demolished in 1750 as part of the construction of Kirtlington Park, another of the works of Lancelot 'Capability' Brown.

Beside the walled garden, turn left to the canal and river where an attractive stone bridge spans both. You cannot reach the canal from the stone bridge, so walk back on a footpath above the canal for a short distance to Northbrook Lock. Cross the lock gates to the canal

Oxford Canal at Kirtlington

towpath and go south for 2.5 miles (4km). The canal has reeds along its banks, and the river flows close by. It is a lovely riverside walk, with more treats in store. At the next lock, Pigeons, the circular walk is completed by crossing over the bridge and walking up Mill Lane back to your starting point. But there are two diversions on the way. First, the Oxfordshire Way signed to Tackley (nearest rail station) curls round the back of the three houses and gives you views of the beautiful garden of the large mill house amid the channels of the Cherwell. Second, along Mill Lane to Kirtlington, you pass a small farm that sometimes serves teas.

Finally, there is Kirtlington Quarry, a local nature reserve. Jurassic limestone cliffs, woodland paths, views over the valley and canalside picnic spots make this a great place for children to explore.

11 River Cherwell

Otmoor and the River Ray To escape the bustle of central Oxford, visit Otmoor beside the Ray, which joins the Cherwell near Islip. You can reach Islip by train from Oxford and Bicester, and walk along the Oxfordshire Way to Noke and Beckley. Alternatively, drive or cycle to Beckley and go down Otmoor Lane to the RSPB reserve. This reserve was created by reclaiming farmland 25 years ago and has become a wonderful place to visit at all times of year. It features waterfowl, marsh harriers, golden plovers, snipe and spectacular murmuration of starlings.

Further upstream on the Ray, the Berkshire, Buckinghamshire and Oxfordshire Wildlife Trust (BBOWT) has acquired water meadows beside the A41 road, 4 miles (6.4km) east of Bicester. These provide protected nesting sites for lapwings, curlews and redshanks. The meadows are managed traditionally, with hay-cutting that encourages wildflowers and insects.

Otmoor

GETTING THERE

BUS SERVICES | Stagecoach 200 Banbury to Charwelton and Daventry; Stagecoach S4 Oxford to Banbury
TRAIN SERVICE | Great Western Railways, Oxford to Banbury
OS EXPLORER MAPS | 180 Oxford; 191 Banbury, Bicester & Chipping Norton; 206 Edge Hill & Fenny Stratford

RESOURCES

Battlefields Trail: *www.battlefieldstrust.com/media/718.pdf*
Bicester Local History Society: *www.blhs.org.uk/uploads/documents/Walks-Cherwell.pdf*
Jurassic Way: *www.ldwa.org.uk/ldp/members/show_publication.php?publication_id=13568*
King's Sutton: *www.kingssutton.org/about-kings-sutton/village-history*
Punt hire: Cherwell Boathouse, *http://cherwellboathouse.co.uk;* Magdalen Bridge, *https://www.oxfordpunting.co.uk*
RSPB Otmoor: *www.rspb.org.uk/reserves-and-events/reserves-a-z/otmoor-reserve/*
Upper Ray Meadows: *www.bbowt.org.uk/nature-reserves/upper-ray-meadows*

River Ock

12

LENGTH: 21 miles (33.8km)

SOURCE: Little Coxwell, near Shivenham

CONFLUENCE: St Helen's Wharf, Abingdon

The Ock is the river of the Vale of White Horse in Oxfordshire. It meanders in a shallow valley between the Berkshire Downs and a low ridge on the line of the A420 road between Oxford and Swindon.

> ### What's in a name?
>
> The Ock's name is said to be derived from a Celtic word meaning 'salmon'. That suggests that it was once larger and faster flowing than it is today.

Source and headwaters Beside a bridle path from Little Coxwell to Longcot, there is a ditch with flowing water in wet weather about where the Ordnance Survey map shows Cock Well. This ditch grows into a small stream that makes a south-westerly loop around Longcot. As it turns east through the Vale of White Horse, it collects water which flows from the springs along the northern edge of the Berkshire Downs.

One group of these springs is in Woolstone, which can be part of an interesting walk from the National Trust's car park for White Horse Hill at Uffington. Walk to the Ridgeway and turn west to Wayland's Smithy. After examining the long barrow and admiring the view, walk down the hill along the d'Arcy Dalton Way, cross the B4507 road and continue along the way to Compton Beauchamp and Knighton. The pale chalky stone of St Swithin's Church at Compton catches your eye. It is amazing that chalk used as a building material can last 800 years.

In Knighton, leave the d'Arcy Dalton Way to follow footpaths on the spring-line to Woolstone, where the White Horse pub welcomes you before you climb up the lane back to the car park. The springs at Woolstone are large enough to create a waterfall and mill ponds.

The village pump at Longcot

Stanford in the Vale to Charney Bassett

The Ock becomes a river requiring a proper bridge for the A417 road at Stanford in the Vale. There is an out-and-back walk that follows the course of the Ock, starting from the High Street in Stanford in the Vale. The route goes along Horsecroft Lane, which becomes a bridle path to Charney Bassett, 3 miles (4.8km) away. St Peter's Church in Charney is in a beautiful place close to the mill stream from the river. The church has a curious stone carving over a doorway (a tympanum), which suggests Saxon origins. The land on both sides of the Ock is largely flat and was marshy in former times. The village place names ending with the letters 'ey' (Charney Bassett, Goosey, Hanney) strongly suggests that these were islands in a network of streams.

Ock Valley Walk

There is a pleasant route along the Ock Valley Walk from the mouth of the Ock at St Helen's Wharf. From the bridge marking the

entrance to the Wilts and Berks Canal, walk beside the old almshouses and St Helen's Church, to a signpost marking the Ock Valley Walk. This walk goes through woodland glades for about ½ mile (0.8km) to Ock Bridge on the Drayton Road (B4017) and there are several paths to vary the return journey. Although there have been plans to restore the Wilts and Berks Canal and a new entrance has been dug to the south of Abingdon, most of the canal has disappeared and there is no old towpath to make a good walk across the Vale of White Horse.

The Ock Valley Walk is part of a 9 mile (14.5km) circular walk that links the Ock to a group of chalk streams that enter the Thames at Sutton Courtenay. Start at the car park at Culham Lock. Cross the Thames on the road bridge and enter the meadow at the gateway on your right side. The path across the meadow can be very wet if river levels are high but there is a lovely sense of space on this island between the natural course of the river and

OPPOSITE *The ford at Stanford in the Vale*

BELOW *Ock Valley River Walk in Abingdon*

12 River Ock

the lock cut. At the far side of the meadow, you can find a path over the weir which has a hydroelectric plant whirring away to make green power. Below the weir are Sutton Pools, rich in fish and birds (cormorants, kingfishers and goosanders) that catch them. The path follows a narrow spit of land between the pools and the stream that powered the paper mills that used to be here.

Leave the river to walk along Church Street, and turn right into Brook Street. When you come to the Mill Brook, turn left and continue south on the footpath at the edge of the meadow until you reach a bridle path. Turn right towards Drayton for ¾ mile (1.2km) to a footpath on the right heading north (about 300 yards/274m) after crossing a lane. Cross the Drayton Road (B4016) to a path that leads you to the Millennium Fields, a park with a pond in Sutton Wick. Continue in the same direction on Sutton Wick Lane to the Abingdon Road. Over the road, take the bridle path signed to New Cut Mill. From the tarmac lane at New Cut Mill (the Cut was the old Wilts and Berks Canal), a footpath goes among recently planted trees beside the river in Ock Meadow Nature Reserve. This leads to a recreation ground and to the Ock Valley Walk in Abingdon. When you get to the St Helen's Church, go along East St Helen's Street to Bridge Street. There is plenty of choice for refreshments here.

From this point, the way back to Culham is simply the Thames Path on the east side of Abingdon Bridge. On the opposite side, at St Helen's Wharf, the entrance to the Wilts and Berks Canal has an elegant iron footbridge. About 1 mile (1.6km) further on, you can see a small inlet on the opposite bank, which is a tentative start to restore the Wilts and Berks Canal. The Thames Path turns left (east) to follow the Culham Cut to the lock and the end of the walk.

Yellow iris

WALK 16 Letcombe Brook

5 miles (8km)

A popular walk is from Letcombe Regis, following the Brook upstream through the nature reserve managed by the Berkshire, Buckinghamshire and Oxfordshire Wildlife Trust (BBOWT) to Letcombe Bassett and climbing to the Ridgeway and Segsbury Camp. There is parking at the village hall in Letcombe Regis and at the Greyhound pub (recommended for lunch before or after the walk). Starting at St Andrew's Church, take the footpath that goes between the retirement home and the Brook to the nature reserve. The path at the upper end of the reserve continues along the side of the valley to Letcombe Bassett, where a small lake marks the source of the Brook. There are watercress beds, so typical of chalk streams, in the lake. In Letcombe Bassett follow the road for about 200 yards (180m) and turn left to go up Gramp's Hill. You will see St Michael's Church, originally Norman, and picturesque cottages. After ⅓ mile (0.5km), fork left to climb up Smith's Hill until you reach the Ridgeway. Turn left (east) until you come to Segsbury Castle, an Iron Age fort with splendid views and masses of colourful cowslips in spring. You can walk around the ancient earth walls of the fort or on the lane though its middle. The lane becomes Warborough Road, which takes you gently downhill back to Letcombe Regis.

Letcombe Brook

12 River Ock

Letcombe Brook Of all the streams that feed into the Ock, Letcombe Brook is one of the longest. It is a fine example of a chalk stream, adorned by a nature reserve on its banks. There is an excellent project to remove weirs and other obstacles from the stream so fish can migrate up to spawn in the clear, shallow waters of the upper reaches.

The walk can be made 2 miles (3.2km) longer by starting in Wantage Market Square (S9 bus services from Oxford). Go past the church (Saints Peter and Paul) to Betjeman Millennium Park, where '… old brick garden walls run down to Letcombe Brook' (an extract from John Betjeman's poem, *Farewell to Wantage* inscribed on stones in the park). Walk through the park to Locks Lane, which crosses a ford over the Brook. Opposite the junction of Locks Lane and the B4507 road, a footpath takes you to Letcombe Regis, from where you follow the main road through the village, past the pub to the church.

Cothill and Sandford nature reserves Sandford Brook is the last sub-tributary to enter the Ock before it reaches the Thames. It drains a group of fens in the Corallian limestone (Coral Rag) hills on the south-west side of Oxford. Wytham, Cumnor and Boars Hills were coral reefs formed 150 million years ago in the sea that covered southern England in the Jurassic Age. When the sea subsided,

Pond in Cothill National Nature Reserve

The bridge and St Helen's Church, Abingdon, where the Ock enters the Thames

fresh water seeped from the limestone to form ponds, which gradually became fens, and the dead vegetation became peat. This has resulted in a group of lowland fens which are rare in southern England. The cluster of fens are the source of Sandford Brook, where there are important nature reserves with open access. The easiest place to start exploring them is to park at Dry Sandford Pit in the small village of Cothill. Walk around the former quarry and see where fossils have been found in the limestone cliffs. To reach the larger Cothill National Nature Reserve, walk from the car park down the road, over Sandford Brook, past the mill to a footpath in the school car park. The signage in these reserves could be better but the ponds, marshes and wet woodland have rare mosses, pennyworts, sedges and more common species: great-crested newts, grass snakes and orchids.

GETTING THERE

OS EXPLORER MAP | 170 Abingdon, Wantage & Vale of White Horse

RESOURCES

Charney Bassett: *http://history.charneybassett.org.uk/buildings/churches/st-peters-church/*
Cothill: *www.bbowt.org.uk/sites/default/files/2018-01/Cothill%20 Wild%20Walk.pdf*
Letcombe Valley Nature Reserve: *www.bbowt.org.uk/nature-reserves/letcombe-valley*

13 River Thame

LENGTH: 40 miles (64km)

SOURCE: 4 miles (6.4km) east of Aylesbury

CONFLUENCE: near Dorchester-on-Thames

The Thame rises in the Vale of Aylesbury, a flat landscape with clay soil and a network of small streams slowly flowing west. These are crossed by the Aylesbury Ring Footpath between Rowsham and Long Marston to the north east of Aylesbury. Somehow one of these streams has been designated as the boundary between Buckinghamshire and Hertfordshire for about ½ mile (0.8km) and as the start of the Thame. The natural state of streams in the area has been much affected by the building of canals and railways. Crossing the Chiltern Hills, the Grand Union Canal is on the watershed between the Thame and the catchment of the River Colne. The canalside village of Marsworth has an enjoyable walk around the lakes built as reservoirs to feed the Grand Union Canal. The lakes attract widgeon and other winter wildfowl. Reedbeds are nesting sites for warblers in summer. The walk can include Bulbourne, where the College Lake Nature Reserve has excellent birdwatching and a visitor centre.

Aylesbury A section of the Round Aylesbury Walk follows along the Thame starting at the modern village of Watermead, where there is an attractive artificial lake. Going west, you find Holman's Bridge where the road to Buckingham (the A413) crosses the Thame. This bridge was the

OPPOSITE *Lake at Watermead*

What's in a name?

The river's name was spelt Tame before the 13th century, like the river in Manchester and similar to the Tamar in Plymouth. Probably all three names are based on a Celtic word Tam, meaning 'a river'. The modern spelling is sometimes confused with the Thames, a muddle made worse by Tudor poets and artists who portrayed a myth that the Thames was formed by a marriage of the Isis (an invented name used for the main river near Oxford) with the Thame.

13 River Thame

Holman's Bridge

scene of the Battle of Aylesbury in the English Civil War. In November 1642, a brigade of the Parliamentarian Army beat the forces in Aylesbury led by Prince Rupert of the Rhine, the commander of the Royalist cavalry. Further south, from Wheatley Bridge to Chiselhampton, the river was an eastern defensive line of the Royalists ensconced in Oxford. The defence was put to the test in June 1643 when Prince Rupert won the Battle of Chalgrove. Returning to the present day, the walk goes along firm paths though grasslands and copses beside the river to the A41 road, which is built here on our old friend, Akeman Street.

Aylesbury to Thame The middle part of the river can be explored using the Thame Valley Walk (TVW), a 15 mile (24km) long-distance path from Aylesbury to the hamlet of Albury near Tiddington. It is not an easy route because there are many stiles, some without dog gates, while parts may be flooded in winter and the signage has not been well maintained. It can be walked in one day or divided into two days using the bus service along the A418, which stops in Upper Hartwell, Thame and Tiddington.

The Aylesbury end of the TVW can be found near Rabans Lane

Industrial Estate. Go to Haydon Mill Farm (SP 793142), where you find the Thame Valley Walk signs. An alternative approach is via the Midshires Way from Upper Hartwell, adjacent to the village of Stone. From the junction of the Midshires Way and the TVW, the path follows the river to the pretty Weir Lodge, where the Thame was diverted to create a lake in Eythrope Park. Eythrope is part of the Rothschild Estate at nearby Waddesdon Manor and is about 2.5 miles (4km) from Aylesbury.

After another 2.5 miles from Eythrope on the west side of the Thame, you reach Nether Winchendon House and its small village, with architecture varying from the Gothic main house to traditional timber-frames. The TVW runs through fields at a distance from the river through Chearsley until it turns down to Notley Abbey, after yet another 2.5 miles.

Weir Lodge at Eythrope

There is a choice after Notley Abbey, either to follow the TVW signs up the hill to Long Crendon or take the direct route of the Bernwood Jubilee Way past a factory to reach the B4011 road at 1 mile (1.6km) from the centre of Thame. This more direct route means you have only a short distance to walk on the verge of the B4011 before you see the TVW sign pointing along the old Thame

13 River Thame

The Thame below Shabbington

Road, now a traffic-free lane. This is 9 miles (14.5km) from Aylesbury and you may be ready to stop at Thame. If so, you have to cross the busy Thame bypass (A418), but it is worth seeing the beautiful St Mary's Church and the surrounding buildings. There is a wide choice of places to eat in the town, a museum, Cuttle Brook Nature Reserve and plenty more besides.

For the remaining 6 miles (9.7km) along the lower part of the TVW, start at the old Thame Road beside the bypass (A418). The last time we visited, the Thame Valley Walk sign had been defaced, but the Bernwood Jubilee Way signs are useful to Shabbington and then you can continue along the TVW, passing The Old Fisherman pub, a good lunch spot. Cross the river to where the path runs along the riverbank. After the TVW leaves the river, it crosses the A418 road to a former railway track. Follow this track and go up a driveway to Home Farm, near Albury, to the Oxfordshire Way. Rycote Chapel, which has wonderful woodcarvings, is open in the afternoons of summer weekends. To complete the TVW, follow the Oxfordshire Way to Albury and on to Tiddington if you want the bus service.

Lower Part of the Thame Waterperry Gardens, a renowned centre of horticulture, is the next place downstream where you can stroll beside the Thame. After enjoying the riverside walks in the gardens, you may like to 'go the extra mile' along the Oxfordshire Way to Bow Bridge over the river to Waterstock, where you can admire a splendid kingfisher sundial on the mill house. When the Thame reaches Wheatley, it has become a substantial river, especially in wet winters when it floods the nearby meadows, giving the appearance of a huge lake. Wheatley was probably the limit of commercial navigation up the river in the Middle Ages, but the construction of mills, such as at Cuddesdon, must have hindered river traffic.

The map shows a footpath from Cuddeson to Stadhampton meeting other paths to cross the river using a ford and stepping stones near Chippinghurst Manor. The stepping stones were the remains of a weir but there is no longer a recognised crossing point. In winter when the river is high, it is unsafe to wade or swim.

Cuddesdon Mill

When the river is low, the ripples on the surface indicate where the stepping stones once lay. However, the river near Chippinghurst Manor, dating from Elizabethan times, is an attractive destination for walks of about 1.5 miles (2.4km) from Cuddesdon, making a circular walk by returning along Denton Lane. The Edward King Chapel in Ripon College in Cuddesdon is stunningly beautiful and open to the public on weekdays.

The Thame has benefitted in recent years from the work of the River Thame Conservation Trust, whose volunteers help monitor water quality and count wildlife along the river.

GETTING THERE

BUS SERVICES | Aylesbury to Oxford, via Thame: Arriva 280 and Redline X20; Oxford to Wheatley: Brookes bus U1; Oxford to Dorchester on Thames: Oxford Bus Co. X38

OS EXPLORER MAPS | 170 Abingdon, Wantage & Vale of White Horse; 180 Oxford; 181 Chiltern Hills North

RESOURCES

Ripon College: *www.rcc.ac.uk/about-us/edward-king-chapel*
River Thame Conservation Trust: *www.riverthame.org*
Ryecote Park: *www.rycotepark.com/rycote-chapel-tours-and-opening-times/*
Thame Valley Walk (TVW): *www.buckscc.gov.uk/services/environment/rights-of-way/walks-and-rides-route-map/*

WALK 17 Dorchester to Long Wittenham

8 miles (12.9km)

The Thame provides an interesting start to a circular walk from Dorchester-on-Thames to Long Wittenham and back along the Thames Path. From the car park at Bridge End in Dorchester, walk up to and around the side of the Abbey. Enjoy the cloister garden beside the Thame before going along Manor Farm Lane to a T junction with a footpath. Turn right to reach the Hurst Meadow, an island in the Thame, bought by local people to protect it from development and turned into a nature reserve. Cross the Meadow to Overy Mill, where an enchanting pool attracts kingfishers. A lane from the mill goes down to the Henley Road where a path has been created by the Hurst Meadow Trust to take you down to the Thames. Turn right on to the Thames Path, which crosses the mouth of the Thame and leads you to Day's Lock.

Below Day's Lock, go over the footbridge to Little Wittenham and walk up past the church to a road junction. Turn right on the road to Long Wittenham. About 300 yards along the road, a pedestrian gate on the left lets you into a long meadow between Paradise Wood and the road. The meadow, the wood and the Wittenham Clumps behind you are owned by the Earth Trust, which provides brilliant conservation work in this area. You are spoilt for choice of good walks on the Earth Trust's land, but to continue this circular walk, follow the path through the meadow to a small car park. From the car park, a footpath brings you to a crossroads in Long Wittenham. Turn right to walk down a lane past a sports field to Northfield Farm. At the farm gate, a footpath on the left side goes to the Thames. You reach the Thames on a boardwalk because these flood meadows do just that! The way back is along the Thames Path, which has been much improved by the River of Life project through the Earth Trust. The creation of backwaters and the planting of trees helps wildlife, provides breeding grounds for fish and reduces the surges of flood water through towns. Back at Day's Lock, cross at the top gates of the lock to a footpath across a meadow to go beside the ancient earthworks called Dyke Hills. A short distance further, you are back at Bridge End.

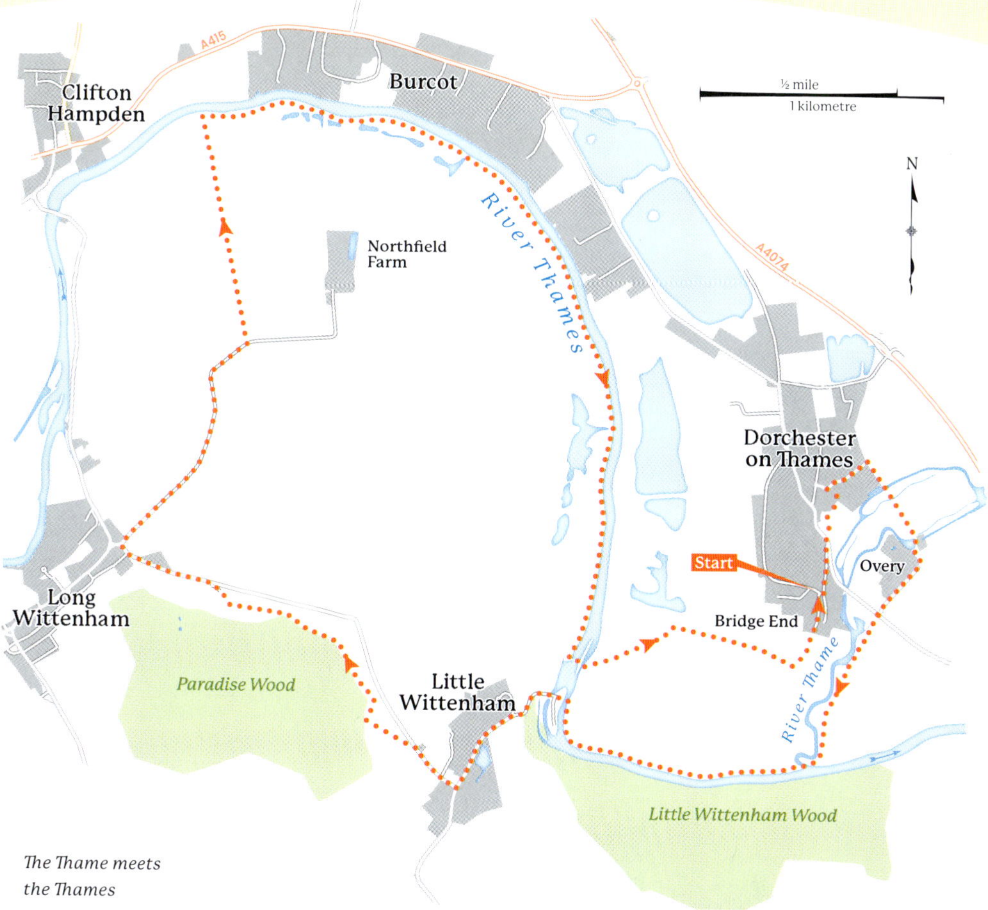
Clifton
Hampden
A415
Burcot
½ mile
1 kilometre
N
River Thames
Northfield
Farm
A4074
Dorchester
on Thames
Start
Overy
Bridge End
Long
Wittenham
Paradise Wood
Little
Wittenham
River Thame
Little Wittenham Wood

The Thame meets the Thames

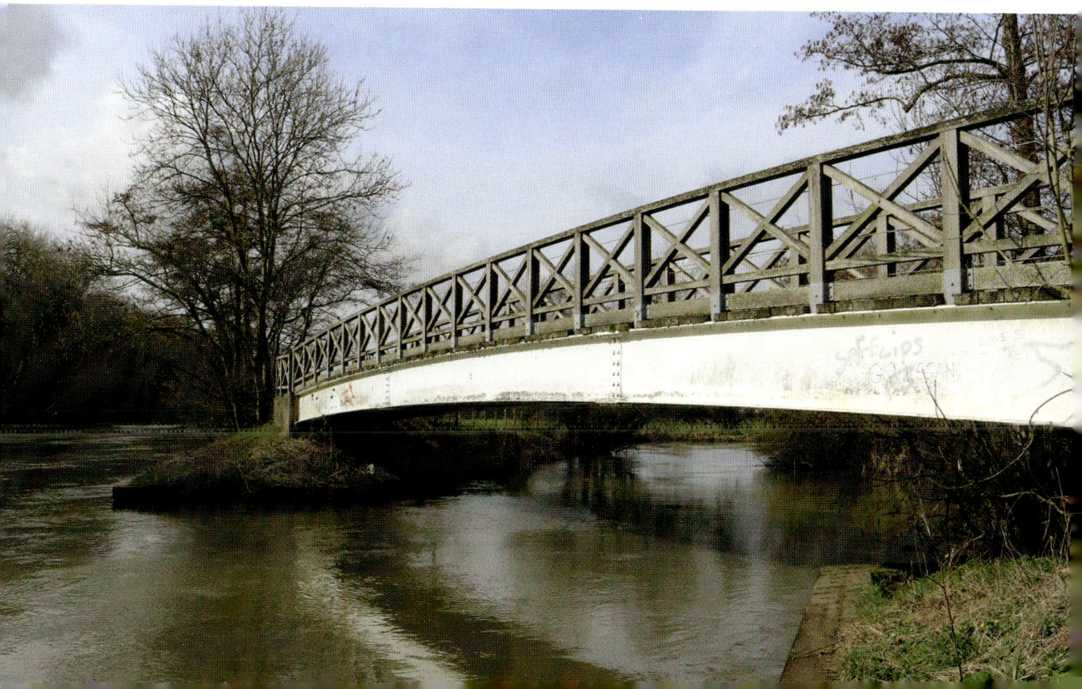

PART 3

The rivers entering the Thames in Berkshire and Buckinghamshire

Waterfall in the Rye, High Wycombe

River Pang

LENGTH: 14 miles (22.5km)

SOURCE: The Ridgeway above Compton

CONFLUENCE: Pangbourne

Until the end of the last Ice Age, about 19,000 years ago, the Pang was joined by the River Kennet at Sulham and they entered the Thames together at Pangbourne. The Pang runs on the south side of the Berkshire Downs from the racehorse villages of East Isley and Compton to the Thames near Reading. Its upper reaches are chalk streams that suffer from water abstraction, like others in southern England. However, it is a pretty river with clear water flowing over gravel beds as it runs east. There are good walks along its banks through small villages and wooded hillsides.

Looking for the source at Compton

The source is the range of springs in the chalk hills above East Ilsley and Compton. The most accessible evidence of origins of the Pang is a ditch on the south side of the High Street in Compton, where there is flowing water after heavy rain. To explore the area where this water rises, there is a 4 mile (6.4km) circular walk to the Ridgeway on Blewbury Down to the north of Compton. Start at Cheap Street in Compton. Walk north, away from the High Street to a bridleway that climbs gently to the Ridgeway. As you leave the village, the view opens up, revealing the river valley on your right-hand side. At the Ridgeway, turn right (east) and cross a bridge over the dismantled Didcot, Newbury and Southampton Railway. When you see the small brick buildings of the water extraction point beside this bridge, continue east along the Ridgeway for about 1 mile (1.6km) to a small copse with pine trees. Turn right where the signpost shows the way back to Compton, at 1.5 miles (2.4km). The Foinavon, formerly the Swan Hotel, and the village shop in the High Street provide refreshment.

Pang near Pangbourne

What's in a name?

The Pang's Old English name was Panganburnan, which is derived from a local tribe, the Paegingas.

The infant Pang near Compton

Back in the village, if you are determined to find running water, follow the ditch along the High Street to the church. Take a footpath heading south across the field opposite the church. The path crosses the Pang (often dry, but clearly a streambed) and goes past the local sewage works. At a distance of ½ mile (0.8km) from the church, you are likely to see running water in the stream as it emerges from the sewage works – an illustration of the effects of water consumption on our rivers.

Woodland and river walk at Hampstead Norreys

As the Pang flows south through Hampstead Norreys, it has cut a steep-sided valley and grown into a river. A very pleasant out-and-back woodland walk 3.5 miles (5.6km) starts at the village hall in Hampstead Norreys, where there is room to park. Walk from the village hall down the playing fields to the gate in the far left-hand corner. A track goes south-east along the edge of Eling Woods to where the river meanders through a water meadow. When the path makes a T junction with a bridle path, turn left down to the ford to see the river. Return to the woods and look for the medieval motte (fort), described on the information board at the entrance to the wood. The bluebells are a splendid sight in spring. Back in the village, a short walk through the churchyard brings you to the community shop and café at the new Manor Barns development.

Between Hampstead Norreys and Bucklebury, the Pang continues south under the M4 motorway, before curving to run east towards Reading. Water flowing from the chalk downs on either side builds up the Pang into a sizeable river by the time it reaches Bradfield.

WALK 18 Stanford Dingle to Bradfield

5 miles (8km)

There is a good circular walk around the Pang Valley between Stanford Dingley and Bradfield. One attraction is that there are no stiles on this walk. Starting at the Bull Inn in Stanford Dingley, go south along the road, over the river, to a track on the left side signposted to Bradfield. Go east along this track for the 2 miles (3.2km) to Bradfield school and village. The Pang runs parallel to the path, flowing through Kimberhead watercress beds. Continue east beside a plantation of poplars until you reach the golf course of Bradfield College. Here, the Pang has a leat (a channel to carry water into the mill, which is now part of the college buildings). There are lovely views over marshland from the path. After this happy passage of walking beside water, you reach the college, an independent secondary school founded in 1850 by the Reverend Thomas Stevens.

The Pang and marshes near Bradfield College

At the road in Bradfield village, turn left over the bridge across the Pang and find a path that goes across a large field where meadow flowers flourish, including poppies and oxeye daisies. When this path reaches Back Lane, cross the road and go up a track for 2/3 mile (1km). At the top of the wooded hill, the climb is rewarded with views of the river valley. When you come to a junction of four paths, turn sharp left and follow the Berkshire Recreational Path through woodland. When this path comes close to a gate into a field, veer right down a path that stays in the wood. You pass a small woodland arena with banks of seats around a fireplace. Climb up to reach a minor road. On the opposite side of the lane is a driveway into Rushall Manor Farm, run by the John Simonds Trust as an educational charity. There is a splendid thatched barn and a car park in the farm that could be another starting place for this walk. Immediately after the car park, find a gate on the right (west) side into a field. Cross the field to Back Lane where a footpath runs west behind the roadside hedge, to return to Stanford Dingley beside the pretty church with a white steeple.

14 River Pang

Moor Copse to Pangbourne

After Bradfield, the Pang curves north through the Sulham Gap towards Pangbourne. The river goes under the M4 motorway to enter Moor Copse Nature Reserve. Moor Copse has a car park beside the A340 (SU 634738). Here, you can walk beside the river as it winds its way through ancient woodland. where alder and birch trees predominate. At the bridge, cross to the path ahead through younger trees to meadows bearing right to complete a circuit of the reserve. If you turn left after the bridge, an unmarked path goes beside the river out of the reserve to Tidmarsh and Pangbourne. However, the last part of the Pang is more easily explored in Walk 19.

OPPOSITE *The Bull at Stanford Dingle*

ABOVE *Pang at Moor Copse*

GETTING THERE

BUS SERVICES | Newbury & District no. 6 goes to Compton and Hampstead Norreys

TRAIN SERVICES TO PANGBOURNE | Great Western Railways between Reading and Didcot

OS EXPLORER MAPS | 158 Newbury & Hungerford; 159 Reading, Wokingham & Pangbourne; 170 Abingdon, Wantage & Vale of White Horse

RESOURCES

Dunlop, Lesley and Greenaway, Dick, *Around the Three Valleys* (The Friends of the Pang, Kennet and Lambourn Valleys, 2011) – useful book for exploring this area

Moor Copse Nature Reserve: www.bbowt.org.uk/nature-reserves/moor-copse

WALK 19 Pangbourne to Tidmarsh and Sulham

3.5 miles (5.6km)

This walk starts from **Pangbourne** rail station. Walk down to the main road and cross to Wharf Lane, where you find a footbridge over the Pang as it joins the Thames. There is a small riverside lawn, privately owned, but public access is permitted to see the Pang enter the Thames below a long weir.

From here, walk to and over the main A329 road to a lane called The Moors. At the far end of The Moors, a footpath leads you between gardens to a meadow with the Pang on your right side. The path goes beside the Pang, crosses a footbridge and runs across another meadow to a drive. It goes around a garden before reaching the main

Millhouse, Tidmarsh

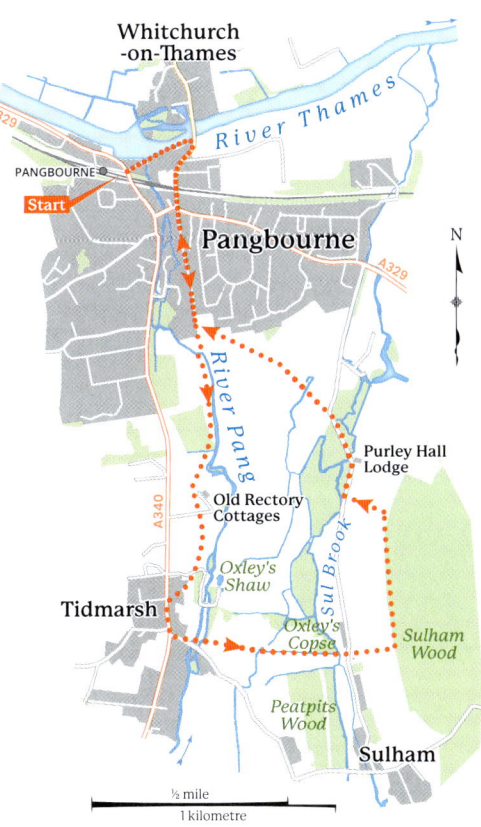

Beech woods at Sulham

road in Tidmarsh. Go along the road to the Greyhound pub and turn left into Mill Lane. In 1918, the Mill House became home to some of the Bloomsbury set, when writer and critic Lytton Strachey lived here with Dora Carrington, who painted local scenes.

Opposite the Mill House in Tidmarsh, a footbridge crosses the Pang and leads across fields beside a pillbox and over drainage channels to reach Sulham Brook. Once over the brook, cross the lane into a field. Walk up beside the hedge to reach the lovely beech trees of Sulham Wood. Turn left and walk for ⅓ mile (500m) to a signpost to turn left again out of the wood across the field. At the lane, turn right, cross Sulham Brook, and find the footpath that leads across the meadows back to Pangbourne.

15 River Kennet

LENGTH: 45 miles (72.4km)

SOURCE: Winterbourne Bassett

CONFLUENCE: Reading

The Kennet is one of the major tributaries of the Thames with a rich history and many enjoyable walks. It rises at Winterbourne Bassett, on the western side of the Marlborough Downs and flows as a crystal-clear chalk stream down to Hungerford. The river becomes muddier when it meanders through clay and gravel between Hungerford and Reading and where side streams flow among flood meadows. It has two significant sub-tributaries, the rivers Lambourn and Enborne.

The Kennet and Avon Canal was constructed in Reading in 1714 and uses the river both as a source of water and a channel on its way to Hungerford. The canal towpath is an excellent way of exploring the Kennet, with a firm surface suitable for cycling (National Cycle Network Route 5, Bath to London). There are car parks and information boards along the way, and trains provide an alternative to cars and an easy way to return to starting points. A canal boat holiday is another delightful way to explore this river.

Walk to the source Avebury, with a large car park, village shop and a pub, is a good place to start exploring the top part of the Kennet. In addition, the National Trust provides a café, museum and guided walks that explore the fascinating surrounding landscape.

Setting off westwards from the Avebury Church along a tarmac footpath, you find a bridge over the young Kennet; sometimes a dry riverbed in summer. Here you can start a 4 mile (6.4km) walk north to the source at Winterbourne Bassett. Take the northward footpath marked as the White Horse Trail to Windmill

What's in a name?

The origin of the river's name is uncertain. Various early spellings include Cynete and Cunnit, similar to Cunetio, which was a Roman settlement near Marlborough.

Kennet Bridge at Berwick Bassett

Hill and when this trail turns west on a track to the top of Windmill Hill, continue northward on a path to Winterbourne Monkton. From this village to Berwick Bassett, the path runs beside the Kennet. At Berwick Bassett, take the lane on the east side of the houses to the bridge near the main A4361 road. Fred S. Thacker, author of classic books about the Thames at the beginning of the 19th Century described the scene in *Kennet Country* as: 'the Kennet Bridge of three round stone arches with a stagnant pool or two in the marshy bed'. In midwinter the river is a bit more convincing than this.

The footpath to Winterbourne Bassett starts at Berwick Church and goes through the site of a medieval village, Richardson, which was abandoned by 1545 when only two people remained eligible to pay taxes. The Winterbourne Bassett Church booklet has an excellent history of the area. The village community bought the pub, now called the Winterbourne, in 2018 to save it from closure and it is a great place to eat before walking back to Avebury. On the way back, you may like to divert to the top of Windmill Hill, a prehistoric meeting place with good views of the north Wiltshire plain. For a longer and more energetic route back, you can climb up to the Ridgeway, walk south to Fyfield Down and turn west to go down the byway back to Avebury, completing a 10 mile (16km) circular walk.

WALK 20 Avebury to Silbury and East Kennet

5 miles (8km)

A circular walk from Avebury follows the Kennet down the White Horse Trail to Silbury Hill and on to the village of East Kennet, returning via Overton Hill. Start in the big National Trust car park beside the A4361. Cross the road to take the footpath on the opposite side, with Silbury Hill in view. This path runs beside the Kennet until you are close to the foot of the hill. Silbury Hill is the largest Neolithic humanmade mound in Europe and is comparable in scale to the pyramids in Egypt. Its purpose is a mystery.

Avebury stones

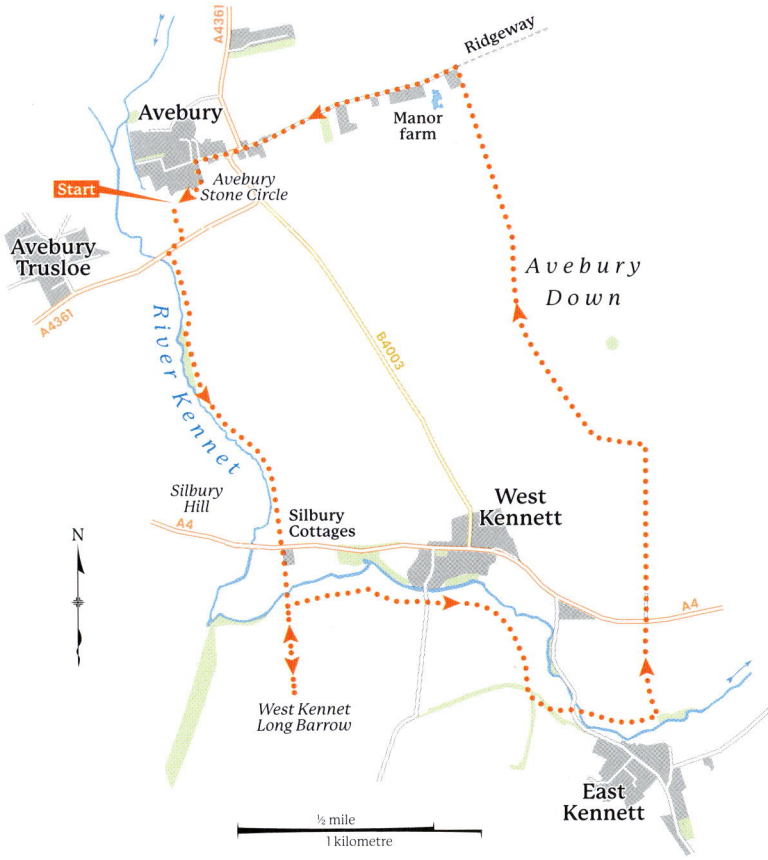

After Silbury Hill, cross the A4 where it lies along the line of the main Roman Road between London and Bath. The footpath on the other side of the A4 takes you to a small stone bridge over the Kennet. If there is water flowing here, it may have come from Swallowfield Springs in the copse that you can see away to the west. A short distance after the bridge, a signpost directs you up the hill to West Kennet Long Barrow, where a super view rewards the climb. Return to the signpost and walk east to the Sanctuary through the meadows beside the Kennet. The Sanctuary is another mystery, a circle originally of wooden posts, then of stones and now of concrete markers. It was a burial site, built before the stone circles at Avebury to which it was connected by an avenue of stones. From the Sanctuary, cross the A4 and walk north on the Ridgeway National Trail. Turn left at the first bridleway that goes to Manor Farm. Turn left again along the lane to Avebury.

133

15 River Kennet

Marlborough At Marlborough, the Kennet becomes a proper river as water that has crept beneath the chalk emerges to join water from several surface streams. It provides an ornamental waterway in the grounds of Marlborough College, as you can see if you walk west on the path from the A345 road bridge to Manton about 1 mile (1.6km).

From Marlborough to Hungerford, there are paths that follow the river past Mildenhall, Axford, Ramsbury and Chilton Foliat. This can make a wonderful 10 mile (16km) walk on the south side of the river but does not have convenient public transport back to the start. From the old viaduct, which carried the former Chiseldon and Marlborough Railway over the river, go along Elcot Lane to a footpath through the site of the Roman town of Cunetio. Walk along Kings Drive from Stitchcombe Farm to a bridle path passing Ramsbury Manor Park, where the river is diverted to make a lake in front of a grand house built in 1683.

Ramsbury and Littlecote Ramsbury, halfway between Hungerford and Marlborough, is a good place to stop for lunch, with two pubs and several shops. Once there was a famous elm tree in the square, so large that its branches touched the surrounding houses. Sadly, the

Kennet at Ramsbury

tree died in 1983 but it has been replaced by an oak. For a quick 1 mile (1.6km) circular walk, start at the square and go along the High Street west towards Marlborough. At the fire station there is a small nature reserve beside the river. Continue along the High Street to Mill Lane, which crosses the river, and walk through the fields on the south of Ramsbury, returning to the village along a road over the river to Scholard's Lane and to the square.

If you continue on the bridleway from Ramsbury on the south side of the Kennet, after 1.3 mile (2km) you find the remains of a Roman villa at Littlecote. There is a beautiful mosaic floor of the former dining room and the outline of other buildings. Littlecote House, now a hotel, has a colourful history. The house dates from medieval times and it is said that Henry VIII courted Jane Seymour here. King James I, Charles II and William of Orange also visited the house. Its most notorious owner was William Darrell, who had a rakish lifestyle. He apparently quarrelled with his neighbours, became the villain of several ghost stories and died in debt in 1589. In the Second World War, the house was the headquarters for the US parachute troops before the D-Day landings.

Leaving Littlecote Park beside the East Lodge, you cross the river to Chilton Foliat and walk along Leverton Lane to Eddington on the outskirts of Hungerford.

Freeman's Marsh at Hungerford

15 River Kennet

Kennet and Avon towpath from Hungerford to Newbury

In Hungerford, the towpath along the Kennet and Avon Canal combines with the Great Western Railway to help the Kennet explorer. It is a pleasure to stroll in one direction, chatting to people, looking for flowers and wildlife, and ride back by train, reviewing the day's walk. The stations are no more than 6 miles (9.7km) apart so the length of the walks can be adjusted to suit your needs. The route is obvious and there are information boards along the way.

For more variety, we suggest three shorter circular walks. The first, is to start walking a mile (1.6km) up the valley of the River Dun to Freeman's Marsh. This is a nature reserve belonging to the people of Hungerford who have held commoners' rights for centuries. Start at St Lawrence's Church, built in 1814 with Bath stone brought along the canal. A path from the churchyard crosses the canal and brings you to the banks of the Dun. Follow the Dun upstream to enter the reserve, and wander through the fields before finding Marsh Lock and the towpath that will take you back to Hungerford.

The second walk is on the east side of Hungerford where there is a 2 mile (3.2km) walk around Hungerford Common, called Port Down. Take a path from the rail station to Park Street, enter through the old gate (or port) of Hungerford, and climb the hill to enjoy the views, before dropping down to Denford Bridge and the canal.

River and canal side by side near Newbury

WALK 21 Speen to Donnington Castle and Bagnor

5.3 miles (8.5km)

This walk combines the best wetlands near Newbury with the superb outlook from Donnington Castle. It uses parts of the Speen Moors Walk and the Lambourn Valley Way, two good trails that start at the Northcroft Leisure Centre. From the leisure centre, walk north past the playground in Goldwell Park to the junction of Speen Lane and Old Bath Road. When you reach the Old Bath Road, note the handsome stone pillar erected to commemorate the turn of the millennium. Go along the Old Bath Road to the modern Bath Road (A4), where a pedestrian crossing takes you to Brummel Road. Walk down Brummel Road, past The Starting Gate pub, to Grove Road, where you turn left and look for a footpath on the right-hand side into the golf course. The golf course surrounds Donnington Grove, a handsome house (now a hotel) built in 1763 in a Neo-Gothic style. The footpath joins the driveway to Donnington Grove and crosses the River Lambourn on a white bridge close to a small marsh beside the river. When the driveway bends left, continue straight on to climb up to the car park at Donnington Castle. From the castle, look

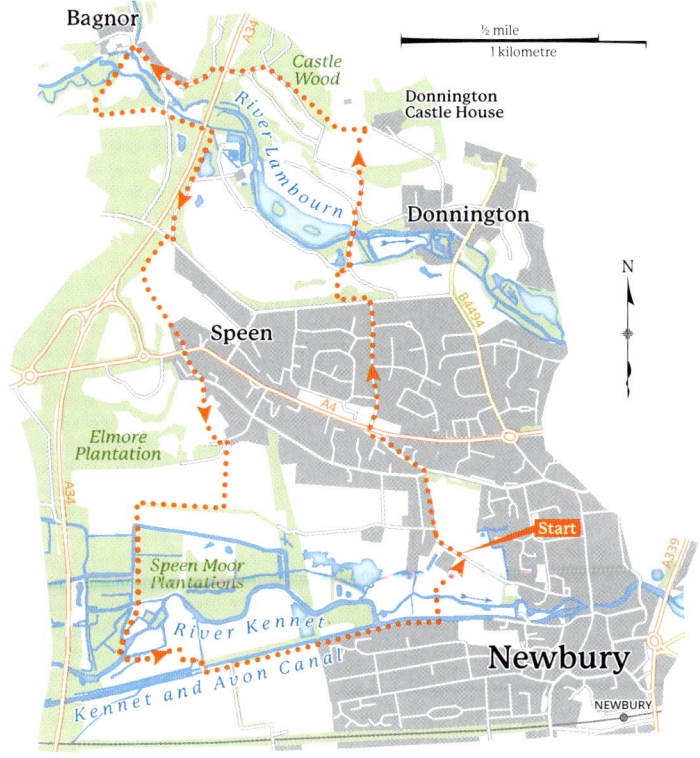

137

Walk 21

Donnington Castle

south across the valley of the Kennet to the North Wessex Downs, where Walbury Hill (974ft/297m) is the highest natural point in south-east England. The castle suffered a long siege in the English Civil War, and the Second Battle of Newbury (1644) occurred in the valley below it.

From Donnington Castle, take the path going west through a wood for 400 yards (366m). When the path ends at a tarmac track by the ninth tee on the golf course, bear left on a path down the edge of the course to a bridge over the A34 road. Here, the path is marked as the Lambourn Valley Trail. On the west side of the bridge, turn left down to Bagnor village.

In Bagnor, walk west along the road towards the Watermill Theatre. The Watermill was converted to a theatre in 1967, originally with a local cast, now enjoying national status. Near the entrance to the Watermill, take the footpath on the left side across Rack Marsh, a nature reserve beside the River Lambourn. Rack Marsh has a wild, ragged look, with tall reeds encroaching on the muddy path. A prehistoric wooden canoe was found here, preserved by the peat. Turn left on the south side of the Marsh to the lane that goes into Bagnor. Turn right at the lane to find the path signed as the Lambourn Valley Way. Follow the Way under the A34 and stay close to the A34 until you reach a field where the Way turns left beside a hedge. Continue into the field and bear left, uphill to Speen village.

In Speen, cross the main road to walk down Speen Lane to the footpath to the village church, signed as the Lambourn Valley Way. A few steps down this path, on the right side, is the Lady Well, which is both an ancient and modern shrine. From the church, follow the Valley Way down a field to a T junction of paths. Turn right on the Speen Moors Walk and follow this where it turns left to cross the marshy land that has a rectangular grid of humanmade channels, built to drain the flood meadows. These and other features are explained in excellent information boards put up by the Thames River Restoration Trust and Newbury Town Council. You will cross the Kennet and reach the canal where you turn left towards Newbury. Walk along the towpath to the wooden Monkey Bridge to cross the canal back to the Northcroft Leisure Centre.

Kennet and Avon towpath, Newbury to Reading Walking from Newbury to Reading, the canal towpath continues to be the best route. The Kennet valley becomes filled with signs of modern life, but the river retains a rustic air, twisting through marshland and supporting wildlife. This is epitomised at Thatcham Nature Reserve, managed by the local council and the Berkshire, Buckinghamshire and Oxfordshire Wildlife Trust (BBOWT).

Central Reading

WALK 22 Thatcham to the River Enborne and Greenham Common

8 miles (12.9km)

Although close to Walk 21, this circular walk has a different feel — more rural and, curiously, more modern. The Nature Discovery Centre, the starting point, is a contemporary building, with excellent educational resources, café and spacious car park. From here, you walk beside the lakes and the reedbeds to the canal at Widmead Lock. Turn left towards Reading and walk to Thatcham station, about 2 miles (3.2km). In early summer, listen for the cuckoos, who will be looking for reed warbler nests. Part of the river flows into the canal at Monkey Marsh Lock. The other part powered the large Chamberhouse Mill, which you pass by crossing the canal and river bridges and taking the lane with this name.

Soon after the mill, the lane does an S bend. Walk up the bridleway for a mile (1.6km), looking back occasionally to enjoy the view of the Kennet valley. In the woodland, which is the eastern part of Greenham Common, cross the road to the farm track opposite. The path skirts a wood and finally veers left to a footbridge over the River Enborne. Walk upstream beside the winding river, looking for buzzards overhead. It is very peaceful and the best part of this sub-tributary. When you reach a lane, turn right over the river on the footbridge beside the ford. Walk up Old Thornford Road to Crookham Common where the Berkshire, Buckinghamshire and Oxfordshire

Thatcham Nature Discovery Centre

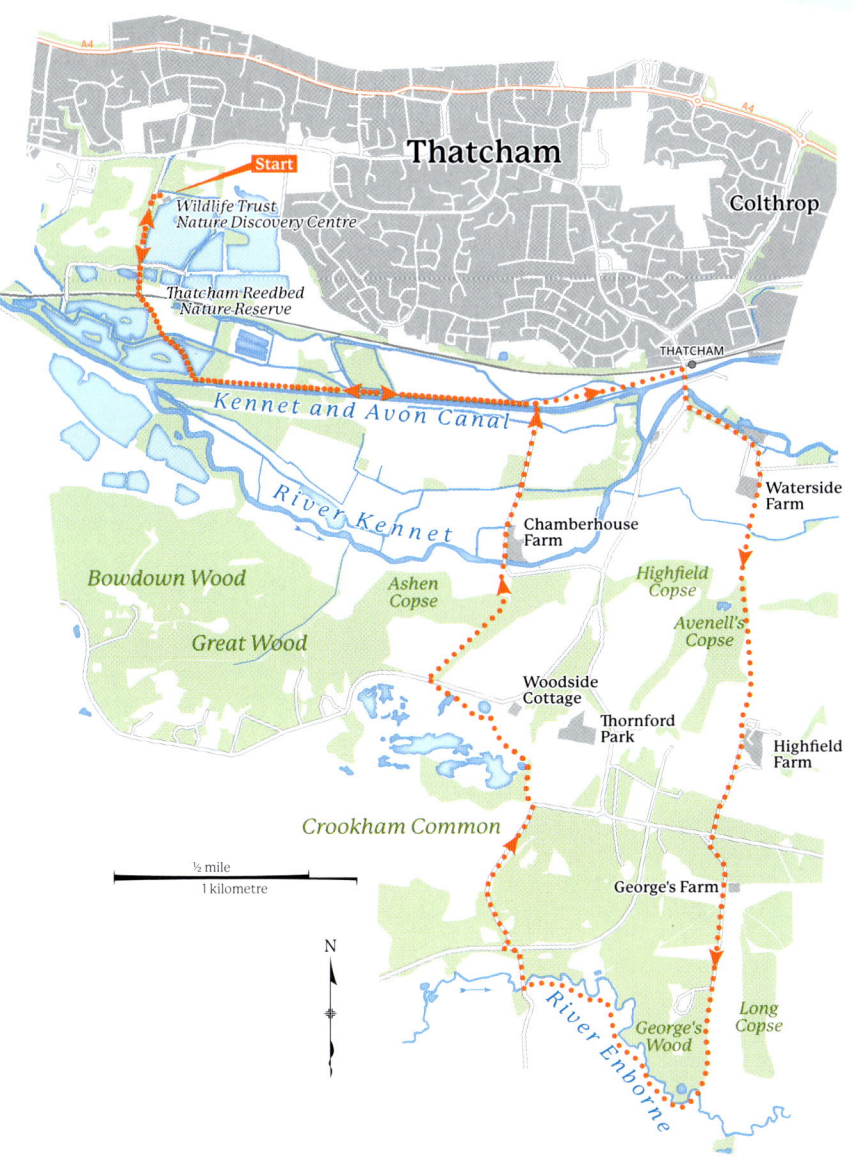

Wildlife Trust (BBOWT) has a super nature reserve created at the end of the runway of the Greenham Common airfield – lots of memories for those people who grew up during the Cold War. Now there are gorse, ponds, cycle paths and a sensible mix of areas where dogs can run off-lead and other places where leads are required to protect ground-nesting birds. On the north side of the reserve, take the bridleway down to Chamberhouse Farm and on to the canal, to complete the walk back to the Nature Discovery Centre.

15 River Kennet

Aldermaston Aldermaston Wharf, with its canalside visitor centre and car park, is a central place to start exploring this section of the Kennet. The wharf is 2 miles (3.2km) away from the village and the Atomic Weapons Establishment that used to be the starting point of protest marches. On more peaceful matters, a walk along the towpath for 2 miles (3.2km) upstream will bring you to Woolhampton and the Rowbarge pub in time for lunch. At Woolhampton, the canal and river have combined, but at Aldermaston the river makes a more southern loop around gravel pits and is joined by the Enborne. Downstream, a 6 mile (9.7km) circular walk includes the canal path between Aldermaston and Tyle Mill, as well as going past Padworth Mill. Tyle Mill was a large flour mill at Sulhamstead that burnt down in 1914. It was later converted to a private house.

Downstream from Tyle Mill the canal uses much more of the original channel of the river. At Theale, there is a picnic area and parking near the swing bridge for a road over the canal. Nearby, at Arrow Head, a side stream called the Holy Brook leaves the Kennet and flows separately into the centre of Reading. Holy Brook was built by the monks of Reading Abbey to supply water for their mills and fishponds. Burghfield village lies to the south of the river beyond the lakes and former gravel pits, now used for sailing and fishing. The Parish Council has produced an online leaflet describing walks around these lakes.

Fobney Island and Reading The final part of the Kennet can be explored starting at Burghfield Bridge close to the Cunning Man pub. Walk along the towpath past Southcote Mill and under a railway bridge to find Fobney Island Nature Reserve. This is a successful example of the restoration of poor suburban fields to good habitats for wildlife. With scrapes and lakes, a hay meadow and reedbeds, it also controls flooding. The paths invite you to wander and look around, and the benches tempt you to relax. Mentally refreshed, you are prepared for the walk beside the river into Reading.

Although there are roads and industry nearby, the riverside path is a beautiful way into the town. In the centre, the imaginative design of shopping centres and office blocks uses the river to

Fobney Island Reserve

enhance the urban space. The last stretch of the Kennet flows around the grounds of the Abbey built by Henry I in 1121, through Blake's Lock, past the riverside museum and under the railway to enter the Thames.

River Lambourn

The Lambourn runs for 16 miles (25.7km) along a pretty valley between chalk downs and enters the Kennet River at Newbury. The river starts from springs and ponds in Lynch Wood on the north side of Lambourn town, but there may not be water flowing on the surface before you reach the village of Great Shefford.

The Lambourn Valley Way starts at Whitehorse Hill above Uffington and can be joined at the marketplace beside St Michael's Church in the Lambourn town centre. The nearby almshouses, founded in 1502, were rebuilt in 1852 with beautiful brickwork in a Tudor style. As one of the older residents said to us: 'They don't build 'em like that these days.'

Almshouse, Lambourn

The upper part of the Lambourn Valley Way is based on a former railway line track built to serve the racehorse farms. In present times, the no. 4 bus service runs at approximately two-hourly intervals along the valley and is a great help for explorers who are unable to perform the two-car trick. For refreshment along the Way there are pubs at Eastbury, East Garston, Great Shefford and Boxford.

In Lambourn, the Way goes through a playing field to the site of a medieval village at Bockhampton and picks up the railway line along the valley to Eastbury and East Garston. In East Garston, the Way follows the village street, where the river is obvious from small bridges at the cottage gates, even when it is dry in summer. Lakes and marshy woodland above the next village of Great Shefford ensure the river gains strength and there is always water flowing here.

After Great Shefford, the Way continues beside the old railway track for another mile (1.6km) to Weston, where it crosses the river beside a mill on the river – another indication of the more reliable water flow in this part of the valley. It is said that the flow of the Lambourn river is close to its natural state because it has not been greatly affected by water abstraction. This is the consequence of

Snowdrops by the Lambourn in Welford

the 1967 to 1976 feasibility studies into using the chalk aquifers of the Berkshire Downs to store water for human consumption in London. In the 1976 summer drought, it was discovered that the Lambourn could contribute little to London's water supplies and it was spared over-abstraction.

The Lambourn Valley Way from Weston to Boxford climbs up the hillside overlooking Welford Park and follows a ridge before returning to the river. Here, you cross the M4 motorway – with its incessant noise – although this 2 mile (3.2km) stretch could be missed out. Welford is worth a visit, especially in February when the park is open to the public, to walk beside the river through woodland carpeted with snowdrops. Henry VIII used Welford Park as a hunting lodge. It was rebuilt in 1652 and remodelled in 1700. The church has a round tower, an unusual feature in this part of the country.

Circular walk from Bangor to Boxford

Local conservationists, Lesley Dunlop and Dick Greenaway describe a good circular walk 4.5 miles (7.2km) from Bangor to Boxford in their book *Around the Three Valleys*. In brief, the route follows a footpath from Bangor to Mount Hill and Boxford Common, along a lane to Boxford, and returns beside the river along the Lambourn Valley Way. En route, enjoy the views from the higher ground, where you can see the river valley curling between the chalk hills. Pause to look at Boxford Church, where there is a charming memorial garden on the riverbank. The path back passes through water meadows, which are being traditionally managed to conserve their rich diversity of grasses and as a special habitat for the rare Desmoulin's whorl snail.

Shaw-cum-Donnington The last part of the Lambourn River can be followed from Shaw House; a splendid Tudor mansion built by wealthy cloth merchant, Thomas Dolman. The river formed part of the defence of the house during the Second Battle of Newbury in 1644. The house is open to the public and is full of interesting history with an excellent café. From the house, walk down Church Road to the pretty mill cottages beside the river. Cross the B4009 road Shaw Hill and walk a short distance along Kiln Road to Riverside Lane. There is a footpath beside the river to the Swan pub on the A4 London Road, only 1 mile (1.6km) from Shaw House. After passing under the road, the Lambourn divides into two channels around the Newbury Manor Hotel to enter the Kennet River on its way to the Thames.

GETTING THERE

BUS SERVICES | Newbury & District no. 4 goes to Lambourn; Wiltshire Connect 110 connects Marlborough and Hungerford; Stagecoach West no. 49 goes Swindon–Avebury–Devizes

TRAIN SERVICES | Great Western Railways between Reading and Hungerford

OS EXPLORER MAPS | 157 Marlborough & Savernake Forest; 158 Newbury & Hungerford; 159 Reading, Wokingham & Pangbourne

RESOURCES

Dunlop, Lesley and Greenaway, Dick, *Around the Three Valleys* (The Friends of the Pang, Kennet and Lambourn Valleys, 2011) – useful book for exploring this area

Greenham and Crookham Commons: www.bbowt.org.uk/nature-reserves/greenham-and-crookham-commons

Lambourn Valley Way: www.westberks.gov.uk/media/36684/Lambourn-Valley-Way-A-Walk-from-the-Whitehorse-Hill-to-Newbury/pdf/Lambourn_Valley_Way_-_A_Walk_from_the_Whitehorse_Hill_to_Newbury.pdf?m=1702030814623

River Loddon

LENGTH: 28 miles (45km)

SOURCE: West Ham, Basingstoke

CONFLUENCE: Wargrave

The Loddon rises at Basingstoke in Hampshire, flows on the east side of Reading and enters the Thames at Wargrave in Berkshire. Its main tributary, the Blackwater, starts near Aldershot in Surrey. These two rivers create valuable green corridors through land that is increasingly covered by roads and towns. Nature reserves and country parks give space to enjoy riverside walks away from the traffic. The Basingstoke Canal started in the town centre and crossed the Rivers Whitewater and Blackwater before joining the Wey Navigation at Byfleet. Between Basingstoke and Reading, the Loddon is best visited using a series of circular walks. From Reading to the Thames, public transport gives opportunities for linear walks.

ABOVE *Loddon near Wargrave*

OPPOSITE *Blackwater at Tice's Meadow*

What's in a name?

Ekwall thought that Loddon was an old river name coming from a Celtic word meaning 'marsh' or 'mud'.

WALK 23 The Basing Trail at Basingstoke

5.7 miles (9.1km)

This walk is a fine combination of human and natural history. It begins at the pedestrian circus where the Loddon emerges into daylight on the east side of the Festival Place at the edge of Eastrop Park. The murals on the walls of the underpass may remind you of the tale of Orpheus and Eurydice, with ideas of underground worlds – only one of the thought-provoking aspects of this walk. This start point is close to the railway station and central bus stops. There are car parks around the route. The leaflet available online (Resources) is helpful.

From Eastrop Park, go south along Eastrop Lane, turn right at the T junction and left at White Hart Lane, signed to The Orchard, which goes to the War Memorial Park. Curve left beside the playing fields to a path under the A30 road to Black Dam Ponds Nature Reserve. These ponds are formed by chalk springs and were once the fishponds in the grounds of Basing House. Walk east to the fields beside the Crabtree Plantation – another nature reserve – to the car park beside the Bolton Arch. This magnificent gateway was once the entrance to Hackwood Park but is now cut off by the M3 motorway. Hackwood House was built to replace Basing House, which was destroyed in 1645 after a two-year siege during the Civil War.

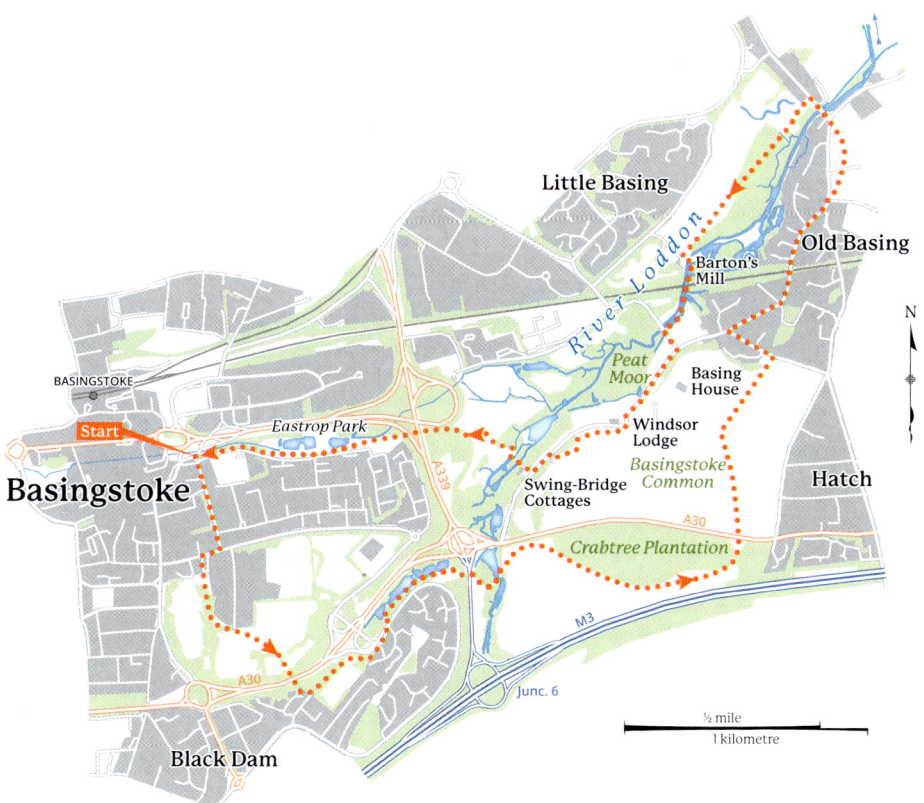

Loddon in Easing Park, Basingstoke

At the Bolton Arch, cross the A30 and walk straight across Basingstoke Common to the siege earthworks around the ruins of Basing House. Bear right to reach Old Basing village hall in Crown Lane. Turn left and then right into the street where the Bakeshop has a great reputation for coffee and pastries. Continue along the street under the railway and beside the park where Cromwell had cannons to attack the Royalists in Basing House. You reach the river at Pygott's Hill where there is a path under the pylons in the Millfield Nature Reserve on the north side of the river. This brings you to the pub at Barton's Mill. From here, the towpath at the start of the Basingstoke Canal leads you past the large Tithe Barn associated with Basing House. Walk along Redbridge Lane to the old lime pits, evidence of the chalk origins of the river, which are now car parks and playgrounds. A path across Peat Moor Nature Reserve leads you to the clear young Loddon. The underpass beneath the busy A33 road brings you back to Eastrop Park.

16 River Loddon

Sherfield on Loddon The village of Sherfield along the A33 road from Basingstoke to Reading is the next place to walk for 4 miles (6.4km) in peaceful farmland beside the Loddon meandering through the rich clay soil. Start near the village green, where there is a pub and café, walk to the roundabout on the main road, which you cross to a footpath that goes over a golf course to Lance Levy Farm. At the farm, take the bridleway that crosses the Loddon to Mill Lane and Hays Farm. Standing on the bridge over the river, you may notice with joy that you can hear only the flow of water – a haven of peace. The way back to Shenfield is along the Brenda Parker Way, a long-distance path named after a stalwart member of the North Hampshire Downs Ramblers group. The Way goes downstream for 2 miles (3.2km) crossing the A33, to Lilymill Farm near the village of Bramley. Mill Lane takes you back from Lilymill to Shenfield.

Stratfield Saye House The next place to walk beside the Loddon is at Stratfield Saye, the country house and park given to the Duke of Wellington in 1817 in recognition of his leadership in the wars against Napoleon. It is open to the public daily in August and the Easter Bank holiday weekend. In addition to the splendid house, paintings and items related to Wellington's life, the grounds are delightful for a riverside walk from the lawn beside the house to the quaint summer house and return through the walled kitchen garden and the grave of Copenhagen, the horse Wellington rode at the Battle of Waterloo.

Swallowfield The village of Swallowfield lies in the triangle of land between the Loddon and the Broadwater, as the River Blackwater is called after it is joined by the River Whitewater. There is a short 1.5 mile (2.4km) circular walk that uses the end of the Blackwater Trail. From the war memorial in the village centre, walk along Part Lane, signposted to Riseley. After about 200 yards (180m) on the right-hand side is Swallowfield Meadow, a local nature reserve bought by the Parish Council in 2003. After ½ mile (0.8km), take a footpath on the left, which goes to the Broadwater. At the road, turn left and walk to Swallowfield Church and continue on a riverside path used by anglers to a brick bridge that leads you back to the centre of Swallowfield.

Reading to Twyford by linear walks using public transport The lower part of the Loddon, to the east of Reading, offers excellent riverside walking with good public transport. The paths are not designated trails, and you will need to use a map and the signposts.

Loddon near Sherfield

WALK 24 Dinton Pastures to Twyford and back

7.7 miles (12.4km)

Although this is a 4 mile (6.4km) walk that can be made in one direction by using public transport from central Reading, we enjoy it as a 'dog bone'; two circular walks around lakes joined by a path beside the Loddon. Starting at Dinton Pastures, walk across the meadows to the large Activity Centre (canoeing, paddle boarding, etc). Cross Sandford Lane into Lavell's Lake Nature Reserve and take the path to the left. The path goes past a bird hide (Bittern), open to the public. On the west side of the lake, the footpath comes to Sandford Lane at a junction of paths. Turn right to take the path beside the river flowing north. This is the middle section that you will walk in both directions. It is the wildest part, where you are more likely to see Loddon lilies growing on the riverbanks or a kingfisher.

About 2 miles (3.2km) from the start, you come to Whistley Bridge. Turn left on the lane and walk to the next path on the right side. This path goes north, under the railway, and turns right to go on the east side of Loddon Lake. Look for a path going off to the right, which

BELOW *Lavell's Lake*

OPPOSITE *Dinton Pastures Lake*

brings you over a weir and past the old Silk Mill, converted into flats. This is close to the centre of Twyford, with its cafés, pubs, buses and railway station an alternative starting point.

To return to Dinton Pastures using a partly different route, walk west along Twyford High Street towards Reading. After crossing the Loddon, which is in three streams at White Bridge, take the path on the left that enters the Charvil Lakes Nature Reserve – the fourth on the journey. Choose the paths that keep you close to the west side of the river until you get to Whistley Mill Lane. Turn left to get to Whistley Bridge and take the path that brought you from Dinton Pastures. When you return to Sandford Lane continue ahead to go up the west side of Sandford and White Swan lakes on a path close to the Loddon. At the far end of the lakes, turn left to get back to the car park.

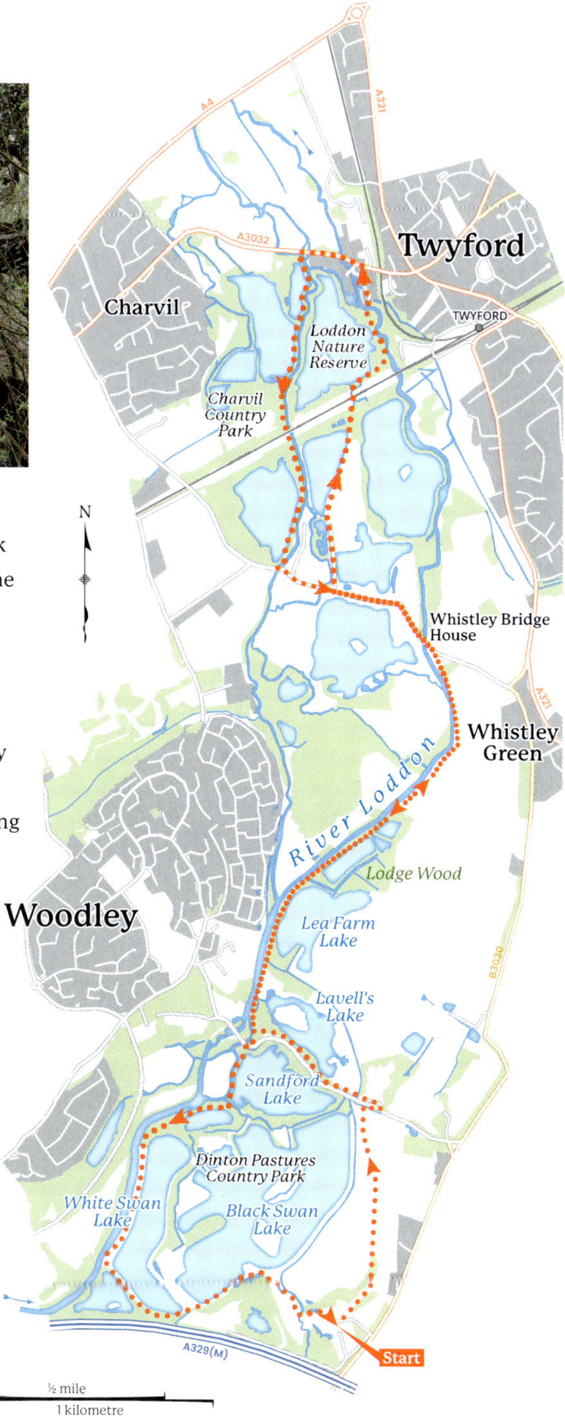

Twyford to Wargrave The last stretch of the Loddon starts at White Bridge at the A3032 road in Twyford, close to the Loddon Nature Reserve. The distance to Wargrave is 2.5 miles (4km). A path across Charvil Meadow follows the river north to the A4 road. On the other side of the A4, the track called Loddon Drive is a public footpath which goes all the way to Wargrave. You cross St Patrick's stream, a side stream of the Thames, and then another channel called Borough Lake. After twisting and turning, the drive crosses the Loddon and goes under the railway, before you arrive at Wargrave station to take a train back to Twyford.

River Blackwater The Blackwater rises on the south side of Aldershot at the Rowhill Nature Reserve, where the source is marked by an information board along the Blackwater Valley Path. The Path follows the river for all of its 23 miles (37km). As the Blackwater flows down from Rowhill, it is on the edge of the village of Weybourne and is little more than 1 mile (1.6km) away from the River Wey in Farnham to the south. But the Blackwater turns north to flow past Aldershot and Farnborough before going west between Sandhurst and Yateley to join the Whitewater to become the Broadwater at Eversley. As described above, the Broadwater enters the Loddon at Swallowfield.

Loddon Lilies near Twyford

The Blackwater forms the county border between Hampshire, Surrey and Berkshire. Its conservation was neglected until recent times when Hampshire County Council and the Blackwater Valley Conservation Trust worked hard to restore the wildlife habitats. There is good coarse fishing in the lakes along the valley and the water quality of the river is good enough for the occasional brown trout. As the fish stocks improve, so otters are returning.

The Rowhill Nature Reserve has 55 acres (22.3ha) of woodland mixed with small meadows, patches of heath and marshes. The Rowhill Nature Reserve Society features a Field Centre beside the car park. It is the first of a chain of reserves along the river and there are enough paths and different habitats to fill an hour of walking. The path in the wet woodland at Rowhill passes a small marshy pond with a sign marking the source of the Blackwater. Two miles (3.2km) along the Blackwater Valley Path is Tice's

The Blackwater looking as dark as its name

Meadow Nature Reserve, which was created from a quarry. It has lakes, reedbeds, gravel islands and grassland, making it a great place for birdwatching.

The 4 mile (6.4km) section of the Blackwater Valley Path from Ash to Frimley can be explored with circular walks because the Basingstoke Canal with its towpath runs parallel to the river with the Blackwater Valley Path. The two waterways are about a ¼ mile (0.4km) apart and are linked by minor roads and paths, so shorter circuits are possible. The paths are also off-road cycleways, so there are plenty of options. The full circuit from Lakeside Park Nature Reserve in Ash along the Blackwater Valley Path to Farnborough North station, returning through Frimley Hatchett Nature Reserve, Frimley Green and back beside the canal is a distance of 8 miles (12.9km). Along the way, you pass through Hollybush Park and Gerry's Copse (a wet woodland nature reserve) beside the Blackwater. The boat centre beside the canal at Mytchett has a popular café and boats for hire. The woodland in the Ministry of Defence land on the east side of the canal and two lakes form good wildlife habitats. The peacefulness of the canal is welcome after walking beside the river close to the noisy traffic on the A331 road.

An alternative to the 8 mile (12.9km) circular walk between Ash and Frimley is an 8 mile linear walk along the Blackwater Valley Path between Ash and Sandhurst, returning by train. After the nature reserves mentioned above, there is Hawley Meadows, 1 mile (1.6km) north of the M3, and Shepherd Meadows with Sandhurst Memorial Park, the few remnants of original flood meadows in the valley. These are vital in holding flood water that pours off the hard surfaces of the roads around them.

Between Sandhurst on the north side and Yateley on the south lie a group of lakes formed by quarrying gravel from the flood meadows. Horseshoe Lake and its neighbour, the Moor Green Lakes Nature Reserve, are excellent, with convenient car parks, good information boards and firm paths – a tribute to the staff and volunteers who work there.

The last part of the Blackwater Valley Path meanders, like the river, from Finchampstead to Swallowfield. The distance is about 5 miles (8km) and there is no easy way to return except by walking back or having a car at both ends. Along the way, Eversley is interesting because this is where Charles Kingsley wrote *The Water Babies* when he was the rector at the church from 1842 to 1875. If using a car, be warned that the fords marked on the map are usually deep in winter and can only be crossed on the footbridges.

River Whitewater The Whitewater rises near Odiham and feeds the Basingstoke Canal. Smaller than the Loddon and the Blackwater, it is a clean chalk stream for most of its length. Its valley is a lovely, peaceful place to walk.

OPPOSITE *Whitewater: Mill and pond at Greywell*

ABOVE *Stratfield Saye*

> **GETTING THERE**
>
> **BUS SERVICES** | Stagecoach no. 14 Basingstoke to Sherfield on Loddon; no. 7 Reading to Swallowfield
> **OS EXPLORER MAPS** | 144 Basingstoke, Alton & Whitchurch; 145 Guildford & Farnham, 159 Reading, Wokingham & Pangbourne; 160 Windsor, Weybridge & Bracknell
>
> **RESOURCES**
>
> *Explore the Blackwater Valley* (5th edn), (Blackwater Valley Partnership, 2012) – available from Hampshire County Council: *www.hants.gov.uk/shop/product.php?productid=16560*
> Basingstoke Canal: *www.hants.gov.uk/thingstodo/basingstokecanal*
> The Basing Trail: *www.hants.gov.uk/rh/walking/basing-trail.pdf*
> Blackwater Valley Conservation Trust: *www.bvct.org.uk; www.bracknell-forest.gov.uk/parks*
> Greywell Moors Nature Reserve: *www.hiwwt.org.uk/nature-reserves/greywell-moors-nature-reserve*
> Stratfield Saye House: *http://wellingtonestates.co.uk/stratfield-saye-house*
> Thames Basin Heath Partnership: *www.tbhpartnership.org.uk/help/*

WALK 25 North Warnborough to Greywell and Odiham Castle

4 miles (6.4km)

Park on the verge before the lift bridge in Tunnel Lane in North Warnborough. Walk to the footpath on the left immediately before the canal bridge. The path goes beside the canal for 100 yards (91m) and goes through the hedge to cross two fields to a lane. Turn right on the lane, which does a double bend. Take the path on the left to enter the Greywell Moors Nature Reserve. This fenland reserve with ponds, marsh and wet woodland is managed by the Hampshire and Isle of Wight Wildlife Trust using Polish ponies to graze the coarse vegetation. The springs that start the Whitewater lie at the southern end of the reserve.

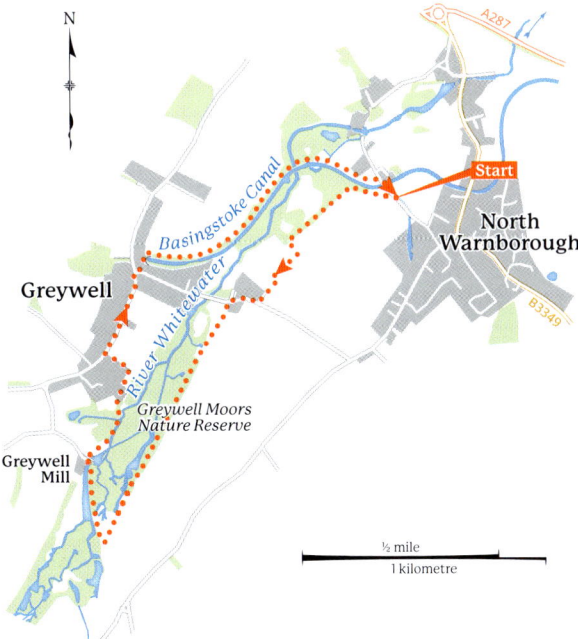

Odiham castle

When you reach the small stream, turn sharp right on to a path that follows the stream down to Greywell Mill, which has a large pond to give a good head of water for its power. Continue to the ancient St Mary's Church with flint walls and a wooden spire. From the church, one path goes straight across the meadow ahead, and another goes left to Greywell village street. Either way, you reach the corner of the meadow in front of the Fox and Goose (recommended for lunch). A few yards past the pub, turn right into a lane and take a footpath on the left bank, which goes over the entrance to the Greywell Tunnel, where the canal went under the hill to Old Basing and the source of the Loddon. Coming down to the canal towpath, the rest of the circuit is simple for the ½ mile (0.8km) back to the lifting bridge at Tunnel Lane. On the way you cannot miss the ruined Odiham Castle, built by King John in 1216. The owners of the castle were unlucky because it was besieged by French knights supporting the English barons in their rebellion against King John. It was granted to Eleanor, King John's daughter and the wife of Simon de Montfort, the Earl of Leicester. Simon de Montfort rebelled against Henry III and was killed by the king's supporters in 1265. It became a hunting lodge but fell into disuse and was a ruin by 1603.

River Wye

LENGTH: 9 miles (14.5km)

SOURCE: West Wycombe

CONFLUENCE: Bourne End

The Wye is one of the chalk streams of the Chiltern Hills that was important in the development of local industries. To quote John Parker, the town clerk of High Wycombe in 1878: 'The river made the mills. The mills made the market and the market made the town.' At least 27 mills have been recorded along the Wye, dating from 1185 to the 20th century. Grinding corn was the primary purpose of many of the mills, but paper-making became a more profitable business in the 18th century and caused pollution that persisted until modern times. This history is described by Charles Rangley-Wilson in his book *Silt Road*, but this title is no longer deserved as the water now runs clear.

The source is in a meadow beside the A40 road on the north side of West Wycombe Park, but this is often dry in summer. A permanent source of running water is the lake in the park, fed by several springs. The water from the eastern edge of the lake cascades to make a wide stream. West Wycombe House and Park were built in the 18th century by Sir Francis Dashwood (perhaps best remembered for founding the Hellfire Club). In summer, when the park is open to the public, it is pleasant to walk around admiring the small temples and following the streams that flow into the lake.

Wye confluence with the Thames

> ### What's in a name?
>
> There is no ancient river name that has been recorded. It was called the Wycombe stream in county records in 1810. By 1910, it was known as the Wye, a name given to it by military cadets making maps for the Ordnance Survey.

WALK 26 West Wycombe

3 miles (4.8km)

Footbridge at West Wycombe

When the park is closed or you want to walk with a dog, there is a good walk outside its boundary which encompasses the upper reaches of the Wye. Start at the car park beside the walled garden at the foot of West Wycombe hill. Walk down to the A40 and turn right (west). After about 200 yards (180m), cross the A40 to Toweridge Lane on the west side of the park. Walk up the lane between meadows that collect water for the Wye. At the top of the hill, turn left on a track running through a belt of trees. There is a fine view of an equestrian statue in the park. The track passes a property called Druid's Hutt, another Dashwood fancy. Bear left along a footpath that descends along a wooded ridge and passes the Sand Banks Nature Reserve. The route rejoins Toweridge Lane, which goes down to the A4010 road. Turn left and after 50 yards (45m), turn left again to an avenue leading to impressive iron gates. Just before the gates, bear right down a slope past some barns and go through the wooden gate to a white footbridge across the Wye. From the bridge, there is a splendid view towards West Wycombe Park. The path goes past a hedge to reach Park Farm Road, where you walk up to the A40 to complete the journey on the pavement back to West Wycombe. There are cafés, pubs, lovely buildings and the Hellfire Club caves in this pretty village. Complete the walk by climbing the hill to St Lawrence's Church and the Dashwood Mausoleum to enjoy the view down the Wye Valley before descending to the car park.

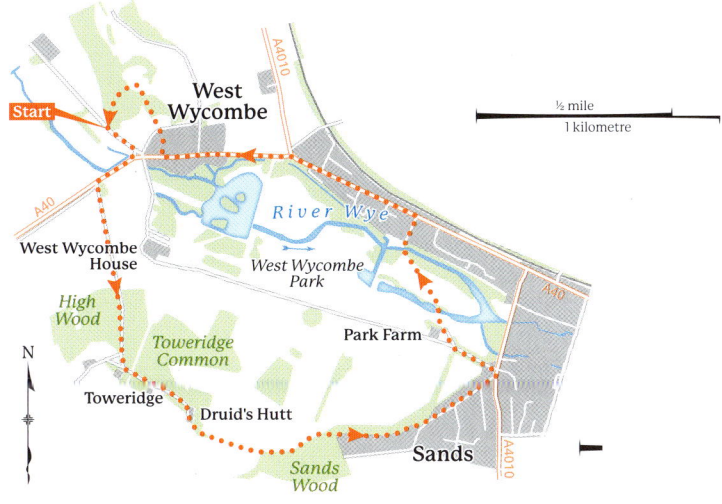

High Wycombe From the bridge where the Wye runs under the A4010, it goes through an urban environment with reminders of its industrial past. Although, the Wye is hidden behind buildings and beneath roads in the centre of High Wycombe, it is a delight to find it near the council buildings and the magistrates' court before it flows under Abbey Way to reach the Rye, where it runs in the open for the rest of its course.

The Rye is a large public area of playing fields, with the Wye running parallel to the A40 on its northern edge. At the north-west corner of the Wye is Pann Mill, which has been conserved as a working flour mill and where you can volunteer to become a miller. If you walk beside the river to the eastern end of the Rye, you can come back along the southern side beside the Dyke. The Dyke is an artificial channel that takes water from the lake in Wycombe Abbey to join the Wye in Loudwater. It has a waterfall, plenty of wildlife and rowing boats to hire at the town western end.

The Wye finds its modern industries in Loudwater and Wooburn Green. It runs beside warehouses, engineering works and playing fields. Exploration requires patience, walking along a main road to find side streets that run down to, or across, the river, and looking for short riverside paths. The best of these is in Wooburn Park, where there is parking. If you walk around the western and northern edges of the playing fields, you find the Wye and a footpath through a nature reserve.

OPPOSITE *Pann Mill in High Wycombe*

ABOVE *West Wycombe Park*

Before reaching Bourne End, the Wye has a short pastoral section beside the A4094, two meadows on one side and a grassy strip with willow trees on the other. The lowest part of the Wye in Bourne End hides behind houses, with high brick walls. Perhaps the best watery connection here is the street, Andrews Reach, named after the builders of slipper launches at Bourne End. The Wye keeps its elusive course to its end, as it joins the Thames where the confluence is partly hidden by a large chestnut tree.

The mouth of the Wye can be seen from Cookham Moor. Exactly opposite the mouth, there is an information board that explains the history and the wildlife of the River Wye.

GETTING THERE

BUS SERVICES | Carousel, no. 40 High Wycombe to West Wycombe; Carousel, nos. 35, 36 & 37 High Wycombe to Bourne End
TRAIN SERVICES | Chiltern Line from London Marylebone; Oxford and Aylesbury to High Wycombe
OS EXPLORER MAP | 172 Chiltern Hills East

RESOURCES

Pann Mill: *www.pannmill.org.uk*
Rangeley-Wilson, Charles, *Silt Road: The story of a lost river* (Chatto & Windus, 2013)

The Wye leaving West Wycombe Park

PART 4

The rivers entering the Thames in Surrey

Winter morning on the Wey at Guildford

18 River Colne

LENGTH: 30 miles (48.3km)

SOURCE: North Mimms Park near Hatfield

CONFLUENCE: Staines

The Colne flows around the north-west of London and reaches the Thames in Staines. It marks the boundary between Buckinghamshire and what was Middlesex, now London. This is the area that the poet John Betjeman called Metroland. A century earlier, the journalist Charles Mackay called the Colne: 'a river of small pretensions to beauty' in *The Thames and its Tributaries* (1840). The best that Mackay could say was that the river was: 'sacred to all the admirers of genius' because the poet John Milton grew up in Colnbrook. Not only does the Colne have chalk streams as sub-tributaries (Chess, Gade, Misbourne and Ver), it is also a vital wildlife corridor amid railways, roads, houses and industrial sites, including Heathrow Airport. The riverside paths are a vital asset for walking, cycling and finding interesting wilderness. The transport systems make it accessible to a large number of people, and yet it gives visitors plenty of uncrowded space.

Upper Colne

The Colne rises from an underground stream and several springs at North Mimms Park, close to the A1(M) road to the south of Hatfield. The underground stream is fed by water that runs into swallow holes at the aptly named village of Water End and by the Mimmshall Brook that runs from South Mimms. This area is an important watershed because the River Lea, which runs around the north-east of London, is only 3 miles (4.8km) away on the other side of Hatfield.

What's in a name?

The name is shared by a river in Essex that flows through Colchester to the North Sea and a Yorkshire river which is a tributary of the River Calder. Also the River Coln in Chapter 7 is sometimes spelt with an 'e'. Perhaps they are all derived from a Celtic word meaning 'the river'. This 'Colne' is obviously the root for place names (Colney Heath, London Colney and Colnbrook).

Broad Colney Lake

A coot at Broad Colney

At Colney Heath Common, the Colne comes above ground and there is usually running water – rather dark because of the peaty soil. It can be followed to the Thames using long-distance paths. Walk across the common, now a nature reserve, to Park Corner and pick up the Watling Chase Timberland Trail to London Colney. The Trail and the river pass Bowman's, Willow and Tyttenhanger fishing lakes. It is quiet until London Colney, where the jollity of families visiting Willows Farm Village and the noise of traffic make you aware of civilisation again.

In London Colney, the river widens into small ornamental lakes divided by a village green where the river is crossed by a ford and a handsome brick bridge. Here, you leave the Watling Chase Timberland Trail and continue on the paths through Broad Colney Lakes Nature Reserve. At Shenley Lane (B5378), a bridle path takes you beside the river under the M25 motorway to Colney Street. On the way, you can see Napsbury Park, once a large mental hospital and now residential apartments. At Colney Street you go through the site of the Handley Page aircraft factories, where passenger planes and bombers were built from 1929 to 1970. Here, also, is Watling Street, the Roman road from London to Wroxeter on the Welsh border.

At this point you have walked about 5 miles (8km) and have choices about which way to continue your walk. If you travelled by car to Colney Heath, it makes sense to return to your car using the same route. If you are using public transport, you can catch a bus from Colney Street, or walk further west along Smug Oak Lane to Bricket Wood train station, about 1.3 miles (2km).

River Colne

Bricket Wood to Rickmansworth Walking beside the Colne between Bricket Wood and Rickmansworth is a mixed bag. The first 5 miles (8km) starts well with a good car park for the Riverside Way – part of the Ver-Colne Valley Walk – near the bridge where Smug Oak Lane crosses the Ver. The signage is clear, the path firm and the river gurgles alongside. The Ver joins the Colne at a ford, which is a lovely spot. Wandering through the fields on a summer's morning to the next ford at Munden House, you can tune out the hum of traffic on the M1 and M25 motorways and enjoy the song of skylarks.

When you reach Watford, the Colne changes from a pastoral river to an urban environment. The riverside parks are municipal in style, but there are features to admire and ponder. The most amusing are the bronze statues of a fisherman at Water Lane and a swimmer at the site of a bathing place. A plaque on one of the railway bridges records that the Colne at Watford was the boundary of the City of London's powers to tax the transport of coal in the 19th century.

Ford across the Colne at Munden, Watford

The Fisherman and the Swimmer at Watford

As you follow the Colne around the south-east side of Watford, you leave the Ver-Colne Valley Walk in a mess of supermarkets and stores. Look for the start of the Ebury Trail near the large railway viaduct to take you to Rickmansworth. This 3 mile (4.8km) path follows the line of a disused railway with a good surface for easy walking and cycling. It curves across the Colne and back to the north side of the valley, runs through scrubby woodland and beside the Common Moor Nature Reserve, crosses the Rivers Gade and Chess, as well as the Grand Union Canal, before ending near the Batchworth Lock Canal Centre.

Rickmansworth to Uxbridge

The Colne Valley between Rickmansworth and Staines was established as a regional park in 1965 and has been saved from the worst effects of metropolitan sprawl. Down to Uxbridge, the Colne winds round gravel pits but keeps returning to the Grand Union Canal, which takes a straight course south. Here is one of our favourite walks, which goes south to Denham Country Park using the Colne Valley Trail and returns along the canal towpath.

WALK 27 Rickmansworth to Black Jack's Lock, near Mount Pleasant

6 miles (9.7km)

Start at the Aquadrome Park at Rickmansworth, where there is a car park, café, playground and toilets. Walk on the north-west side of Bury Lake, which is used for watersports, to find a path beside the Colne. Continue on the north-west side of the next lake, Stocker's, which is a nature reserve and excellent for birdwatching. At the western end, cross the Colne using the bridge on the right side. You come to Springwell Lane and turn left to the towpath near Springwell Lock. Cross the bridge and walk up the lane, looking for the Colne Valley Trail sign on the right side. After ¼ mile (0.4km), at a group of barns, keep right (not the Hillingdon Trail that veers left). The trail gives you views over the canal and the large sewage works. Beside the works is a large reedbed, a nature reserve that you will see more closely on the way back. After a short woodland section the trail becomes Summerhouse Lane, which descends to the canal and the Hillingdon Narrowboats, a community boating charity. Continue along Summerhouse Lane to Park Lane in Mount Pleasant. Turn left and then right to Jack's Lane. At about ½ mile (0.8km) along Jack's Lane and 3 miles (4.8km) from the start, you come to a bridge (no. 178) over the canal beside Black Jack's Lock. Cross to the canal towpath and start your return to Rickmansworth. Who was Jack? A miller who lived here a long time ago who gained his name through being cruel to his donkey – or so it is said.

Bury Lake, Rickmansworth Aquadrome Local Nature Reserve

As you walk back, you have the river on your left side. You come to the Coy Carp, a pub at the Coppermill Lane bridge, and pass the lovely reedbeds that you saw on the way down. After Springwell Lock, the canal bends east and you stay on the tow path until you reach the Aquadrome Park and the end of the walk.

Colne near Harefield

Denham to Staines If you continue south from Black Jack's Lock, the canal towpath is the easier way because the Colne Valley Trail is affected by the building of the HS2 railway. When you have been under the viaduct of the railway line from Marylebone to the main towns in Buckinghamshire, you find Denham Country Park on your right side, with several paths from the towpath. There is a visitor centre and café in the park, which could be the destination of a 6 mile (9.7km) linear walk from Rickmansworth.

Shortly before the A40, a path takes you away from the canal in an easterly direction to the Shire Ditch, a side stream which is the county boundary between London and Buckinghamshire. The path beside the Shire Ditch leads to Alderglade Nature Reserve and to Fray's River, a side stream that once powered mills in Uxbridge.

Downstream from Uxbridge, the Colne divides into a complicated pattern of side streams and secondary rivers, including the Duke of Northumberland's and the Longford rivers (both humanmade), the Wraysbury and Ash rivers, and the Colne Brook.

City of London boundary marker beside the Colne

To follow the rivers from Uxbridge to Staines, go along the Colne Valley Way where it leaves the Grand Union Canal below the Waterloo Bridge and goes westward along Culvert Lane to the River Colne. The London Loop signs are a useful indicator to this cross path. The Way is marked by handsome wooden posts. The path goes through woodland and beside meadows until you reach the Grand Union Canal. Turn west beside the canal for ⅓ mile (0.5km), to find the Colne Valley Way going south through a more industrial area near the Colne Brook and under the railway to Thorney Park Golf Club. This attractive green space makes you realise the pressure on wildlife caused by human activity, including Heathrow Airport, motorways, enormous reservoirs, waste tips, gravel pits, railways and warehouses.

Another dogleg westward along Thorney Mill Road takes you over the M25 to a path that reconnects to the Colne Brook before crossing the M4. Soon you arrive in the village of Colnbrook for a halfway break at about 7 miles (11.3km), as well as shops and hotels for refreshments and several unspoilt buildings along the main street. Aircraft dominate the next mile (1.6km), but it is good

Spring morning, Grand Union Canal at Denham

to go through Arthur Jacob Nature Reserve and Poyle Poplars Woodland. Birdsong and the rustling poplar tree leaves give relief.

Next is Wraysbury Reservoir and road bridges over the M25 junction 14. The marking of the Colne Valley Way is not obvious, but the signs to Staines are clear. Now that you are on the east of the M25, you meet the Colne again and its attendant Hithermoor Stream, which is a flood relief channel running through a park where there is good riverside walking. Continue on the Colne Valley Way to the King George VI Reservoir. From the reservoir behind its high embankments, look for a footpath across Staines Moor. At southern side of Staines Moor, the bridge bearing the Staines bypass has murals on its walls and the path brings you into the older part of Staines around St Mary's Church. From there, it is a short distance to the banks of the Thames. Walk downstream on the embankment to find a pelican statue beside a bridge over the mouth of the Colne. Staines derives its name from being the place where the London Stone, or Stane, marked the upper limit of the fishing rights of the City of London and of the Port of London until 1908.

River Ver The Ver is the first sub-tributary to join the Colne and is a beautiful chalk stream named after the Roman settlement Verulamium, now the city of St Albans. The source near Markyate is usually dry but there is running water at Redbourn. The Ver Valley Society has been successful in protecting the river and produced excellent guides to walks beside the river, including the River Ver Trail and eight circular walks (Resources).

175

WALK 28 St Albans to Childwickbury and Redbournbury

7.5 miles (12km)

This walk is based on no. 5 of the Ver Valley Society circular walks mentioned above. Start at the car park beside the Verulamium Museum in St Albans. Go down St Michael Street to the old bridge and ford across the Ver. Pass the former mill house in Branch Road and cross Redbourn Road. Turn left. Walk through the play area to a driveway to the golf club. Along the driveway, take the bridle path on the left signed as the Hertfordshire Way. Follow the Way up the hill and through a wood which has a fine display of bluebells in the spring.

Childwick Bury Manor, the large house and park, belonged to the filmmaker Stanley Kubrick. The route goes through a group of estate buildings at Childwick Green. The small church, St Mary's, is a 'chapel of ease' for the estate workers to worship without the long walk to the St Albans Cathedral and Abbey Church. Continue along the tarmac driveway to Harpenden Road (A1081). Turn left. Using the good path along the wide verge for ½ mile (0.8km) to Beesonend Lane.

Beesonend Lane is quiet, leading straight down to a ford across the Ver to Redbournbury Mill, which was badly damaged by a fire in 1987 but has been restored with help from volunteers. It is open on Saturday mornings and Sunday afternoons. Even when it's shut, it's worth crossing the river to admire the conservation that has kept a watermill working here for at least 500 years. Return to the east side of the river to go back to St Albans on the Ver-Colne Valley Walk. You are likely to see herons beside the river, and a kingfisher if you are lucky. The walk through flood meadows is always beautiful, with buttercups galore in summer. Water voles have been reintroduced to the river here. After another mill house at Shafford, you cross the Redbourn Road and enter flood meadows in the Gorhambury Estate. Soon you cross the river and take the track going between two fields. At the top of the track turn left and walk along the avenue, with a fine view of the abbey. The avenue is close to the line of the Roman road, Watling Street. At the end of the avenue the Roman theatre is on the right side. Cross over to St Michael's Street and the car park.

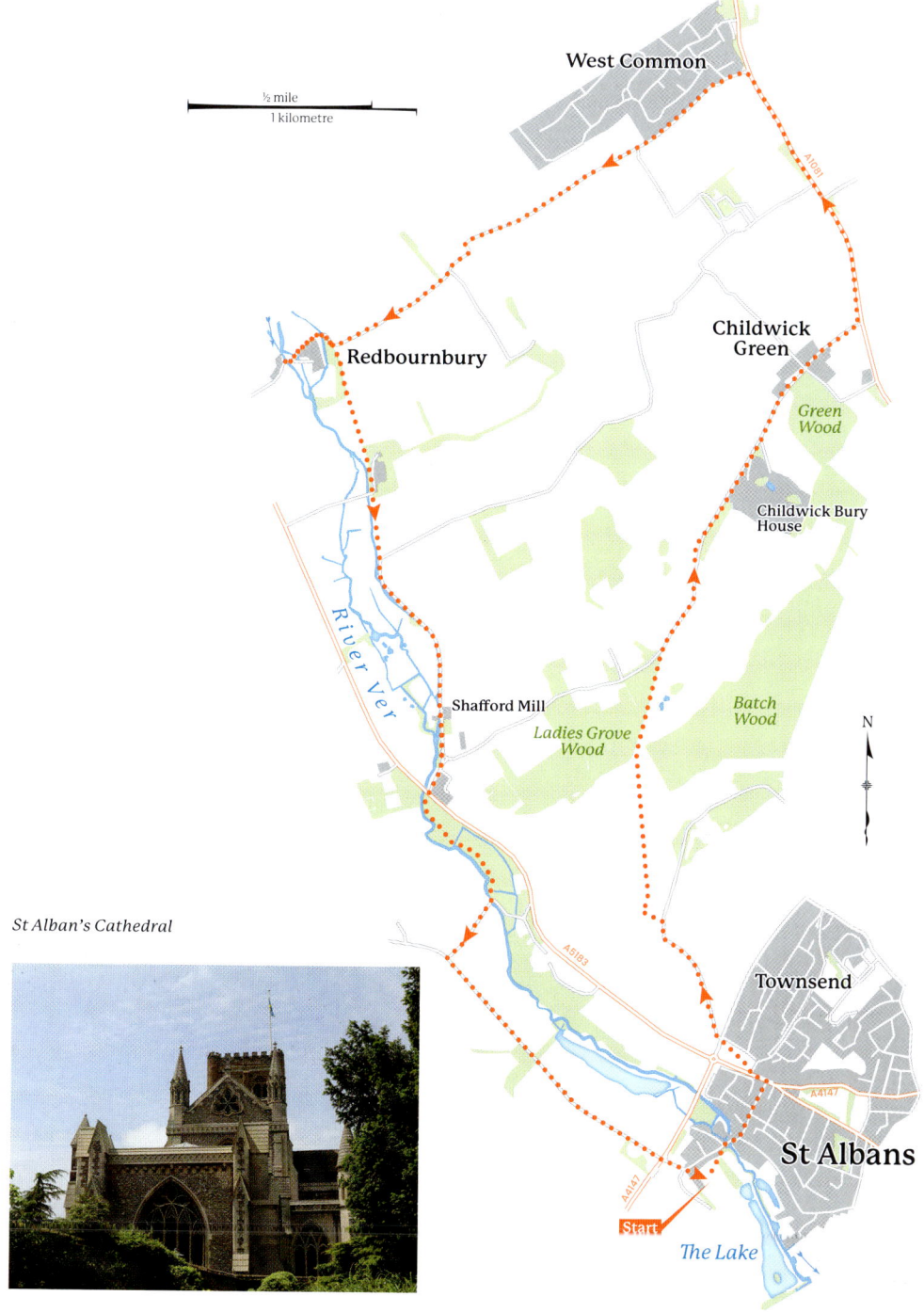

18 River Colne

Rivers Gade and Bulbourne The Gade flows from Gaddesden near Berkhamsted to join the Colne at Rickmansworth. The Grand Union Canal uses its water and its valley to climb up to Hemel Hempstead and then follows its tributary, the Bulbourne, through the Chiltern Hills to Tring, as mentioned in Chapter 13. The Grand Union Canal towpath is the best way to explore the Gade and Bulbourne, with railway stations at Watford, Hemel Hempstead and Tring. The features are similar to those encountered along the Colne, a mixture of lovely countryside, fascinating history and dull urban patches. The Bulbourne is 7 miles (11.3km) long and flows into the Gade at Two Waters in Hemel Hempstead. From this confluence to the Colne at Rickmansworth is another 9 miles (14.5km). A mile (1.6km) downstream from Tring railway station you enter the Bulbourne Valley at Cow Roast, which is a crossroads in time and space. The hamlet's name is a corruption of 'Cow Rest', where drovers stopped on their way when taking cattle to London. The excavation of the canal-boat marina revealed evidence of a pre-Roman iron

The Grand Union Canal at Bulbourne

industry and a Roman town. Akeman Street, already encountered at other tributaries, lies under the A4251 from Tring to Hemel Hempstead. The West Coast main train line from Euston, London, to Scotland runs along the side of the valley. In modern times, the river starts to flow on the surface between Cow Roast and Northchurch.

Three miles (4.8km) down the valley is Berkhamsted, a market town since Saxon times where the large Norman castle used the Bulbourne for its defensive moats. Then, the river and canal are out in countryside again until they enter Hemel Hempstead and join the Gade. In its upper reaches above Hemel Hempstead, the Gade is a more typical Chiltern river, with chalk springs, watercress beds and memories of trout. Gadebridge Park has waterside picnic places with walks in open space. Box Moor and the land around Two Rivers was a marsh until canal building improved the drainage. The Box Moor Trust has conserved the water meadows that were bought by local people in 1594 to prevent enclosure.

From Hemel Hempstead to Rickmansworth, the Gade changes from a chalk stream to a real river meandering through fields and woods, sometimes close to the canal and sometimes at a distance. One of the larger loops makes a feature in Cassiobury Park, the 190 acre (76.9ha) public open space at Watford. On the west side of the Gade, the Herts and Middlesex Wildlife Trust has made a nature reserve. A short walk of less than a mile (1.6km) on the west side to the river and canal takes you to Whippendell Wood, which is full of bluebells in the spring. The lowest reach of the Gade flows through Croxley Common Moor, a piece of wilderness surviving amid urban sprawl, a place to walk among unmown grass and wildflowers.

River Chess The Chess flows for 10 miles (16km) from Chesham to Rickmansworth. The name is derived from Chesham, which was a significant settlement in Saxon times. It appears to have suffered less from water abstraction because it runs well in most conditions. The Chess Valley Walk is a wonderful linear walk from Rickmansworth railway station to the Chesham station, connected by the Metropolitan Line of the London Underground (Getting there).

WALK 29 Chess Valley at Chenies

6.8 miles (10.9km)

Instead of the whole length of the Chess Valley, we have a circular walk that visits some of the best places. Start at the Green in Chenies (TQ 015984) and take the path beside the village school. This path gives you a view of the Manor's beautiful gardens before you turn right and then left to walk to Walk Wood, with great views of the valley on the way. The path goes into a field on the edge of Little Chalfont. Stay close to the edge of the wood until you reach a sign showing the link to the Chess Valley Way on the right. Go down through the beech wood and over the meadow to Latimer, where the large Latimer House was used to hold senior prisoners of war, including Rudolf Hess. Follow the Chess Valley Way signs downstream. You pass a 'lost' church, explained on an information board, and the tomb of William Liberty, a relative of the Liberty's of London family, built in an isolated spot so his body parts would not mix with anyone else on the Day of Resurrection. Frogmore Meadows Nature Reserve is a fine set of flood meadows with scabious and southern marsh orchids. At Sarratt Bottom, the watercress beds are a small remnant of what was a flourishing business in the Chilterns. The Way becomes a small lane. Turn right at the T junction and

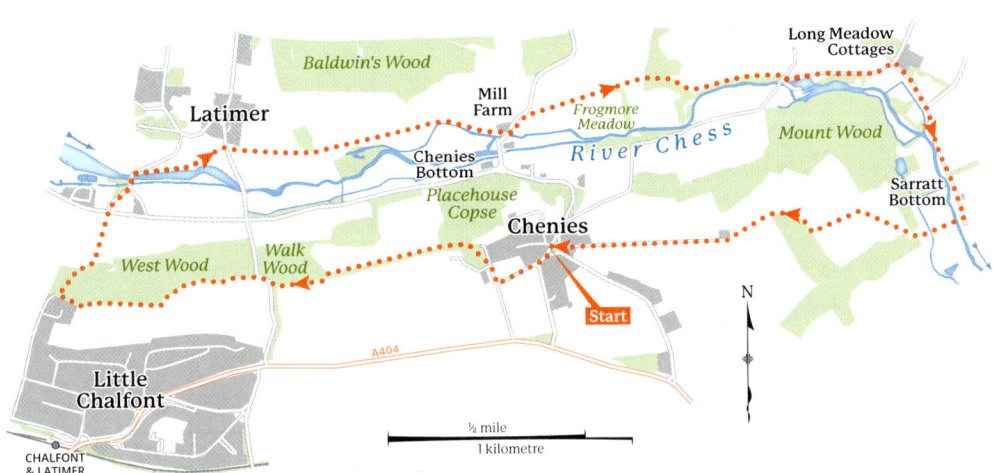

Latimer House in the Chess Valley

continue beside the river until you come to a crossing of paths. Turn right over the river and through the marsh to another meeting of paths. Take the path angled to the right shown by a finger called 'Chenies half mile'. This brings you back to the starting point. For refreshment, try the Bedford Arms Hotel, the Red Lion pub or the café in the garden centre on the main road.

18 River Colne

River Misbourne The Misbourne rises from springs near Great Missenden and flows to Denham, a distance of 16 miles (25.7km). The section between Amersham and Chalfont St Peter is a 'perched river', so called because it is perched above the usual water table and its water may sink to flow underground. In summer, it is quite usual to find running water above Amersham, but a dry riverbed from the waterworks below Amersham to the lake in Chalfont Park. The depth of the valley between the hills suggests that once the river was more substantial.

The South Bucks Way follows the Misbourne from Great Missenden to Chalfont St Peter, and from Denham to the confluence with the Colne. The best part starts in Little Missenden

Misbourne near Amersham

at St John the Baptist Church, which has a display of local history. Follow the South Bucks Way signs downstream to the cricket field on the edge of Old Amersham. The large house you see along the way is Shardeloes, built in the 18th century. During the construction of the house and lake, coins and broaches were found dating from AD 220, another sign of Roman villas beside Thames tributaries. Trains between Great Missenden and Amersham, and buses between Amersham and Chalfont St Peter, can help with linear walks along the South Bucks Way.

GETTING THERE

TRAIN SERVICES | The Colne valley is well served by trains from Central London (Paddington, Marylebone, Euston, King's Cross) and the Metropolitan Underground Line

OS EXPLORER MAPS | 172 Chiltern Hills East; 173 London North; 181 Chiltern Hills North; 182 St Albans & Hatfield

RESOURCES

CHESS

The Chess Valley Walk: *www.chilternsaonb.org/wp-content/uploads/2021/12/Chess-Valley-Walk-Leaflet-For-Web.pdf*

COLNE

Boxmoor Trust: *www.boxmoortrust.org.uk*

Colne Valley Way: *www.gps-routes.co.uk/routes/home.nsf/RoutesLinksWalks/colne-valley-way-walking-route#*

Croxley Common Moor: *www.croxleycommonmoor.org.uk/index.html*

Stocker's Lake: *www.fosl.org.uk*

Watling Chase Timberland Trail: *https://ldwa.org.uk/ldp/members/show_path.php?path_name=Watling+Chase+Timberland+Trail*

MISBOURNE

Misbourne Walks: *www.chilterns.org.uk/wp-content/uploads/2021/09/misbournewalks.pdf*

VER

Redbournbury Mill: *www.redbournburymill.co.uk*

Ver Valley Society walks: *www.riverver.co.uk/walks/*

River Bourne

LENGTH: 13 miles (21km)

SOURCE: Virginia Water (North Bourne) and Bisley (South Bourne)

CONFLUENCE: opposite Hamhaugh Island near Shepperton

The Bourne is usually described as a river with two arms, named North and South. The North Bourne is the easier to explore because it has a definite starting point and it grows to be large enough to be marked by a double line on Ordnance Survey maps before it enters the Thames. The South Bourne is more of a challenge, as we explain below.

The North Bourne in Chertsey

What's in a name?

Ekwall lists 15 English rivers called Bourn(e) or Burn, the latter being the older word used for a stream. All are small tributaries of larger rivers. There are many more with 'bourne' preceded by a qualifying word, for example, Winterbourne.

North Bourne

The North Bourne is formed by streams in Windsor Great Park running into Virginia Water. The lake was created in the 1750s by building a dam that became the Cascade at the south-eastern corner of Windsor Great Park. Firm paths around the lake make a popular walk of 5 miles (8km). If you start at the car park beside the A30 and walk clockwise around the lake, you quickly come to the Cascade. Next are the ruins of Leptis Magna, whose stones were brought from Libya in 1816. There are fine views of the lake from the south shore before you reach the Five Arch Bridge that crosses an arm of the lake to the northern shore. Passing lakeside houses and crossing the next arm of the lake, you enter the Valley Gardens. In spring, the rhododendrons give a splendid show of colour. In all seasons, zigzag paths entice you to admire the exotic shrubs and trees. Then, an enormous totem pole from British Columbia catches your attention, before you turn right at the top of Wick Pond to return to the starting point and refreshments at the lakeside café. It was unkindly described by the 19th-century travel writer John Murray as 'a place full of artificial prettinesses in that boasted taste which, for want of a better name, we may

Five Arch Bridge at Virginia Water

19 River Bourne

Pylons stride over Chertsey Mead

denominate the Grand Cockney', *A Picturesque Tour of the River Thames in its Western Courses*, 1845. John Murray also wrote: 'But water in every landscape is pleasing and compensates for many defects', which is one of our themes.

At first, the river runs through the privately owned Wentworth Golf Course and Country Club, after which it is buried under the junction of the M3 and M25 motorways and emerges beside the gravel pits at the southern end of Thorpe Park. Happily, a public riverside walk exists in the middle of Chertsey. Between the Staines Road (A320) and Free Prae Road, the Bourne runs through a strip of parkland for a mile (1.6km). There are paths on both sides, including the National Cycle Network Route 4. With trees, grassy areas, seats and fishing platforms, this is a pleasant place for a stroll. For dog owners, office staff taking a lunchtime break and parents with small children, riverside walks in towns are a precious resource. The Ramblers Association has a local health walk that includes this part of the Bourne. The town centre and Chertsey station are close and the River Bourne Health Club has plenty of parking space. Route 4 continues east towards London for ½ mile (0.8km) on the minor roads and comes to Chertsey Meads, where we start another of our favourite walks.

WALK 30 Chertsey Meads to Weybridge

5 miles (8km)

Chertsey Meads is one of more than 150 nature reserves with public access close to the Thames. Start at the car park after the last building on the left side of Mead Lane, Chertsey. Go to the left of the children's playground to find a path that goes to a footbridge over the river entrance to Bates Wharf. After the marina, bear right through the car park beside the riverside apartments to a path beside the Thames. Walk up to Chertsey Bridge and cross the river to Dumsey Meadow which, like the Chertsey Meads, is a vital flood meadow. Dumsey has never been artificially fertilised nor ploughed and is the only such meadow beside the Thames in Surrey. The Thames Path stays close to the river for 1.5 miles (2.4km) to Shepperton Lock. You pass an eclectic array of houseboats before more conventional riverside homes. As you reach Shepperton, the houses you see on the opposite bank are, in fact, on an island (Pharoah's) only accessible by boat.

The interest in access across the river becomes personal after Shepperton Lock: the only way to complete the circle is to take the ferry across to the Weybridge side. Enjoy a coffee or ice cream from

Walk 30

the café while waiting for the boat. After crossing, you leave the Thames Path to walk beside the mouth of the Wey. The path becomes Thames Street, where a path on the right, before the Old Crown pub, is signed to the Wey Navigation. Follow this path and you come to an arching footbridge looking down into Thames Lock, the start of the Wey Navigation, one of the first canals with locks build in England, and opened in 1653. Walk along the towpath for 1 mile (1.6km) to where the canalised part of the Wey goes right and the original river comes under the Weybridge. As you approach the Addlestone Road, you cross a stream, which is the South Bourne entering the Wey.

At Addlestone Road, turn right and right again, to walk along Weystone Road. Cross the larger Weybridge Road (A317) and continue on Hamm Court Road. When you reach the Hamm Court entrance with its forbidding notices, turn left on to a footpath in woodland that brings you to the southern end of Chertsey Meads. The electricity pylons striding north are a useful navigation aid. Follow the paths beneath them until you reach a small river in a belt of trees. This is the North Bourne, which has been joined by the Woburn Park Stream bearing some of the water from the South Bourne. After crossing the Bourne, there are numerous paths, open grassland and the hard-surfaced east-west track across the Meads to bring you back to the car park where you started. Unfortunately, you cannot follow the North Bourne to its confluence with the Thames because this is hidden by the privacy of Hamm Court.

The South Bourne at Heather Farm

South Bourne The South Bourne rises from springs in the rifle ranges at Bisley. There is no definite starting place and several streams including Trulley Brook at West End and Mill Bourne at Chobham could be regarded as significant sources.

There are no riverside paths that follow the South Bourne for more than a mile, but we found two nature reserves with attractive walks. The first is Chobham Water Meadows, starting at the car park in Chobham High Street. If you bear left on entering the meadows, you find the Mill Bourne flowing east. There are paths on both sides of the stream, but the one on the south side runs for a mile to a T junction of paths. The path to the right is interesting because it leads to Emmett's Mill, but it is badly overgrown. Turning left takes you over the Chertsey Road and on to lanes that climb up to Chobham Common, which is a large national nature reserve with fine walks over sandy heathland.

The simple way to go is to return to the water meadows and walk beside the ash and oak trees on the south side of the meadows, finishing at the delightful dog-friendly café near the car park.

Heather Farm The South Bourne flows along the western side of Horsell Common where a nature reserve, Heather Farm, has been created by the Horsell Common Preservation Society. The reserve has water meadows, heathland and wet woodland with well-made paths and good signage. The information centre, café and large car park make this a popular day out for families. Wildlife attractions include the flowers (yellow toadflax, purple loosestrife) and birds (skylarks, blackcaps, Dartford warblers). A circular walk of 4 miles (6.4km) goes along the river to McLaren Park with its striking Technology Centre. This is well described on information boards and leaflets available near the main car park. The walk takes you from the busy area around the information centre and playground to spacious meadows and quiet woods, where you can sit at the water's edge in peace.

As it flows north, the South Bourne passes the east side of Addlestone. At Hamm Moor, it contributes water to the Woburn Park stream and turns east to enter the Wey at Weybridge.

19 River Bourne

GETTING THERE

TRAIN SERVICES | Virginia Water and Chertsey are served by South Western Railway from Waterloo and Reading, on a loop between Staines and Weybridge

OS EXPLORER MAP | 160 Windsor, Weybridge & Bracknell

RESOURCES

Chertsey Health Walk: *www.walkingforhealth.org.uk/content/18b-chertsey-and-river-bourne*

Chertsey Meads: *https://www.runnymede.gov.uk/explore-borough/suitable-alternative-natural-greenspaces-sangs/7*

Heather Farm: *https://horsellcommon.org.uk/heather-farm*

LEFT *Horsell Common*

BELOW *Cascade at Virginia Water*

20 River Wey

LENGTH: 35 miles (56.3km)

SOURCE: Alton (north branch) and Black Down near Haslemere (south branch)

CONFLUENCE: Weybridge

The Wey drains a large area of Surrey and North Hampshire, set in the wonderful scenery of the Surrey Hills. It has two branches: the north branch flows from Alton through Farnham to join the south branch at the beautiful village of Tilford. The Wey flows on to Godalming, Guildford and close to Woking, before joining the Thames below Shepperton Lock.

The lower part of the Wey was used to make one of the earliest canals in England, now owned by the National Trust which ensures that the towpath is in good order to explore the river below Godalming. The upper parts can be explored using excellent walks in the Surrey Hills.

RIGHT *Lammas Lands Godalming*

OPPOSITE *Eashing Bridge*

What's in a name?

The name comes from Old English with various spellings (for example, waie), with meanings of movement and transport.

Alton: one of two sources The source of the north branch is marked by a sign on the New Odiham Road (B3349) on the west side of Alton, rising from a spring in marshy ground below a chalk slope. When you cross the road into the flood meadows, you find the streambed in a semi-wild area of ponds. The stream runs along Tanhouse Lane into the centre of Alton. The river disappears into culverts under the town centre and reappears at Kings Pond, named after a local man, William King, who dammed the river to power his paper mill. From Kings Pond, the river flows north-east beside the railway embankment and can be followed along footpaths for 1 mile (1.6km) to the edge of the town. You walk through a residential area to Anstey Mill Lane, before following a footpath in woodland on Lynch Hill overlooking the river to the Upper Neatham Mill.

Farnham to Tilford Farnham is the main town on the northern branch of the Wey. Gostrey Meadow, a riverside park in the centre of the town, offers a gentle stroll from the war memorial to the Maltings – the Wey water was well known for making good beer.

There is a super walk of 4 miles (6.4km) that follows the Wey from Farnham to Tilford, with several return choices that require more walking and catching a bus. From Farnham train station,

20 River Wey

follow the first mile (1.6km) of the North Downs Way until it crosses the river at Moor Park, which was rebuilt in the 1680s by Sir William Temple, who employed Jonathan Swift, author of *Gulliver's Travels*, as a secretary. In the middle of the 19th century, Moor Park was leased to Dr Edward Lane, who ran a hydrotherapy spa here. Charles Darwin, the naturalist who wrote *On the Origin of Species*, also visited and commented in his diary that: 'The country is very pleasant for walking.' In 1897, the owner Sir William Rose stopped the public walking through the park by locking the gates. The local

Waveney Abbey beside the Wey

residents objected and a crowd gathered and forced the gates open. Fortunately, today, you can walk without hindrance.

Turn south off the North Downs Way on to a spur of the Greensand Way, the Moor Park Heritage Trail, through woodland above to the river. The land on either side is managed for wildlife within the Moor Park Nature Reserve. You pass Mother Ludlam's Cave, formed by a spring that has washed the sandstone out of the cliff. There is a legend that an old woman lived in the cave and lent kitchen utensils to poor people.

Soon after the cave, you come to a road that goes down to Waverley Mill Bridge and Waverley Abbey. Divert to Waverley Abbey, built by Cistercian monks in 1128, which adds 1 mile (1.6km) but is worthwhile. Back at Waverley Mill Bridge, go up the road that bends right for about 200 yards (180m), looking for a byway/bridle path on the right. This path continues the off-road route for another 1.5 miles (2.4km) to Tilford. It goes through woodland looking down on the river. At Sheephatch Lane, there is a lovely drystone wall that we saw being built. When asked how he learnt the skill, the builder replied, 'The wonders of YouTube!' Tilford has a flourishing village shop that serves snacks and a pub, The Barley Mow, overlooking the village green. Children can swim and paddle in the ford beside the car park while adults watch cricket on the green.

To return to Farnham from Tilford, walk up the street past the shop and waterworks, then turn right down Whitmead Lane. At the lodge to Whitmead House, turn left on a bridleway to Charleshill, a hamlet 1.5 miles (2.4km) from Tilford Bridge. On the way you can see the bare sandstone and signs of quarrying in the bank beside the path. Looking down on the right side there are glimpses of the Wey in the valley below.

At Charleshill, there is a pub called The Donkey and a bus stop for the service between Guildford and Farnham (no. 46, two hours between buses).

Another way of returning from Tilford is to take the first part of Walk 31, below, until you reach Frensham Little Pond. From there continue along the road, which becomes Priory Lane to the village of Millbridge 2 miles (3.2km) from Tilford where there is an hourly bus service (no. 19) to Farnham.

WALK 31 Tilford to Frensham Little Pond and Pierrepoint Farm

5.5 miles (8.9km)

Start at Tilford Bridge where there is car parking beside the river. Walk up the east side of the village green. The striking black and white building overlooking the green is the Tilford Institute, designed by architect Sir Edwin Lutyens and used as the cricket pavilion. At the top of the green, the footpath goes behind a hedge to a car park, where byways cross the road. Turn right (west) along the track that leads to Frensham Little Pond, which was created in the Middle Ages as a fishpond and is good for birdwatching all year round. At the Little Pond Nature Reserve, turn left to follow the paths around the pond to return to the car park. Walk a short way along the track back towards Tilford to a footpath on the left that goes down to a ford across the south branch of the Wey to Pierrepoint Farm. The farm is being managed in a sustainable way and has a small brewery and café. The path continues over Tankersford Common – lovely heathland – to a lane. Turn right to go down the lane, right again to the medieval bridge, built by the monks at Waverley Abbey, and you are back to Tilford village green.

Tilford Institute and the River Wey

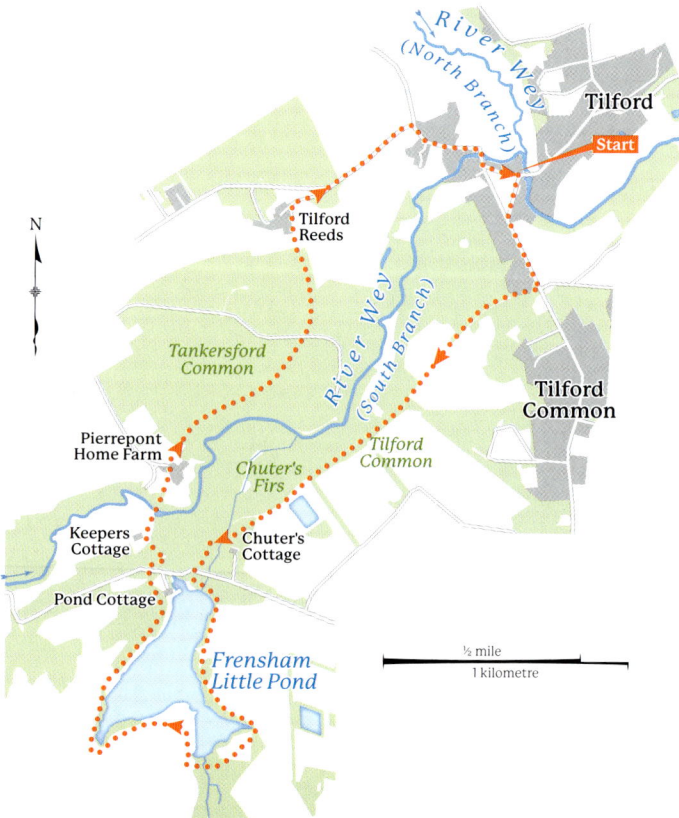

South branch Following the south branch of the Wey upstream from Millbridge, there is good walking on Frensham Common to the Great Pond and back via the Little Pond. At Liphook, the flood meadows have been restored to make Radford Park Nature Reserve, on the banks of the river. At Shottermill, near Camelsdale, the National Trust has two old mill ponds and a trail around the wooded hills of Marley Common.

Frensham Little Pond

WALK 32 Camelsdale to Black Down, including the south branch source

6 miles (9.7km)

To find the source of the Wey's south branch on Black Down near Haslemere, start at Bell Vale Lane on the east side of Camelsdale. The infant Wey chuckles beside the lane as you walk to Valewood Park. At the end of the lane, take the bridle path alongside the National Trust sign to go south along the valley for 1 mile (1.6km) to reach Fernden Lane at Wadesmarsh Farmhouse. Walk for a mile along the lane, passing small lakes, and turn right to Cotchett's Farm. Here, the Wey is a small trickle of water emerging from a spring into a trough beside the lane. Another National Trust sign tells you that you have reached Black Down. Summon up your strength to climb the grassy path to enjoy the magnificent views from the Temple of Winds at the top of the hill. To return, follow the Serpent Trail along the ridge and go down the Sussex Border Trail back to the head of Bell Vale Lane.

ABOVE *Source of the south branch at Black Down*

Downstream from Tilford To explore downstream along the Wey after the north and south branches have joined, you can walk the south side of the river from Tilford to Elstead, a distance of 3 miles (4.8km). From the car park where the byways cross the road from Tilford village green, the path eastwards signed to Stockbridge Farm brings you to a fishing lake. The track continues through woodland to Westbrook Farm and a lane into the hamlet of Elstead. Walk through Elstead to the medieval stone bridge where the Farnham Road crosses the Wey. At the bridge, a bench in the shade of a weeping willow looks over the river for a rest before walking back. Close by is The Mill pub and flood meadows in Thundry Meadows Nature Reserve.

WALK 33 Godalming to Guildford

5 miles (8km)

The walk from Godalming to Guildford is simple using the towpath beside the Wey Navigation. Start at the Jack Phillips Memorial Park in Godalming, which is close to the town centre, the train station and a car park. Phillips was the young radio operator aboard the *Titanic*, who stayed at his post transmitting SOS messages until the liner sank. His memorial, the beautiful Cloister Garden near the Borough Road Bridge, was designed by Gertrude Jekyll. Walk beside the river to the Town Bridge at the lower end of the park. Continue by crossing the bridge to the Lammas Meadows, named after the tradition of cutting the hay on Lammas Day (1 August). At the first lock, Catteshall, it is worth stopping for a cup of tea and a chat at the Farncombe Boat House to learn more about the Wey Navigation. From here, the towpath goes for 20 miles (32km) to the Thames.

The path and the Wey Navigation soon leave the houses of Farncombe and passes through peaceful fields. On the opposite side at Unstead Lock is Peasmarsh, a wetland between the river and the canal, which

Footbridge near Godalming

come together near the former railway bridge, now a cycle path. On the opposite side is the entrance to the Wey and Arun Canal, which was once an inland waterway connecting London and the south coast. At Broadford Bridge, you can divert to Shalford village to look at the watermill if it has reopened after renovations. The diversion leads to an interesting (meaning wet in places!) way across Shalford Water Meadows to return to the towpath at St Catherine's Lock. The lock is named after a nearby chapel on the Pilgrims' Way from Winchester to Canterbury. In early morning sunshine, the next part can be one of the most beautiful riverside walks, framed by a line of trees and lush green fields on the opposite bank. At the end of this reach, the Wey Navigation turns left to enter Guildford, where two bridges mark the town centre. If you have time, visit the National Trust's Dapdune Wharf to learn about the history of the Wey Navigation and see barges and their gear. You can return by bus or train (Getting there).

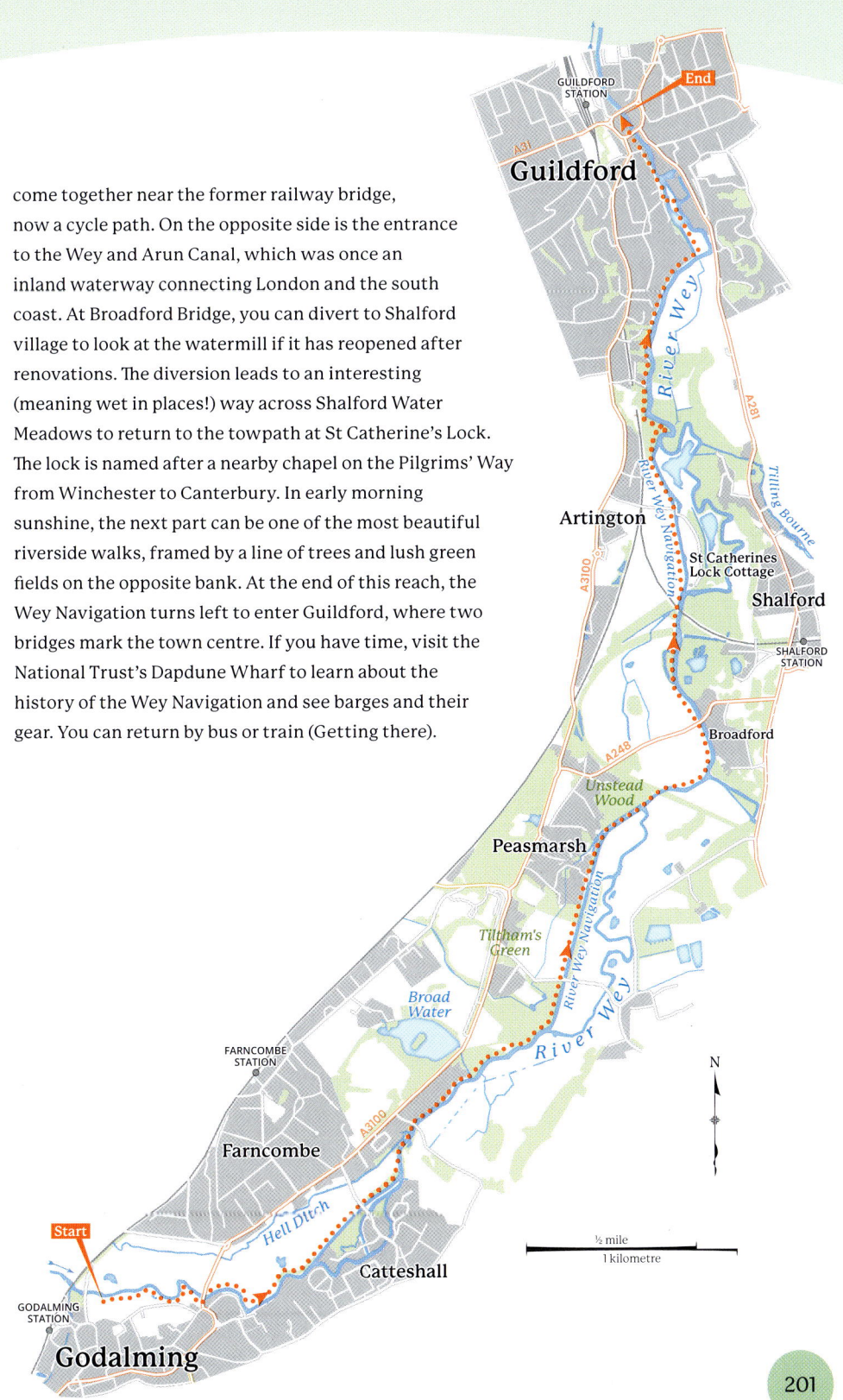

20 River Wey

Guildford to Weybridge There are two circular walks, both of 3 miles (4.8km), which offer an alternative to a longer linear walk.

Wisley Many visitors to the Royal Horticultural Society Garden Wisley must have looked through the boundary fence, seen the Wey and had a passing thought about where it might flow. A footpath crosses the northern part of the gardens. If you follow this path for 1 mile (1.6km) upstream, you come to Ockham Mill. Walk from the mill to a driveway with a right of way that goes straight to the Wey Navigation. Go along the towpath for ½ mile (0.8km) to Pyrford Lock and The Anchor pub. Turn east on to a footpath across fields and you come to Wisley Bridge and the lane that leads back to Wisley.

Wey Island When the natural River Wey leaves the navigation

Weybridge

channel near Wisley, it creates a large island between the two watercourses, which reunite at the edge of Weybridge. Wey Island includes the town of Byfleet and the former Brooklands airfield and racing circuit. The northern part of Wey Island has remained as flood meadows with a 3 mile (4.8km) walk on the footpaths. Starting at Weybridge Town Lock, walk along the footpath beside Wey Meadows private road to a mobile home park. The footpath goes on to Wey Island Trust on the banks of the river and crosses the island through Wey Manor Farm to New Hall Lock on the Navigation. Returning along the towpath you see the large mill, converted to flats, at Coxes Lock before you reach Weybridge.

And lastly, the path from Weybridge to the Thames is part of Walk 30.

GETTING THERE

BUS SERVICE | Stagecoach no. 70 Guildford to Godalming

TRAIN SERVICES | South Western Railways from London Waterloo serving towns beside the Wey, including the line between Godalming and Guildford

OS EXPLORER MAPS | 145 Guildford & Farnham; 160 Windsor, Weybridge & Bracknell; OL 33 Haslemere and Petersfield

RESOURCES

National Trust – Black Down Trail: *www.nationaltrust.org.uk/black-down/trails/black-down-trail-shottermill-to-marley-common-and-cognor-wood*

National Trust – River Wey and Godalming Navigations: *www.nationaltrust.org.uk/river-wey-and-godalming-navigations-and-dapdune-wharf*

Radford Park: *https://bramshottandliphook-pc.gov.uk/facilities-open-spaces/radford-park*

River Wey north branch: *www.weyriver.co.uk/theriver/wey_north_A.htm*

River Wey south branch: *www.weyriver.co.uk/theriver/wey_south_a.htm*

Waverley Abbey: *www.english-heritage.org.uk/visit/places/waverley-abbey/history*

River Mole

LENGTH: 50 miles (80.5km)

SOURCE: Rusper

CONFLUENCE: East Molesey

The Mole is a long Thames tributary of 50 miles (80.5km) on the south-west side of London. It starts from small streams between Horsham and Crawley on the Surrey–Sussex border, which flow into a culvert running under Gatwick Airport. From Gatwick, the river turns north-west to the gap between Dorking and Box Hill, where it may disappear underground during dry summers. It gains force approaching Leatherhead and adds to the attractions of Cobham and Esher. It reaches the Thames in East Molesey opposite Hampton Court.

The river is unjustly immortalised in Alexander Pope's poem *Windsor Forest* in which he wrote in 1713: 'sullen Mole that hides his flood'. This attractive river is not sullen. Charles Mackay writes warmly about the Mole, who was rude about the Colne: '... and if

Cuckoo Flower (Lady's Smock) on the banks of the Mole

What's in a name?

The name Molesey comes from Mull's Island, but the river was once known as the Emel, meaning 'misty'. This name is echoed by the River Ember, a large side stream at the lower end of the Mole.

Stepping Stones, Box Hill

the most sullen man in England would, as we did, take a day's ramble upon its banks, he would, if he had any soul at all in him, be cured of his sullenness for a month at least, by the contemplation of its woodland treasures, its sylvan nooks, and its simple, sequestered, and elegant villages.' Mackay describes a journey from Hampton Court to Dorking along the Mole, crossing via the Hog's Back to Guildford, and coming back to the Thames along the Wey. In the two centuries since Pope and Mackay walked this way, the growth of towns, roads and Gatwick Airport have altered the landscape, but the river continues to offer a refuge from the hubbub of modern life.

The first part of the Mole roughly follows the border between Surrey and Sussex but it is too small to be the county boundary. To meet the Mole when it is more than a stream that can be jumped across by any fit person, find a footpath close to the bridge along Mill Lane in Horley on the north side of Gatwick Airport. Here is a meadow where anglers stand between clumps of blackthorn or in the shade of the oak trees. The footpath follows the river for ½ mile (0.8km) to St Bartholomew's Church and Ye Olde Six Bells pub near the A23. The Mole Gap Trail is the only path that follows the river for more than a few miles. However, several circular walks offer every chance of curing sullenness.

WALK 34 Brockham Village Circular Walk

5 miles (8km)

The first of these circular walks around the Mole starts at the village green in Brockham, claimed to the best place to watch traditional village cricket in England. The route begins near the Inn on the Green, with a restaurant called the Grumpy Mole. Take the lane leading to the animal rescue and turn left down to the river. Follow the Greensand Way signs near the river to St Michael's Church, Betchworth, 1 mile (1.6km) away. From there, walk along Wonham Lane, which curves around Wonham Manor and its deer park. Opposite Wonham Mill, now converted to luxury flats, take the footpath beside a stream that runs to the Mole, still a small river, at Rice Bridge. Cross the bridge and walk up the right-hand path, which goes due west. A mile further, turn right when you come to a lane, and look for a kissing gate in the hedge opposite a house with a gargoyle on its chimney stack (Snowerhill Farm). Through the gate, a footpath goes across grassland to a ridge with views across the Mole valley towards the chalk cliffs on the far side of the M25. Bear left along the ridge to a beacon and follow the path over a small lane to the side of a wood. Take the path to the right descending to School Lane in Brockham and to the green. There is a popular café on the west side of the green in what was once the village reading room.

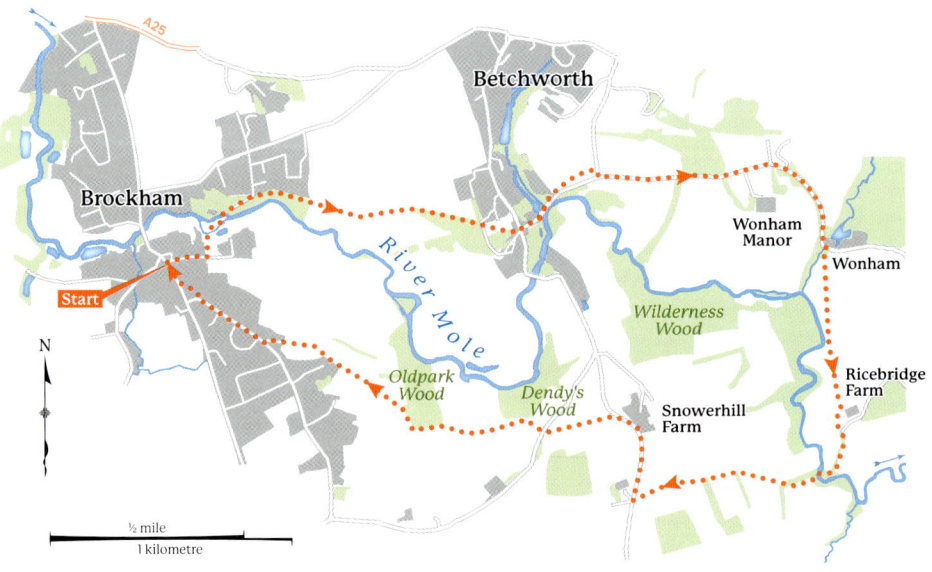

Box Hill At Box Hill near Dorking, the National Trust has well-marked paths with leaflets available at the visitor centre. The Riverside Walk and the Stepping Stones Walk include the banks of the Mole. The climb up from Burford Bridge to the top is rewarded with magnificent views of the valley, and you can pause to imagine the scene of the picnic in Jane Austen's novel, *Emma*. Thinking of food and other necessities, there are refreshments at Burford Bridge and the visitor centre.

View over River Mole towards Brockham

WALK 35 Dorking to Leatherhead, via Box Hill and the Mole Gap Trail

5.7 miles (9.1km)

For this walk, park at Leatherhead, catch the train to Dorking, and walk back. Walk out of Dorking train station, turn left and go through the car park to Lincoln Road. Turn left under the railway bridge and right along the path beside the railway. At a T junction of paths, turn left and take the path on the right that goes to Swan Mill Gardens. This residential road takes you to Pixham Lane. Turn right, go under a railway bridge and take Leslie Lane on the left. A path on the left leads down through trees to a meadow and to Castle Mill. Turn left to cross the Mole and left again so you are walking north, close to the river. After these detailed instructions from Dorking, the route becomes more obvious and more interesting.

The path beside the river is part of the National Trust Riverside Walk. On the riverbank, there are the remains of Second World War concrete defences. The path enters a wood and climbs across the slope of Box Hill with views down to the river. At the junction of paths turn left to take the Stepping Stones walk down to the river. You cross the river either using the stepping stones – fun on a hot day – or the bridge a short distance downstream. Continue north on the path through the meadows, staying close to the river as it curves round to Burford Bridge. There is a subway with a gorgeous mural under the busy A24 road. On the far side, turn left for a short distance to turn right along Westhumble Street. You pass the Stepping Stones pub (open from breakfast onwards). When you have crossed the railway, the path on the right side is the Mole Valley Trail (MVT). Pause to admire the gateway to Camilla Cottage, which was built by Fanny Burney, a successful novelist and playwright in the late 18th century.

The MVT stays close to the railway until both have crossed the Mole, which turns left at Cowslip Farm to the river. As you cross, look up to see Norbury Park on the top of the hill, which was built with landscaped grounds in the 18th century and is now owned by Surrey County Council. The woods are managed as a nature reserve. There is a picnic area at the top of the slope with a lovely view over the valley to Box Hill. After 400 yards (366m) in the woods, take a right turn where a bridleway crosses the footpath. This should be signed as the

Rail Bridges over the Mole in Leatherhead

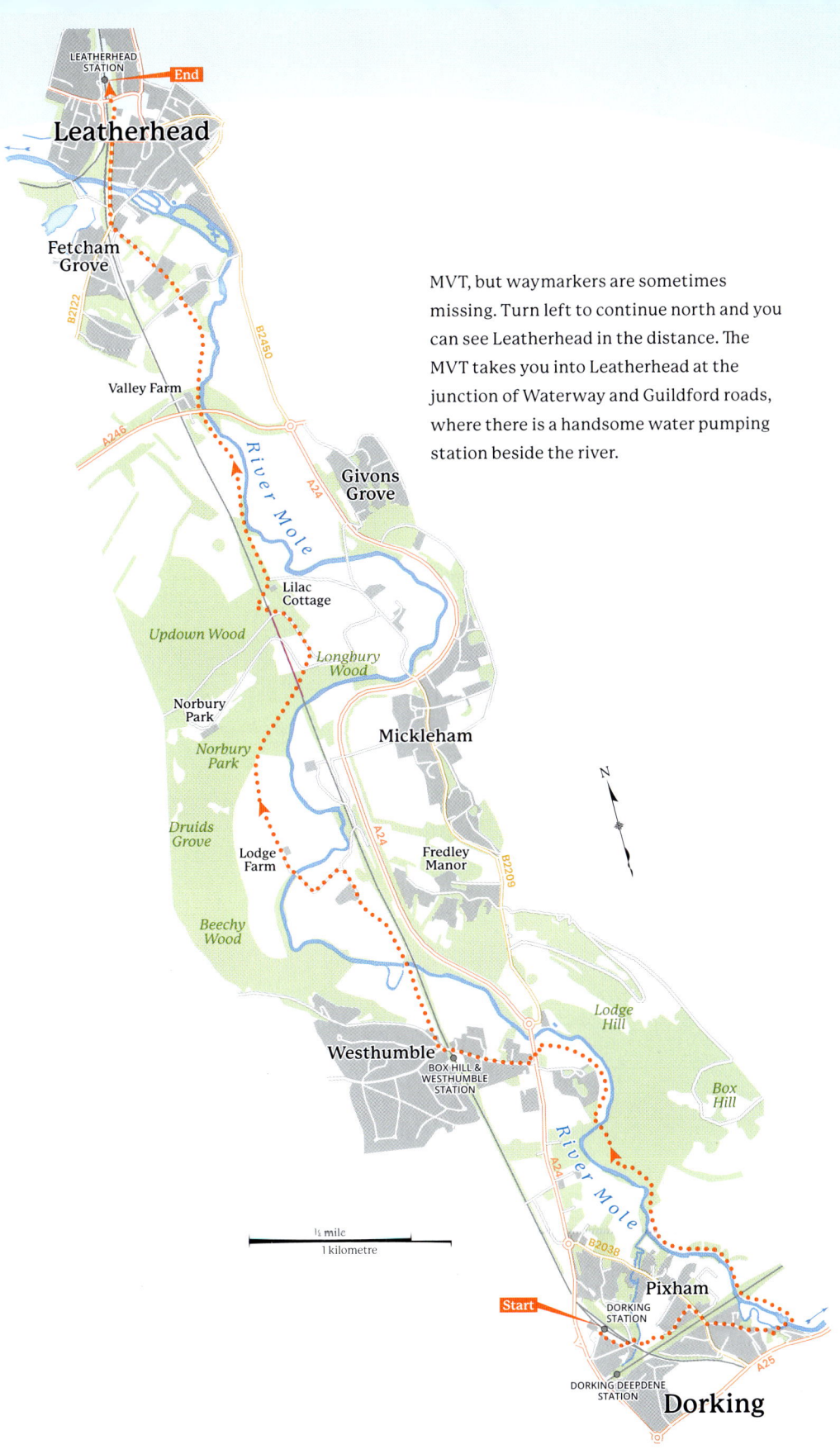

MVT, but waymarkers are sometimes missing. Turn left to continue north and you can see Leatherhead in the distance. The MVT takes you into Leatherhead at the junction of Waterway and Guildford roads, where there is a handsome water pumping station beside the river.

21 River Mole

Short circular walk – Leatherhead and Fetcham A 3 mile (4.8km) walk downstream from the Leatherhead pumping station follows Mill Lane under the railway viaduct to a footpath that leads to a lake and playing fields behind the fire station. Keeping close to the rail embankment, you enter a quiet housing estate. Walk along Cannon Grove and Cannon Way to a path that goes under the railway to Mole Road and River Lane, which takes you to the Mole in a small wilderness around a weir and continues through fields to a main road, the A245. Turn right towards Leatherhead. If the gates are open, you can walk into the grounds of Randalls Park Crematorium and Cemetery and follow paths that run parallel to the main road. At the far eastern end of the cemetery, a footpath goes from the A245 to fields beside the Mole and the route back to the town.

ABOVE *Town Bridge at Leatherhead*

WALK 36 Cobham Circular Walk

4 miles (6.4km)

The Mole describes a large curve on the south side of Cobham and a circular walk explores this bend of the river. Starting from St Andrew's Church in the centre of Cobham, walk down Bridge Road to Downside Bridge. The name originates from the Downe family who lived in Cobham Park in the 13th century. There is a story that the first bridge here was built by Matilda, Queen of Henry I, because her maid-in-waiting had drowned in the ford. A similar story is told of Bow Bridge across the River Lea. Soon after the bridge, a footpath on the right side crosses the field to a row of oak trees and passes close to the riverbank, and stiles between the fields ahead. In April, you may find the delicate cuckoo flowers (lady's smock).

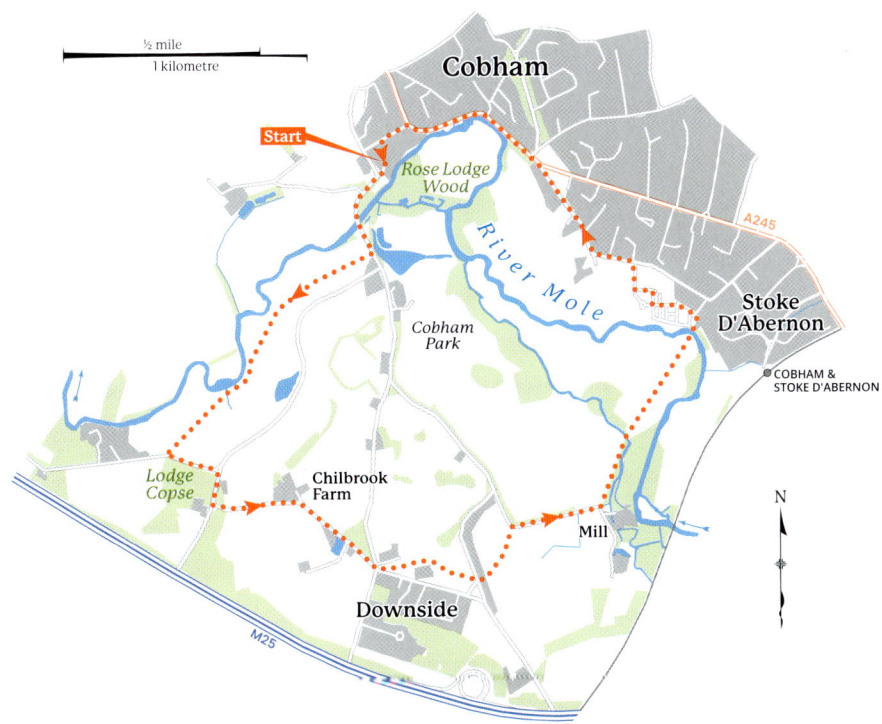

Walk 36

Mole at Cobham

Reaching Poynters Road, turn left to walk down to Ockham Road (also called Plough Lane). Turn right and then, left into Chilbrook Road to Downside Common. The Cricketers pub on the north side of the common is the midpoint of the walk. Beside St Michael's Chapel and a white water pump on the far side of the common, a bridle path leads to Cobham Park Road and north through water meadows to a footbridge over the Mole. Here, you can wander through Cobham Cemetery, where there is a beautiful mausoleum on the riverbank belonging to the McAlpine family, who gave money to restore the cemetery chapel. Tilt Road and the A245 Stoke Road take you back to Cobham along a lovely riverside path passing a watermill. After the Riverside Gardens, turn into Church Street to reach St Andrew's Church again.

Painshill Park and West End

Painshill Park is an 18th-century park beside the Mole on the north-west side of Cobham. Now restored and owned by Elmbridge Borough Council, it offers pleasant walks around the lake and through the landscaped gardens.

In contrast to the orderly design of Painshill Park, West End Common is a wilderness of flood meadow and woodland. Lying between the Mole and the A307 Portsmouth Road between Esher and Cobham, this rough ground has a network of paths between streams and ponds. There are two car parks and the centre of Esher is only 1 mile (1.6km) away. On the opposite side of the road is Claremont Landscape Garden, also owned by the National Trust, with a large lake, landscaped gardens and a Palladian mansion. Walk north through West End Common to reach the village green, complete with pond and cricket pitch. A short distance further, the Mole flows through West End Recreation Ground with a riverside walk.

Pond at Esher

21 River Mole

Esher to Molesey

If there were a direct bus service between Esher and Hampton Court, there would be a very tempting 3 miles (4.8km) walk from Esher to the Thames. However, there is enough variety in the paths along the route to make a return 6 mile (9.7km) walk to explore this last section of the Mole and its large side stream, the River Ember.

Start from the A244 bridge at West End Recreation Ground and walk along the drive to South Weylands Equestrian Centre. The footpath goes around the farm, past Hersham Golf Club, under a railway and beside the river, which has been straightened and embanked. After ½ mile (0.8km) the Mole leaves the Ember to meander between muddy banks on the west side of the Island Barn Reservoir. A footpath follows the Mole behind a caravan park to Molesey Heath Nature Reserve. Walk across the Heath to reach the Dead River that runs into the Mole. Turning east on a path beside the Mole, you come to Cow Common and East Molesey. The Mole and Ember come close together and create a spit of residential land called Molember. Once reunited with the Ember, the Mole goes under the A309 road and Hampton Court train station to enter the Thames. To reach the confluence, walk along Molember Road and cross the A309 to a path beside Kingston Grammar School. It takes you the last 300 yards (275m) to Ditton Field, on the banks of the Thames opposite Hampton Court Palace.

River Ember at Molember

GETTING THERE

OS EXPLORER MAPS | OL34 Crawley & Horsham; 145 Guildford & Farnham; 146 Dorking, Box Hill & Reigate; 160 Windsor, Weybridge & Bracknell; 161 London South

RESOURCES

London's Lost Rivers – River Mole: *www.londonslostrivers.com/river-mole.html*

Mole Gap Trail: *www.alltrails.com/trail/england/surrey/mole-gap-trail--2*

National Trust – Box Hill Riverside Walk: *www.nationaltrust.org.uk/box-hill/trails/box-hill-riverside-walk*

To the Source of the River Mole: *https://moleriver.wordpress.com/page/4/*

PART 5

The rivers entering the Thames in West London

Brentford gauging locks

River Hogsmill

LENGTH: 6 miles (9.7km)

SOURCE: Bourne Hall Park, Ewell, Surrey

CONFLUENCE: Kingston upon Thames

The Hogsmill was once a Surrey chalk stream flowing from a village pond in Ewell to the county town, Kingston upon Thames. Since 1965, when Kingston and Surbiton became part of Greater London, it has become a London river. Fortunately, it has escaped being buried beneath culverts. Rivers open to the sky in urban areas are vital green corridors for wildlife. Its compact length offers an excellent river trail, which is a delight to explore.

What's in a name?

The name is said to come from John Hogg, a successful business man who owned watermills in Kingston in the 12th century.

Naming the river after a mill owner shows the historical importance of water power. From Tudor times, mill owners added paper-making, pounding coconut fibres and producing gunpowder to the traditional business of grinding flour. On an aesthetic note, the Hogsmill inspired two famous Pre-Raphaelite artists. William Holman Hunt married at Ewell and produced *The Hireling Shepherd* on the meadows beside the Hogsmill. The doorway in Holman Hunt's famous *The Light of the World* is believed to be based on a workmen's hut in gunpowder mills at Worcester Park. John Everett Millais used the Hogsmill for the background of his romantic painting of the drowned Ophelia.

OPPOSITE *Winter sunlight on the Hogsmill*

BELOW *Frosty Hogsmill*

WALK 37 Riverside Walk from the source to the Thames

8 miles (12.9km)

Of the 33 Thames tributaries, the Hogsmill has the best riverside trail. The trail goes through green spaces close to the river for most of its length, it can be walked in half a day and it is well signed. It is section eight of the London Loop. There are several guides available online. We recommend the one produced for Transport for London by the Inner London Ramblers, updated in 2023 (Resources). We mention the highlights and suggest a slightly different route near the middle of the walk.

The trail starts at the pond in Bourne Hall Park, close to the Spring Tavern. William the Conqueror was said to have watered his horse at this pond – a story that resembles the legend of Julius Caesar and the source of the Ravensbourne (Chapter 27). The park dates from the 18th century when a country house was built here. It became a girls' school in 1923 when it was named Bourne Hall. Epsom and Ewell Borough Council acquired the park in 1945, preserving the waterside green space. The house was replaced by the modern building that houses a museum, a library and facilities for the arts. At the pond, look for the green London Loop signs, which you find along the route. On leaving the main park, cross the road to a narrow park between the river and the Kingston Road. The large brick building where you turn left across the river is the former Upper Mill, which ground corn until 1953.

Bourne Pond (the source of River Hogsmill)

After the low railway bridge you enter Hogsmill Nature Reserve. You may notice the absence of litter, thanks to the volunteers who look after the river and monitor its quality. New reedbeds are being created to filter water that runs off nearby roads before it enters the beautifully clear stream. Pass the stepping stones and continue with the river on your left side until you cross at the next bridge. At the playground, you cross back again to the east side and continue north to Ruxley Lane and ½ mile (0.8km) further to the major Kingston Road.

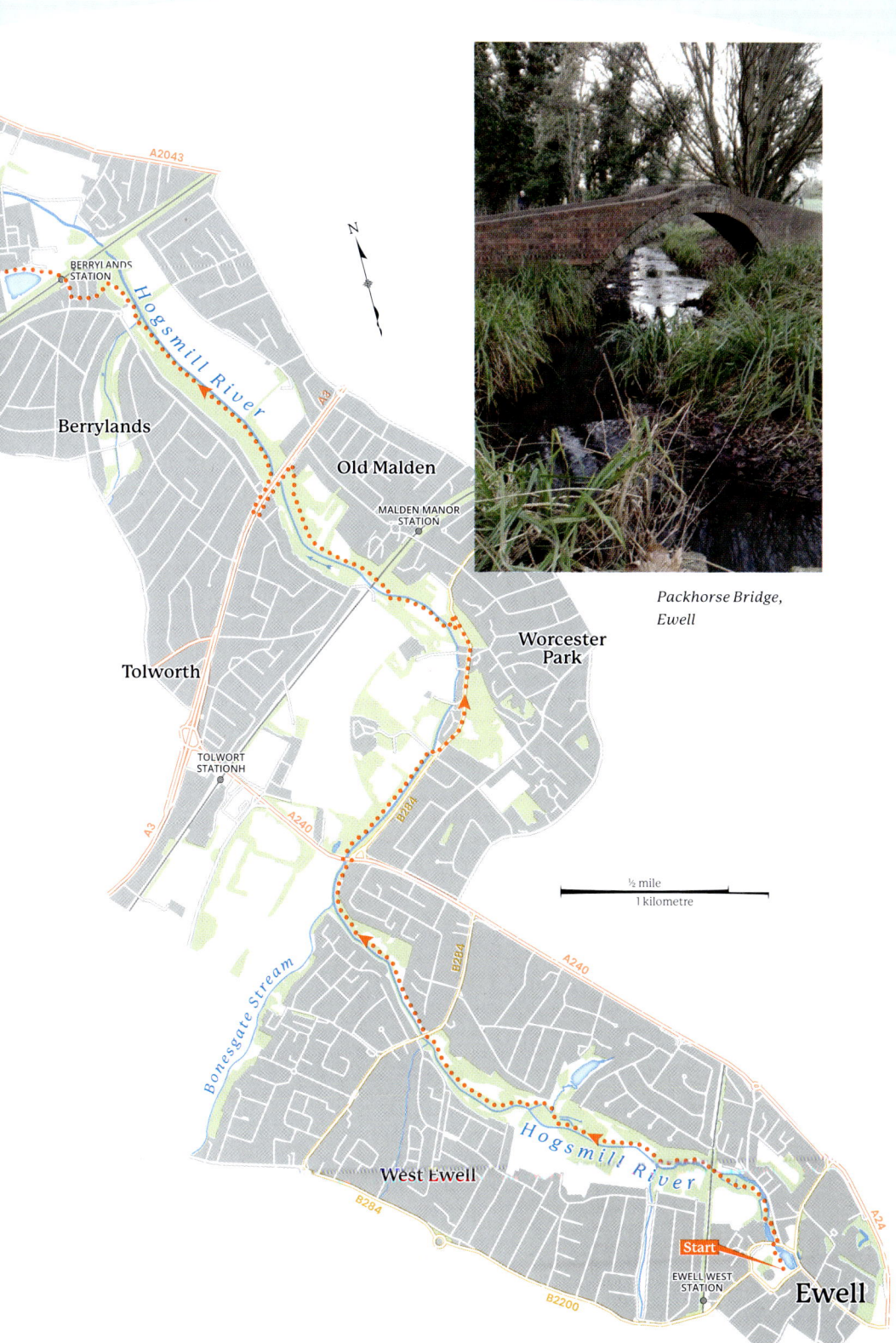

Packhorse Bridge, Ewell

Walk 37

ABOVE *Clattern Bridge in Kingston*

BELOW *The Hogsmill joins the Thames*

After crossing Kingston Road, turn left over Worcester Park Road and the river to the footpath between the go-karting track and the river. This path ends with a bridge over the river to The Hogsmill pub. This is open all day and is a welcome place for a mid-walk break. At this point the guides tell you to leave the river and go up Cromwell Road, whereas the Old Malden Road stays close to the river. This was because the pavement along the Old Malden Way is narrow in places. However, there is a new path between the river and new houses in Gunpowder Road (in memory of the mill here), which takes you some of the way along Old Malden Road. Further on, the pavement will be improved as more new houses are completed. Past the point where Old Malden Road becomes Church Road, there is a footpath on the left, signed as London Loop, which goes down to and along the river. This was where Millais drew inspiration for his famous Ophelia painting.

The path goes back to, and stays on, the east side of the river before the railway bridge until you reach the A3 Kingston bypass. Turn left up to the subway and right to return to the river. What a relief it is to find peace in the Hogsmill River Park Nature Reserve for the next ½ mile (0.8km). The route leaves the river to go around the large sewage treatment works in Lower Marsh Lane, where you pass the Berryland pub, cafés and the Berryland train station. Thereafter, the trail follows along urban streets with two historic features to see, the Saxon Coronation Chair and the ancient Clattern Bridge, before you and the Hogsmill reach the Thames.

Other walks Other walks at Ewell include the shorter Hogsmill Valley Walk, which is about 1 mile (1.6km) and takes only 30 minutes, with interesting features, including an eel pass and eel monitoring station; a wide variety of birds to spot at Knight's Park; the river's aquatic fauna; and Charter Quay Artificial Wetland Area.

The Ewell Trail takes walkers around the village, visiting more than 20 historical features, including the source of the Hogsmill. There is a short route of 1 hour and a longer route of approximately 1.5 hours. Free maps, provided by the Ewell Rotary Club, can be picked up from the library in Bourne Hall.

Local nature reserves include Horton Country Park, Epsom Common and Berrylands Nature Reserve.

GETTING THERE

BUS SERVICES | Many bus services stop in Ewell: the 293, 406, 418, 467, 470, E5 and E16. The 406 goes directly from Kingston (Cromwell Road bus station) to the Spring Tavern in Ewell

TRAINS | to Ewell West train station from Waterloo, Dorking and Guildford, and to Ewell East station from London Victoria, Dorking and Horsham

OS EXPLORER MAP | 161 London South

RESOURCES

Ewell to Kingston Hogsmill River – London Loop: *www.tfl.gov.uk/modes/walking/loop-walk.*

Inner London Ramblers – London Loop (Ewell to Kingston Bridge): *www.innerlondonramblers.org.uk/images/RingandLoop/guides/LL08-ewell-to-kingston-bridge-May23.pdf*

Hogsmill, Kingston: *https://www.epson-ewell.gov.uk/residents/venues-sport-and-leisure-facilities/parks/local-nature-reserves/hogsmill-local-nature*

River Crane

LENGTH: (including Yeading Brook): 15 miles (24km)

SOURCE: Ickenham

CONFLUENCE: Isleworth

The Crane and its main tributary, the Yeading Brook, make one river, so we started our exploration in Ickenham. The name changes at Hayes, where the Crane takes another 8.5 miles (13.7km) to reach the Thames. When the river reaches Hounslow Heath, it is deflected to an easterly course through Twickenham beside a ridge of higher ground that includes Strawberry Hill. The Crane is also fed by the Duke of Northumberland's River, a humanmade channel drawing water from the Colne near Heathrow. The Duke of Northumberland built Syon House in Isleworth in the reign of King Henry VIII, and made his river to power his mills and irrigate his fields.

Yeading Brook at Ickenham Marsh

What's in a name?

The river is named after the manor of Cranford, the Cranes' Ford, which was mentioned in the Domesday Book. Yeading Brook is derived from the Anglo-Saxon 'Geddi's settlement'.

ABOVE *Crane Park Island Nature Reserve*

Ickenham to Cranford Park The Yeading Brook can be followed from Ickenham Marsh Nature Reserve to Cranford Park using the Hillingdon Trail. Ickenham Marsh lies between Ickenham Village and RAF Northolt airfield and has good information boards, firm paths and clear water without much litter. The Hillingdon Trail and the river go under the A40 to Gutteridge Wood and Ten Acre Wood nature reserves. The Trail has a short road section followed by a large expanse of grassland, Yeading Brook Meadows, the fourth nature reserve along the river. At the east end of the meadows, the Trail reaches the Grand Union Canal and follows the towpath to Bull's Bridge in Hayes. Where the brown Hillingdon Trial signs show a foot and cycle bridge over the busy A312, you can see the Crane flowing from Minet Country Park. Along the appropriately named Watersplash Lane, the Hillingdon Trail ends by passing through a tunnel under the M4 motorway to enter Cranford Park.

Cranford Park The history of Cranford Park is told on the good information boards where the manor house once stood, in a moat filled by water from the river. All that remains are the 18th century stables, an attractive river bridge, St Dunstan's Church and 144 acres (58ha) of grassland. The park is large enough to offer a 2 mile (3.2km) walk on both sides of the river. Go on one side to Cranford Lane at the southern end, cross the river and return along Avenue Park. This is a better walk than trying to follow the river via the London Loop, which goes to Hounslow Heath on busy roads and under the aircraft landing at Heathrow.

WALK 38 Crane Park and Kneller Gardens

5 miles (8km)

The best walking beside the Crane is in Crane Park and Little Crane Park, which have paths on both sides of the river. Start in Kneller Gardens, which is close to Whitton station (trains to Waterloo). Starting from the café and WCs in Kneller Gardens, go upstream past the tennis courts and over Meadway. This part of the path is shared with cyclists but there is plenty of width. After walking under trees, you emerge into a small field with a carved wooden bench overlooking the river. There are more wood sculptures of animals along the walk. If you stay close to the river, you find the pedestrian tunnel under Chertsey Road (A316) to enter Crane Park. The signs to the Shot Tower guide you through the park. The Shot Tower, once used for making lead shot by dropping lead from a height into water, is the last remnant of an ammunition factory on the site. It is an information centre, has a pop-up café and is next to the entrance to the Island Nature Reserve. On the island, you can admire the reedbeds and coppiced willows, look out for heron and little egret, and listen for woodpeckers. Continue along the well-made paths of Crane Park to Hanworth Road, which could be another starting point with good bus services.

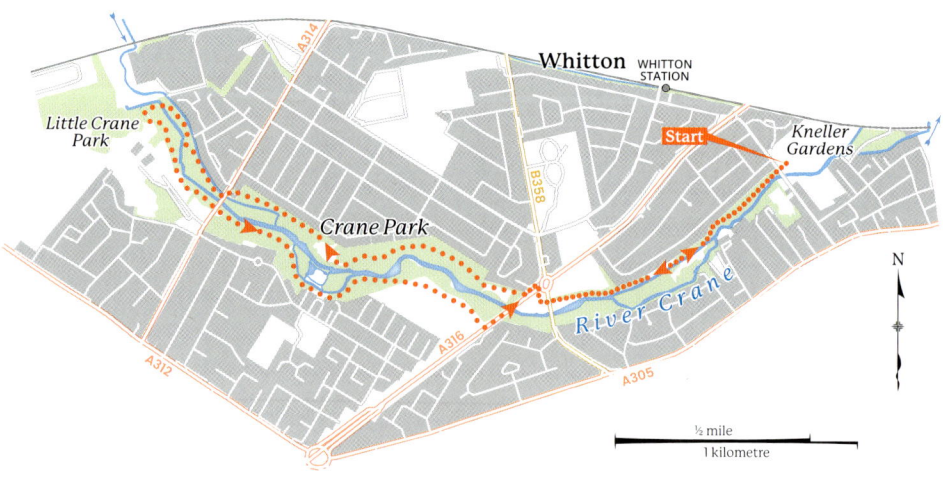

ABOVE *Bench by the River Crane walk*

Across Hanworth Road, on the east side of the Crane, is Little Crane Park, which is a typical wet woodland — muddy paths, fallen trees and lots of puddles. After ½ mile (0.8km), cross the footbridge on the left side. This is the top end of the walk. Take the first grassy path on your left to go downstream. Here, you are on a London Loop trail which goes back to Crane Park staying on the south-west side of the river until you reach Chertsey Road. Turn left to reach a pedestrian crossing at the roundabout. Return to Kneller Gardens along the path where you started the walk.

Down to the Thames At the downstream end of Kneller Gardens, the Duke of Northumberland's River takes a separate course to the Thames. There is a 5 mile (8km) circular walk to the Thames using the River Crane Walk and returning on the Duke's River Walk. The walk is mainly on pavements but has points of interest, including Mereway Nature Park, where rough grass and wild shrubs abound; the Thames at the Richmond Lock and its tidal gates; Isleworth Ait, where the Crane enters the Thames; the famous London Apprentice pub; Mogden Sewage Treatment Works; and Twickenham rugby union stadium.

ABOVE *Stables at Cranford Park*

GETTING THERE

TRAIN SERVICES | TfL from Paddington to Hayes and Harlington is closest to Cranford Park; South Western Rail from Waterloo to Hounslow and to Twickenham

TUBE | Piccadilly Line to Ickenham station

OS EXPLORER MAPS | 161 London South; 172 Chiltern Hills East; 173 London North

RESOURCES

Crane Park Island Nature Reserve: *www.wildlondon.org.uk/nature-reserves/crane-park-island*
Cranford Park: *http://cranfordparkfriends.org/*
Crane River Partnership: *http://cranevalley.org.uk/*
The Crane River Walk: *www.carfreewalks.org/walks/230/the_river_crane_walk*
Friends of the River Crane Environment: *www.force.org.uk/*

River Brent

LENGTH: (including Dollis Brook): 24 miles (38.6km)

SOURCE: Hendon

CONFLUENCE: Brentford

The Brent is formed by two streams, Dollis Brook and Mutton Brook, meeting in Hendon in north-west London. Dollis Brook is the larger stream and is regarded as the upper part of the Brent. This adds a worthwhile extra 8 miles (12.9km) to explore. Flowing through Barnet, Finchley, Hendon, Wembley, Ealing and Hounslow, the Brent is a defining feature of North London.

Downstream, the Brent has a commercial character from its close relationship with the Grand Union Canal, built at the beginning of the 19th century. The development of Middlesex to an urban county resulted in the dense network of railways –

Brent joins the Thames

What's in a name?

According to Ekwall, the name Brent referred to the Celtic goddess, Brigantia. Possibly it meant 'Sacred Water'. Certainly, it is an example of river worship.

Dollis Brook at Barnet

overground and underground – that help you to explore the Brent. There are two linear paths, Dollis Valley Greenwalk and the Brent River Park Walk, which take you through the best parts of the Brent catchment. Within the Brent River Corridor Improvement Plan is a proposal to make a riverside path 24 miles (38.6km) long, from High Barnet to Brentford (Resources).

Dollis Brook: from Mill Hill to Brent Cross

Dollis Brook rises in Moat Mount Open Space to the north of Mill Hill. It can be followed closely by the Dollis Valley Greenwalk, which has attractive wooden signposts. The green London Loop signs are also useful indicators of the right path. The first 3 miles (4.8km) to Barnet Playing Fields fit Betjeman's words, wending their way through the meadows between Totteridge and Chipping Barnet.

From Barnet Playing Fields to the junction with Mutton Brook, Dollis Brook is fed by springs and streams and grows into a river. The Greenwalk becomes a firm path linking green spaces from the hay meadows of Brook Farm and Whetstone Stray to the Riverside Walk in Woodside, Oakdene Park and Windsor Open Space. These make a good riverside walk of 5 miles (8km). If you want to make a shorter walk, there are Northern Line train stations close by, signed from the path. At Mutton Brook, the Dollis Valley Greenwalk goes east to end at Hampstead Heath Extension. The London Loop path goes west beside Dollis Brook as it becomes the Brent near the North Circular Road at Brent Cross.

The Welsh Harp

Between Brent Cross and Perivale, the Brent has few riverside paths. It is partly enclosed in culverts under roads and railways, and you must pound the streets with no signs of natural water if you try to follow its course. However, the Welsh Harp (or Brent) Reservoir is a glorious contrast with its lakeside paths, waterbirds and excellent sailing facilities. Built in 1834/5, to supply water to the Grand Union and Regent's Canals, it has been used for recreation for much of its existence. The name comes from the Old Welsh Harp Tavern on the Edgeware Road, where the owner, William Perkins Warner, arranged day and evening entertainments beside the lake, *The Jolliest Place That's Out*, in the words of the 1860s music hall song. Despite its chequered and noisy history of collapsed dams, powerboat racing, and seaplane trials, the Welsh Harp is a haven of peace within 10 miles (16km) of central London.

The Welsh Harp

WALK 39 Horsenden Hill to Brent River Park

8.3 miles (13.4km)

Ealing Borough has lots of green spaces and makes good use of them. One of the best is the Brent River Park, which is explored on this walk. Rail stations at Greenford, Hanwell and Perivale are close to the route, but we start at the car park opposite the Ballot Box pub

The Gruffalo Trail at Horsenden Hill

in Horsenden Lane North. Follow the path signed to Paradise Fields across the playing fields to the Paddington Canal. Cross the footbridge over the canal to enter Paradise Fields. Since October 2023, there has been a beaver colony in this nature reserve. It will be exciting to see how the colony has developed by the time you are reading this!

Leaving Paradise Fields, you enter the Westway Cross Shopping Park where the Greenford Road (A4217) goes under a railway bridge. Greenford station is close by. Go under the railway following the green Capital Ring signs. Turn left down Bennet Avenue to a path that leads to a foot and cycle bridge over the A40. This brings you to Perivale Park, which has areas of lovely wildflower meadows and sports facilities. When you reach a stream, stay on the east side until you cross a footbridge over the Brent. Turn right and walk beside the river to the Ruislip Road. Over the road, you enter Brent River Park, where the route goes beside the river for the next mile (1.6km). You walk through Bittern's Field, a restored landfill site, where in early spring the blackthorn blossom is beautiful. After Bittern's Field, cross to the west side of the river. Near the southern end of the park, the spire of St Mary's Church, Hanwell, soars above the trees. Head towards the church to cross the river and walk up the steps out of the park.

From the church, go along Church Lane until you come to Madge Hill on the left. Take the track which is also a cycle path until you reach a road, High Lane. Continue north on this road passing Mayfield School, where you re-enter Brent River Park on the east side of Bittern's Field. Go straight on until you reach Ruislip Road, which you cross into Perivale Park. Turn right, keeping to the footpath between the river and the Ruislip Road for ½ mile (0.8km). After going under a railway bridge, take the path on the left hand into Longfield Meadows. After crossing the river, take the gravel path that goes beside the river to the north-east corner of the meadows at Stockdove Way. Walk along Stockdove Way, and cross Argyle Road to continue east on Perivale Lane. When you reach the Premier Inn hotel, make a short diversion to look at St Mary's Perivale, a pretty 12th-century church with a white tower, and used for wonderful chamber concerts.

Walk 39

The rest of the route is straightforward. Go north on Church Lane to the bridge over the A40. There you are at Horsenden Lane South, which takes you past Perivale station, over the canal, past the visitor centre at Horsenden Hill (car park, café, WCs, craft shop, canoe centre, Gruffalo Trail and super views from the top of the hill). Finally, you arrive back at the Ballot Box pub, which was originally built as a polling station for people living on barges.

The Brent in Perivale

Hanwell to Brentford

The Brent River Walk from Hanwell goes under the magnificent Wharncliffe Viaduct, which carries the Great Western Railway. There is a story that while on her way to Windsor, Queen Victoria asked for her train to stop on the viaduct so she could enjoy the view of the Brent Valley. An older form of transport comes to the fore when the river joins the Grand Union Canal at Hanwell Locks. The canal towpath provides easy walking with interesting information boards. The scenery becomes increasingly urban as the river passes under the M4 motorway and enters Brentford, where there has been a crossing over the Brent since Roman times. Nevertheless, the waterside paths are peaceful and the architecture is good, especially at Brentford Gauging Locks where cargoes were measured for the canal tolls. The final ½ mile (0.8km) follows the Thames Path, until you reach the River Thames opposite Kew Gardens.

GETTING THERE

TRAIN SERVICES | South Western Rail Waterloo to Brentford; TfL Paddington to Hanwell

TUBE | Northern Line to Barnet, Finchley and Brent Cross; Central Line to Perivale and Greenford

OS EXPLORER MAPS | 161 London South; 173 London North

RESOURCES

Brent River Corridor Improvement Plan: www.thames21.org.uk/wp-content/uploads/2014/05/brent_river_corridor_improvement_plan_final_2014.pdf.

25 Beverley Brook

LENGTH: 9 miles (14.5km)

SOURCE: Cuddington Recreation Ground, Worcester Park

CONFLUENCE: Putney

Beverley Brook in Richmond Park

The Beverley Brook starts near the Surrey–London border and flows north through two of London's largest green spaces, Wimbledon Common and Richmond Park. The name acquired literary fame in the 2011 fantasy novel *Rivers of London* by Ben Aaronovitch, in which one of the main characters is Beverley Brook, the daughter of Mother Thames.

The 6.5 mile (10.5km) Beverley Brook Walk is a linear walk with public transport at both ends. It starts at New Malden train station (National Rail from Waterloo) and is on the 213 and K1 bus routes. The northern end is on the Thames Embankment, near to Hammersmith and Putney Bridge underground stations. The trail is marked by a distinctive deer symbol and is well described in a leaflet provided made by Merton Council.

Another local walk is the Barnes Trail, a circular walk beside the Thames that visits the nature reserve at the Leg o' Mutton Reservoir. The Wildfowl and Wetlands Trust London Wetland Centre at Barnes has excellent walks around its lakes.

GETTING THERE

OS EXPLORER MAP | 161 London South

RESOURCES

Beverley Brook Walk: www.merton.gov.uk/beverley_brook_walk.pdf

River conservation: South East Rivers Trust, Thames21, Friends of Richmond Park, Wimbledon Conservators and the Wildfowl & Wetlands Trust

What's in a name?

The Beverley Brook's name comes from Beavers Ley, meaning 'a place where beavers live'.

WALK 40 Richmond Park to Putney and back to Wimbledon, using a bus from Putney to Wimbledon

9.2 miles (14.8km)

As an alternative to the linear Beverley Brook Walk, we like a circular walk that suits people coming by car or public transport. The starting point is Roehampton Gate in Richmond Park with car parks, café, WCs and East Sheen railway station nearby. Walk out using the Roehampton Gate and turn left on to a path beside the park wall. Turn right after the path crosses the Brook and walk beside the Brook through Palewell Common and its allotments to Hertford Avenue. Turn right at Upper Richmond Road and cross to Priests Bridge Road, the way the clergy took between the parishes of Mortlake and Wimbledon. After rejoining the main road, turn left along Vine Road on the western edge of Barnes Common. Cross Station Road to the path on Barnes Common. At the bridge between Barnes Common and Barnes Green, turn sharp right at the bridge to follow the diagonal path across the Common. In summer, look out for the uncommon burnet rose. Another diversion is the old Barnes Cemetery, which is wonderfully overgrown, where crumbling headstones are carved with poignant inscriptions.

Windmill, Wimbledon Common

With the Brook visible on your left, walk on to Lower Putney Common, where chiffchaffs spend the summer in the hawthorns. Take the footbridge over the Brook and turn right to reach the Thames at the Ashlone Wharf, Putney. A fish pass has been installed here for eels to swim up to spawning grounds in the Brook. Walk along the embankment, past rowing clubs and cafés to Putney Bridge. Cross Putney High Street to catch a no. 93 bus to Wimbledon Common. Get off the bus at Queensmere Road and look for the green Capital Ring signs. The path across the Common passes the Windmill and the Queen's Mere (lake) in Putney Vale. Walk on until you reach Beverley Brook at a footbridge, which is dedicated to Chris Brasher, Chris Chataway and Roger Bannister, who trained here when they were preparing to run the first four-minute mile. Don't cross the bridge. Instead, walk beside the Brook using the signposted Beverley Brook Walk to cross the Kingston Bypass (A3) and Roehampton Vale to enter Richmond Park at Robin Hood Gate. Turn right across the car park to a path beside the Brook, which goes back to Roehampton Gate.

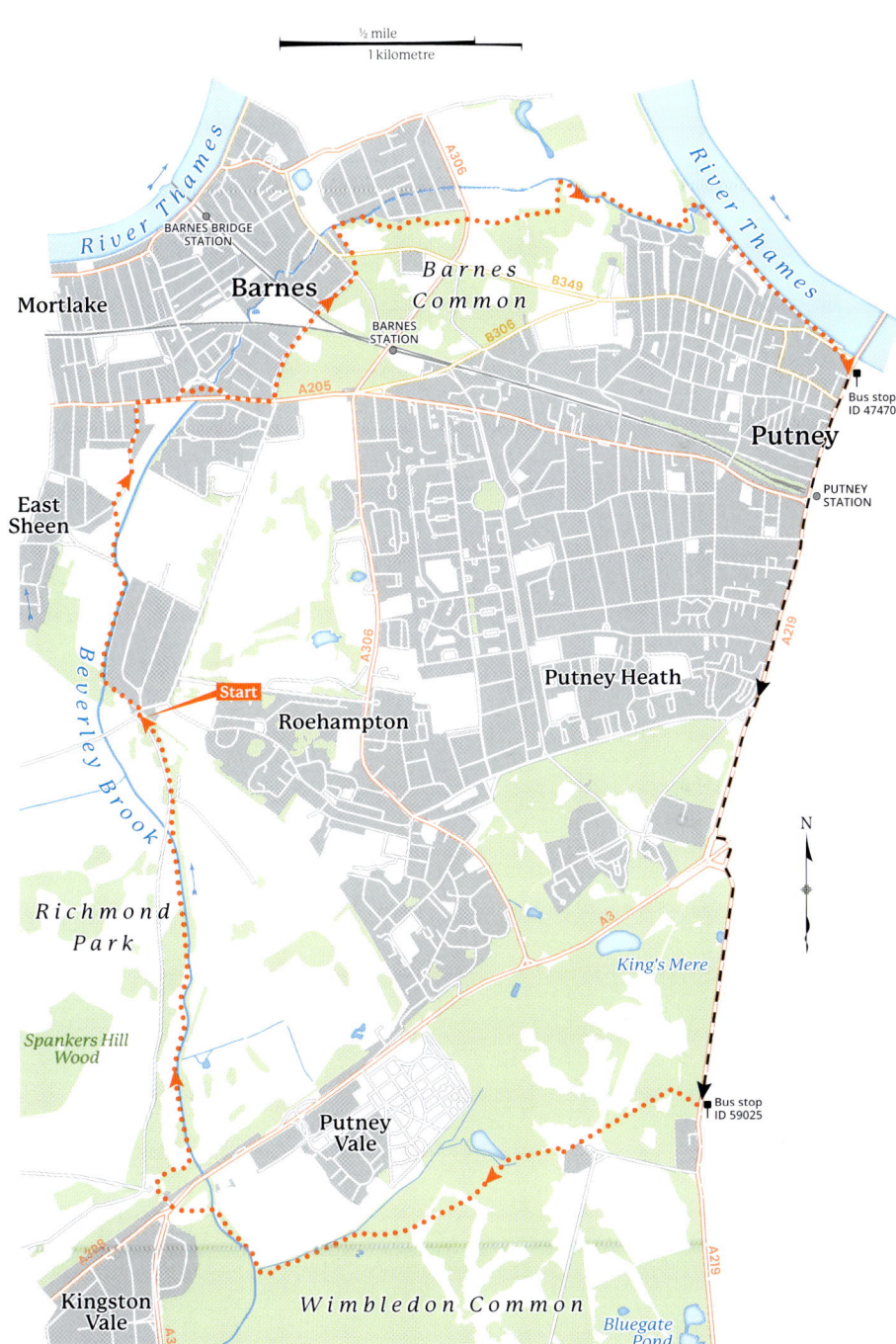

The Thames at Putney Embankment

River Wandle

26

LENGTH: 12.5 miles (20km)

SOURCE: Waddon Ponds in West Croydon and Carshalton Ponds

CONFLUENCE: Wandsworth

The Wandle is a super river to explore, being long enough to fill a day of walking and having lots of interest to attract you back again. The mixture of historic buildings, parks and nature reserves amid the suburban streets and industrial sites is most appealing.

The Wandle Trail follows the entire length of the river and is a designated walk and cycle route of 14 miles (22.5km). Most of the first half of the trail makes one of our favourite walks on pages 244–5. The route is well signed by large Wandle Valley plaques designed in the style of textile designer, artist and writer, William Morris, discrete waymarkers showing a watermill wheel, and conspicuous signs for National Cycle Network Routes 22 and 75.

Morden Hall to the Thames

Leaving Morden Hall Park, you pass Deen City Farm, where children can handle farm animals. Downstream, Merton Abbey Mills have used the river for centuries, most famously for the factory established by William Morris to make his ever-popular fabrics. A craft market continues to practise his tradition today.

Crossing Merton High Street, you are back among the grassland and trees of Wandle Park and Wandle Meadow Nature Park. The trail now enters a more industrial area, with traces of the old Surrey Iron Railway, opened in 1806. Here, horse-drawn trucks carried goods from the factories, mills and breweries beside the Wandle to the Thames.

There is one more nature reserve, the Lower Wandle and the

Wandle Valley plaque

What's in a name?

The name comes from Wandsworth (Wandelesorde in the Domesday Book) meaning 'the enclosure of a man called Waendel'. Seven mills are mentioned, which are likely to have been on the Wandle and to have lasted nearly a thousand years.

The Wheelhouse at Merton Abbey Mills

playing fields of King George's Park to relieve the built environment, before you pass the shops and apartment blocks of modern Wandsworth to reach the Thames and the end of this delightful trail.

GETTING THERE

TRAIN SERVICES | trains to East Croydon run from London Victoria, London Blackfriars and London Bridge. Trains to Wandsworth run from Waterloo
TRAM | Croydon Tramlink runs from Wimbledon to Addington
TUBE | Merton (Northern Line) is the nearest station to Morden Hall
OS EXPLORER MAP | 161 London South

RESOURCES

Deen City Farm: *https://www.deencityfarm.co.uk*
Morden Hall Park: www.nationaltrust.org.uk/morden-hall-park
South East Rivers Trust: www.southeastriverstrust.org
Wandle Trail Guides:
www.merton.gov.uk/leisure-recreation-and-culture/tourism-and-travel/local-attractions/the-wandle-trail
http://wandlevalleypark.co.uk/wp-content/uploads/2017/05/Wandle-Trail-Map-Interactive.pdf

WALK 41 Waddon Ponds to Morden Hall

The Canon Bridges Bridge in Beddington Park Lake

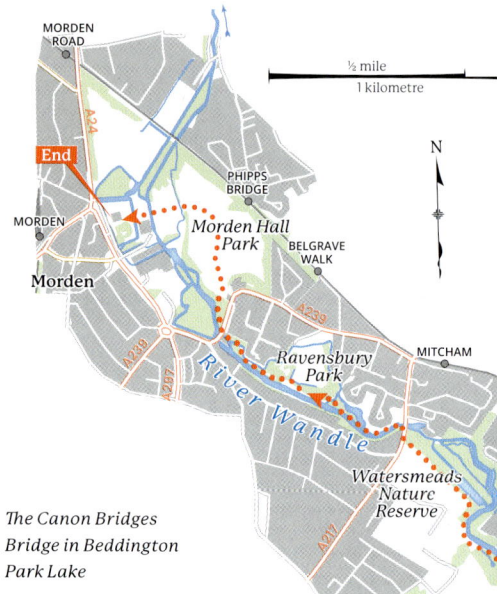

6.5 miles (10.5km)

This walk explores the upper half of the river from Wandle Park to Morden Hall. There is a large car park at Morden Hall and a direct Tramlink from Phipps Bridge to Wandle Park. Start at the Wandle Park tram stop, walk along Vicarage Road, turn right at Waddon Road, continue across Purley Way to Mill Lane and Waddon Ponds. There is a steady stream flowing from the northern end of the ponds to run west beside Richmond Green to Beddington Mill, a large flour mill in medieval times but now an apartment block. Carew Manor in Beddington Park is where Henry VIII wooed Anne Boleyn. The Wandle is a major feature of the park and is enhanced by a terracotta bridge built by a clergyman, Canon Bridges (but of course!), who bought the estate from the Carew family in 1859.

At the west end of Beddington Park, the river has been dammed to make a mill pond that has become the ornamental Grange Lake. From here, the trail leaves the river to go past Elms Pond and through the Grove to Carshalton Ponds. These ponds are fed by springs that make a second source of the Wandle. Nearby stands the grand Carshalton Water Tower, built in the early 18th century to supply fountains and baths. It is open to visitors on Sunday afternoons in summer.

The humanmade splendour continues to the Carshalton part of the river where it starts as a canal, an 18th century term for long rectangular ponds in landscaped gardens. Walking beside the canal, you follow the trail under the railway to Wilderness Island, a nature reserve in the triangle of land between the two arms of the river. Exploring Wilderness Island means leaving the trail – an example of why the Wandle will draw you back for more visits. In this area, the river water is clear and fast flowing, as well as being delightfully free of litter. This is largely due to the monthly clean-ups by volunteers of the South East Rivers Trust.

The next large green space is Poulter Park, once the grounds of Bishopsford House, which was destroyed by fire in 2001, but is now used for sports fields and public gardens. Adjacent to the park is Watermeads, a wetland nature reserve that was acquired in 1913 with funds raised by Octavia Hill, one of the founders of the National Trust. The river and the trail enter Ravensbury Park, where there was once a manor house. From Ravensbury Park, cross Morden Road near the Surrey Arms pub to end the walk in Morden Hall Park, where the National Trust provides a wide range of activities, from photography courses to BioBlitz weekends among the gardens and reedbeds.

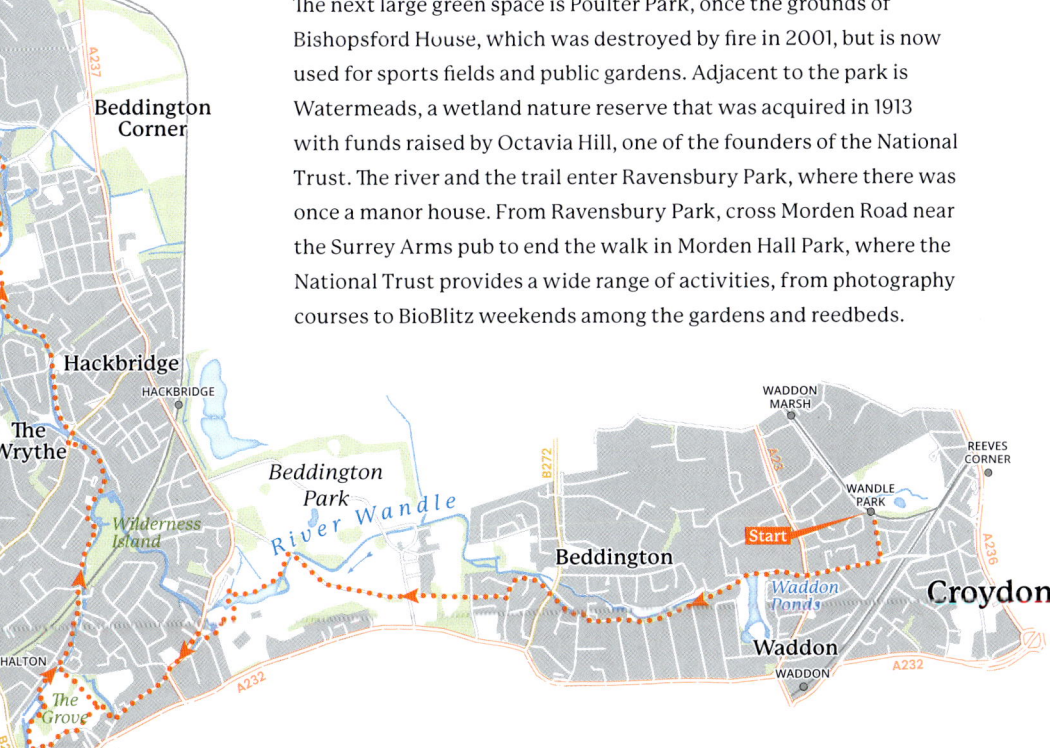

PART 6

The rivers entering the Thames in and near East London

Lake in Wanstead Park

River Ravensbourne

27

LENGTH: 11 miles (17.7km)

SOURCE: Keston

CONFLUENCE: Deptford

The Ravensbourne begins as a chalk stream in Bromley (south-east London) and ends as a tidal creek in Deptford. It has a northerly course through Beckenham, Catford and Lewisham. It is a joy to explore because it has few culverts and its water is clear. The upper reaches are best explored walking around parks but the lower half has an interesting riverside path.

Deptford Creek at low tide

What's in a name?

It is said that the names of the river and its source are derived from the invasion of Britain by Julius Caesar in 54 BC. When camped nearby, the Roman soldiers saw a raven that showed them where water could be found.

WALK 42 Keston Common

3 miles (4.8km)

Keston Common is popular with walkers. It has attractive and varied wildlife habitats – woods, heath, ponds and fens – which were studied by Charles Darwin when he lived in the nearby village of Downe. It is on the London Loop trail and is part of the Three Commons Circular Walk of 5 miles (8km), which starts at Hayes railway station. The Friends of Keston Common have a leaflet that describes the connection between Darwin and the wildlife that you may see along the walk (Resources).

Start at the car park in Westerham Road, which is beside the source of the Ravensbourne at Caesar's Well. Walk from the Well past the chain of ponds on your left side to Fishpond Road. Turn left to find a path that goes down to the next pond. Cross below this pond to have the stream on your left side. The woodland path takes you through alder and sweet chestnut trees in Padmall Wood, close to Croydon Road on the north side of the Common. Turn left to walk through more open ground and then, bear right to go up the wooded hillside to a playground and school. If you are ready for refreshment, go along Lakes Road to the cafés and pubs in Keston village.

Caesar's Well

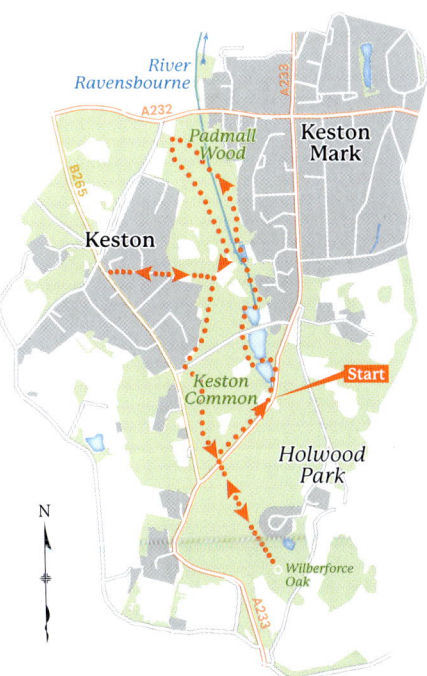

Walk 42

Wilberforce oak

Keston ponds

When you return to the Common, start on the London Loop path, which goes to the car park, and bear right to pass the bogs where Darwin studied sundew plants. Beyond the bogs, you come to heathland with birch trees and heather. The London Loop at the south end of the Common crosses the Westerham Road, where the path goes along the edge of Holwood Park, once the country house of William Pitt, the Younger (British Prime Minister 1783–1801, 1804–1806). About 500 yards (450m) along the path, there is a clearing where the trunk of a dead oak tree stands. The Wilberforce Oak is where William Wilberforce (another British politician, 1759–1833) talked to William Pitt about his 'intention to bring forward the abolition of the slave trade' in 1788. When the old oak was dying, one of its acorns was planted as a replacement. And when the younger tree was blown down by the fierce storm in October 1987, its acorns were grown to make a second replacement. The remaining dead trunk provides life to insects and other invertebrates. It is good to conserve memories, as well as wildlife.

We suggest you return along this path to the start of the walk, perhaps thinking of Darwin who must have walked this way from Downe.

Bromley and Beckenham Place Park

Between Keston and Bromley, the Ravensbourne flows through meadows and woods. Richmal Crompton, who wrote the *Just William* books, lived and taught in Bromley. You can imagine boys exactly like her fictional hero and his gang of 'outlaws' exploring the network of paths here.

Beckenham Place Park is the largest green space in Lewisham, with the Ravensbourne River on its eastern flank. From the south-east corner of the park, near Ravensbourne station on Crab Hill, you can walk through the meadows beside the banks of the rivers on a path signed as Ravensbourne Green Way.

From the lake, the Capital Ring Walk winds up the hill on the northern side of the park up to the Palladian mansion, which is now a community centre for arts and crafts. From the mansion and the lake, paths lead back to the gates on the west side of the railway at Ravensbourne station.

Waterlink Way from Lower Sydenham to Deptford

From Beckenham to Bellington, the Ravensbourne flows through a built-up area with few opportunities to walk beside it. However, the River Pool, a tributary of the Ravensbourne, starts a good riverside path, the Waterlink Way, which is also National Cycle Network Route 21. The path has a distinctive logo embedded in the surface of the path. The distance is 6 miles (9.7km), but the walk can be divided into three equal sections by stopping at Catford and Lewisham.

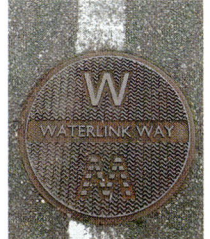

Waterlink Way sign

Start at Lower Sydenham railway station on a path to Southend Lane (A2218) where you can enter the Riverview Walk, the first park along the way. A cheerful mural near the entrance promises wildlife along your route. Next comes the River Pool Linear Park, where willow trees, reeds and rough grass provide excellent cover for birds, amphibians and insects. The River Pool joins the Ravensbourne where the Waterlink Way passes between the two railway stations in Catford.

Between Catford and Lewisham, the Ravensbourne flows for 1 mile (1.6km) through Ladywell Fields. The Lady's Well was a physic well used for medicines in the Middle Ages. As remarkable is the Lewisham Elm, a full-grown tree that resisted the fungal Dutch elm disease, which killed almost all of the mature elm trees in Britain.

27 River Ravensbourne

ABOVE *Ladywell Park*

LEFT *Mural along the Waterlink Way*

After strolling through this large open space close to Lewisham Hospital, follow the streets away from the river until you reach Cornmill Gardens. The name is a reminder of the watermills along the Ravensbourne until the 19th century. The Domesday Book recorded 11 mills in Lewisham and one in Bromley. After Lewisham, the Waterlink Way goes beside the Docklands Light Railway (DLR) at Brookmill Park with a nature reserve and ornamental gardens.

Where the Ravensbourne becomes tidal, its name changes to Deptford Creek. Deptford was once a Royal Dock. Here, Francis Drake was knighted by Queen Elizabeth I when he returned from his circumnavigation in 1580. The Thames Path completes the riverside walking between Deptford Bridge and the River Thames.

GETTING THERE

BUS SERVICES | 320 Catford to Downe gives access to upper reaches of the Ravensbourne

TRAIN AND DLR SERVICES |

Hayes (Kent): Southeastern Rail from Cannon Street

Catford and Ravensbourne: Thameslink from Blackfriars to Bromley South

Lewisham: DLR and Southeastern Rail from London Bridge

Lower Sydenham: Southeastern Rail from Charing Cross and Cannon Street

Greenwich: DLR and Southeastern Rail from London Bridge

OS EXPLORER MAPS | 147 Sevenoaks; 161 London South; 162 Greenwich & Gravesend

RESOURCES

Friends of Keston Common: *https://friendsofkestoncommon.chessck.co.uk/About%20us/KestonHolwoodTrail*

The Londonist article: *https://londonist.com/london/great-outdoors/weekend-walks-the-river-ravensbourne-from-catford-to-the-thames*

Three Commons Walk: *https://ldwa.org.uk/ldp/members/show_path.php?path_name=Three+Commons*

Walk Around London: *http://walkaroundlondon.com/waterlink-way-from-new-beckenham-to-deptford-creek/*

River Lea

28

LENGTH: 42 miles (67.6km)

SOURCE: Leagrave near Luton

CONFLUENCE: Bow Creek, East London

The Lea is one of the largest Thames tributaries, flowing east from Bedfordshire through Hertfordshire before going south on the east side of London to join the Thames at Trinity Buoy Wharf, close to the East India Dock. The Lea has a long-distance path that can be completed in sections, and several shorter walks for day trips and family outings. It offers a wide range of riverside industry and history, plus wildlife and picnic spots, well served by train stations and car parks.

The source of the River Lea

What's in a name?

The name has been recorded through history with more than 25 different spellings, as seen in Leyton (East London) and Luton (at the source). Lea and Lee are both used today in official titles. One convention is to use Lea for the river and Lee for the canal. Some people say that the name is Celtic, meaning 'bright river'; others say it means 'flow' or 'current'.

History

The Lea was a strategic boundary between the Anglo-Saxon kingdoms to the west and the Viking territories to the east, known as the Danelaw. Nowadays, it separates Essex from London. Of specific historical interest is Waltham Abbey, where King Harold II was buried (reputedly) at the Church of the Holy Cross and St Lawrence after his death at the Battle of Hastings in 1066.

The Lea has been navigable since Roman times. Records reveal there were cargoes of grain and flour transported from Ware to London in 1220. Through the Middle Ages, millers who wanted weirs to power their mills argued with boatmen who wanted free passage. The Lee Navigation (canal) was built in 1571–1581 with improvements, particularly better and bigger locks, up to the 1920s. Commercial use declined in the middle of the 20th century, but today it is a popular recreational waterway.

Hertford Castle

28 River Lea

ABOVE *The River Lea begins slowly*

OPPOSITE *The River Lea with canal boats*

The Lea is an important part of London's water supply. An extra channel, the New River, was made in 1613, drawing clean water from the Lea at Hertford. Now, there is a chain of large reservoirs between Waltham Abbey and Walthamstow.

The Lee Valley Park was Britain's first regional park established by an Act of Parliament, in 1966. It stretches 26 miles (41.8km) from Ware in Hertfordshire to the Thames in London. The park is a unique blend of countryside, nature reserves, urban green spaces, heritage sites, sports facilities, and overnight accommodation including campsites.

The Lea Valley Walk is a 50 mile (80.5km) long-distance path that was opened in 1993, three years before the Thames Path was inaugurated. It follows the whole length of the river and is clearly marked by Swan signs.

The Lea became world famous in the London 2012 Summer Olympics, which improved public access to the river, the Navigation, and the outdoor spaces for visitors and local residents. The Olympic Park changed the face of the area between Hackney Wick and Bow, including new walking and cycling paths, as well as bringing more people to enjoy its many local landmarks.

The Upper Lea There are plenty of short walks to complement the long Lea Valley Walk. The first 5 miles (8km) from the source to Luton Airport is a good example. It starts in Leagrave at Well Head in Waulud's Bank – a Neolithic mound and ditch. The walk includes Leagrave Marsh, which provides habitat for a diverse range of wildlife, including grey heron, cormorant, tufted duck, lapwing and swans, as well as several rare plants, such as the marsh bedstraw and common twayblade. The walk passes through Wardown House, where there is a boating lake, mini golf and beautiful gardens. It is home to the Luton Museum and Art Gallery, which has fine collections of decorative art, natural history, archaeology, local history and much more. The walk also passes St Mary's Church, 1121, one of the finest medieval churches in England. The walk skirts Someries Castle, built around 1448 making it one of the earliest surviving brick buildings in England, and ends at the rail station beside Luton Airport, where a train can take you back to Leagrave.

WALK 43 Hertford to Rye House

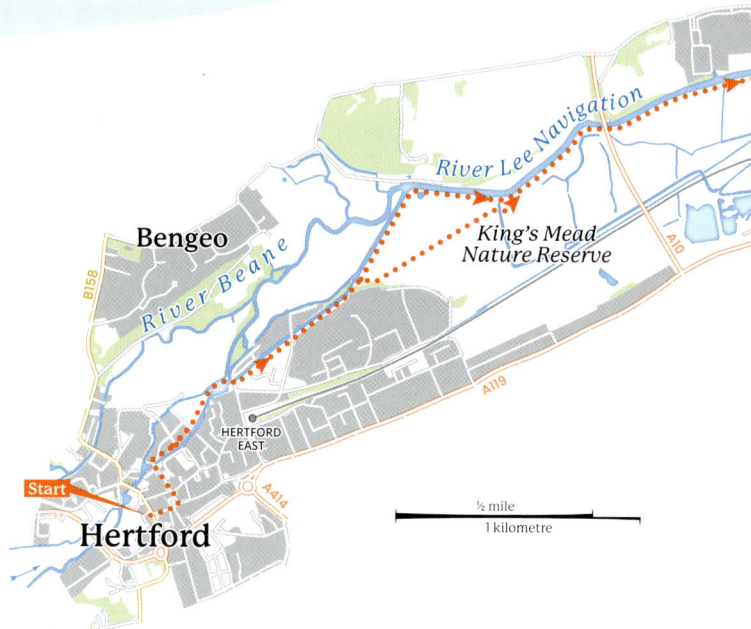

7 miles (11.3km)

The first 7 miles (11.3km) of the Lee Navigation, from Hertford to Rye House, is one of the best explorations along the Lea, including one railway branch line, two stately homes and three nature reserves. Hertford East and Rye House stations provide an easy return on this linear walk. There is a way back beside the New River for the stronger walkers. Start from Hertford Castle, a royal palace until the reign of James I. Walk via Castle Street and the town centre to Bull Plain, which leads to the head of the Lee Navigation where the river tumbles down the Castle Weir into the canal basin. As you walk, watch out for the elusive but colourful kingfisher.

The basic route is along the canal towpath, but there are a couple of variations to consider. The first of these is at Hertford Lock, where the King's Mead, one of the largest nature reserves in Hertfordshire, lies to the right of the Navigation. There is a path that cuts straight across this flood meadow, where many rabbits can be seen, and offers a close look at the birds, insects and flowers. Where the meadow path rejoins the towpath, they cross the beginning of the New River taking water

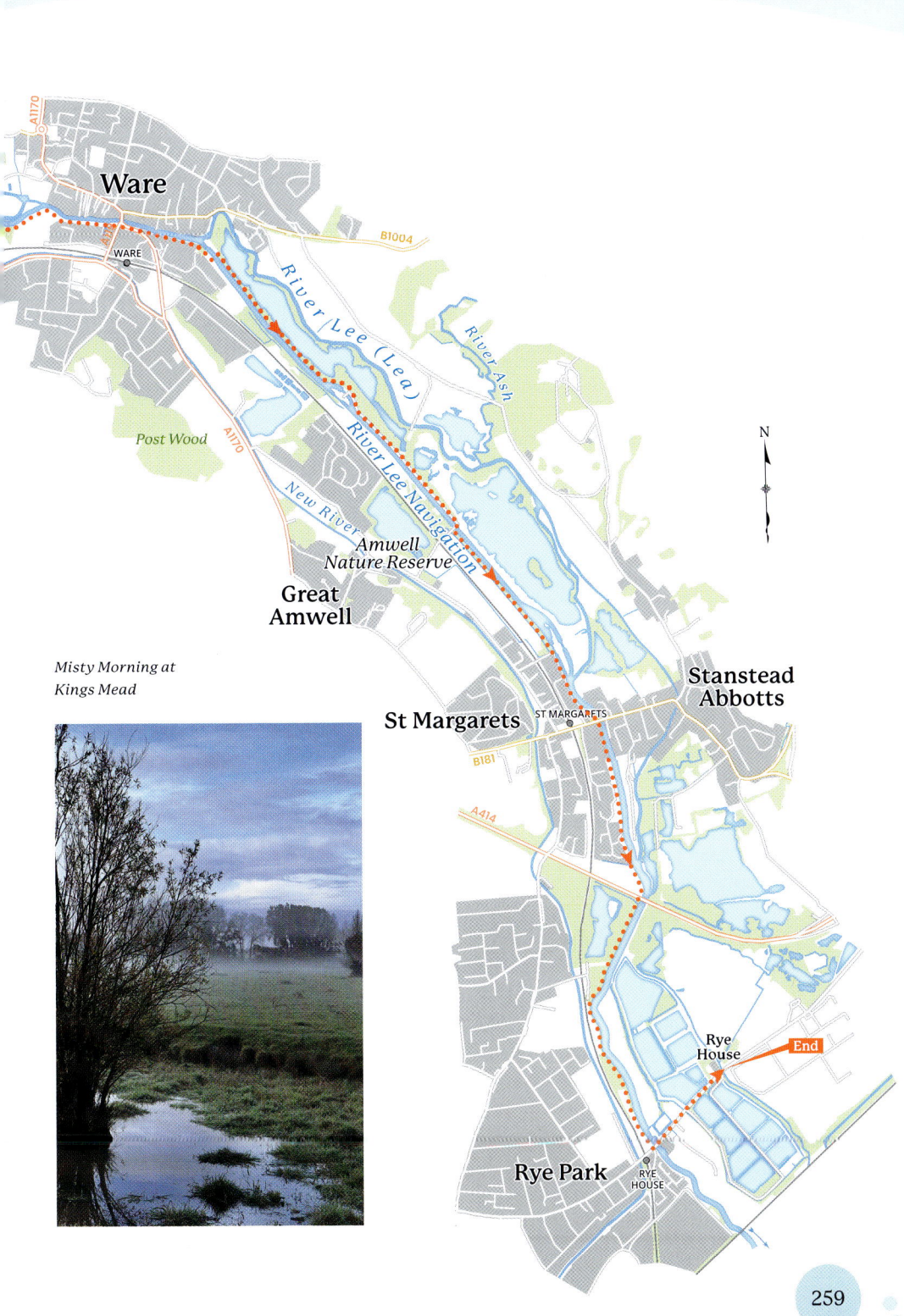
Misty Morning at Kings Mead

Walk 43

from the Lea. Through Ware, the river is the Navigation. Look out for the Gazebos of Ware, extraordinary and beautiful bay windows that lean over the water. They were first built 200 years ago, as quiet retreats from the busy High Street, which was once the main road from London to York and Scotland.

As you leave Ware on the towpath, you come to a footbridge to Tumble Lake and a sign inviting you to a 'pop-up' café on the opposite bank. Our second variation is from the café (recommended) along the path on the east side of the Navigation. The path is wider than the towpath, less busy and has views of the lakes (former gravel pits). The last and biggest of the lakes is Amwell Nature Reserve, with bird hides and a super viewpoint. From this point, cross back to the towpath for the last 2 miles (3.2km) to Rye House Bridge.

Rye House train station and the New River are close to the canal bridge on the west side. The lane on the east side passes: the Rye House pub; the Rye House Gatehouse — all that remains of the grand manor house which became a Victorian workhouse; a car park, which you can use for your visit; and last but certainly not least, the Royal Society for the Protection of Birds Rye Meads Nature Reserve.

OPPOSITE *Gazebo at Ware*

BELOW *Rye House Gatehouse*

Hoddesdon to Waltham Abbey

The River Stort joins the Lea at Hoddesdon, close to Rye House. It is also navigable and has a towpath that takes you to Bishop's Stortford 14 miles (22.5km) and a railway to bring you back. It is a peaceful alternative to the lower parts of the Navigation. Below the Stort–Lea confluence, the Lea Valley from Hoddesdon to Waltham Abbey is deservedly named the River Lee Country Park. The lakes and side streams are great places for fishing. This must have inspired the writer, Izaak Walton, who came fishing here when he lived in London. In *The Compleat Angler*, he wrote: 'rivers and the inhabitants of the watery element were made for wise men to contemplate and fools to pass by without consideration.' A good motto for the river explorer.

WALK 44 Cheshunt, Fishers Green and Waltham Abbey

5 miles (8km)

Of three possible starting points, the Lee Valley Country Park car park in Willow Road, Cheshunt (next to the Herts Young Mariners Base) is the one we chose. This is close to Cheshunt train station. From the car park, turn left at the canal towpath and walk past the Young Mariners Lake on your left to the first canal bridge. Cross the Navigation into the nature reserve and turn left to walk north beside Seventy Acres Lake, where there extensive reedbeds. Follow the path around the top of the lake to the Wildlife Discovery Centre, which has a very good bird hide and information. Continue on the lakeside path

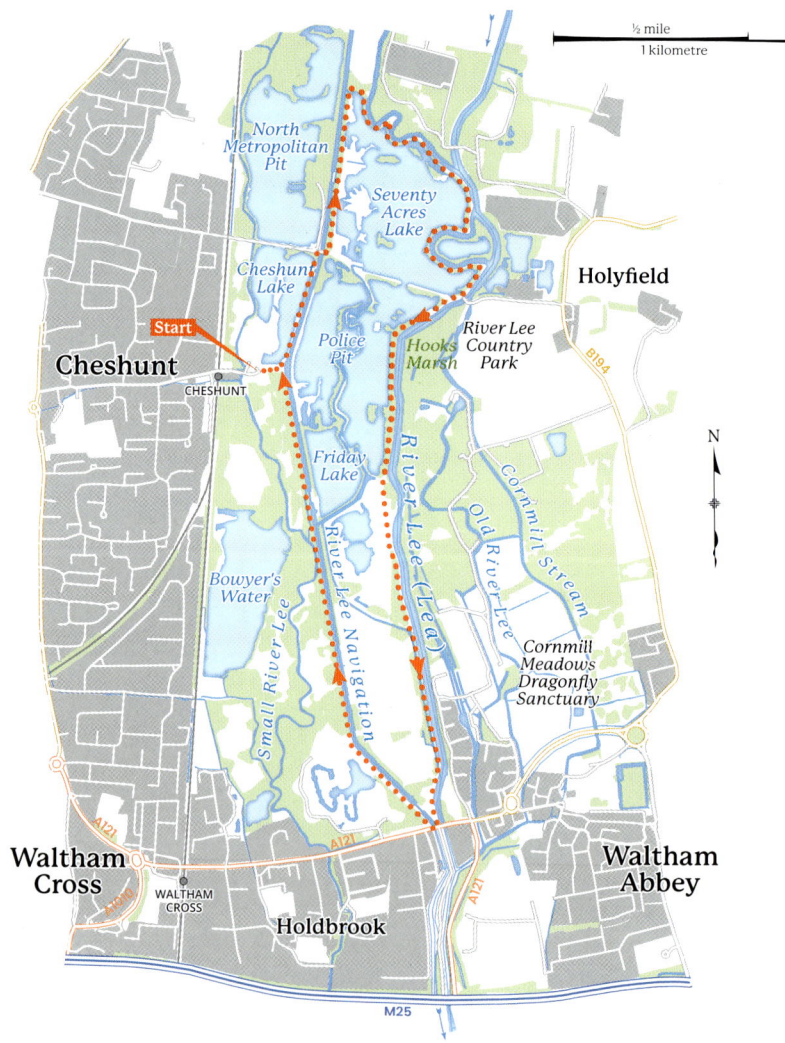

southwards. After the lakes, you cross a path to the Fisher Green car park, another starting point. Stay on the southward path, also a cycle route, which has the Horsemill Stream on its left (east) side. You pass interesting wood sculptures including a Viking ship. The buildings you see on the far side of the Horsemill stream are the Royal Gunpowder Mills, which has a museum. When you reach Highbridge Street, the road to Waltham Abbey (another start point), turn left if you want to see the Abbey or the Gunpowder Mills. Otherwise turn right to the Lee Navigation and walk back along the towpath to Cheshunt.

Viking ship sculpture at Waltham Abbey

28 River Lea

Waltham Abbey to Tottenham Going south from Waltham Abbey, the Lea River and Lee Navigation flow side by side under the M25 motorway and then separate to make a large island at Enfield. This was the site of the Royal Small Arms Factory, makers of the Lee Enfield rifle. The island is now a residential village. The separation becomes wider by the two large reservoirs, King George's and William Girling, for the next 3 miles (4.8km) to Edmonton, with the river on the east side and the Navigation and path on the west. Things are more interesting around Tottenham, where marshes, flood meadows and industrial heritage have been conserved.

Heat and Power Project, Edmonton Eco Park

WALK 45 Walthamstow Marshes to Hackney Marsh

6 miles (9.7km)

This is an enjoyable walk down the towpath of the Lee Navigation and up beside the River Lea. Start at Clapton Station (trains from Liverpool Street) in Hackney. The car park in Coppermill Lane in Walthamstow is another possible starting point. From Clapton Station, walk down Gunton Road and cross the green to Lea Bridge Road. Go to the bridge beside the Princess of Wales pub and join the Navigation towpath. Here is the Docklands Canal Boat Trust whose boat is adapted for people with disabilities. Go down the towpath, to cross the canal on the Pond Lane Flood Gates and pass the Middlesex Filter Beds, which are now a nature reserve created on old sewage works.

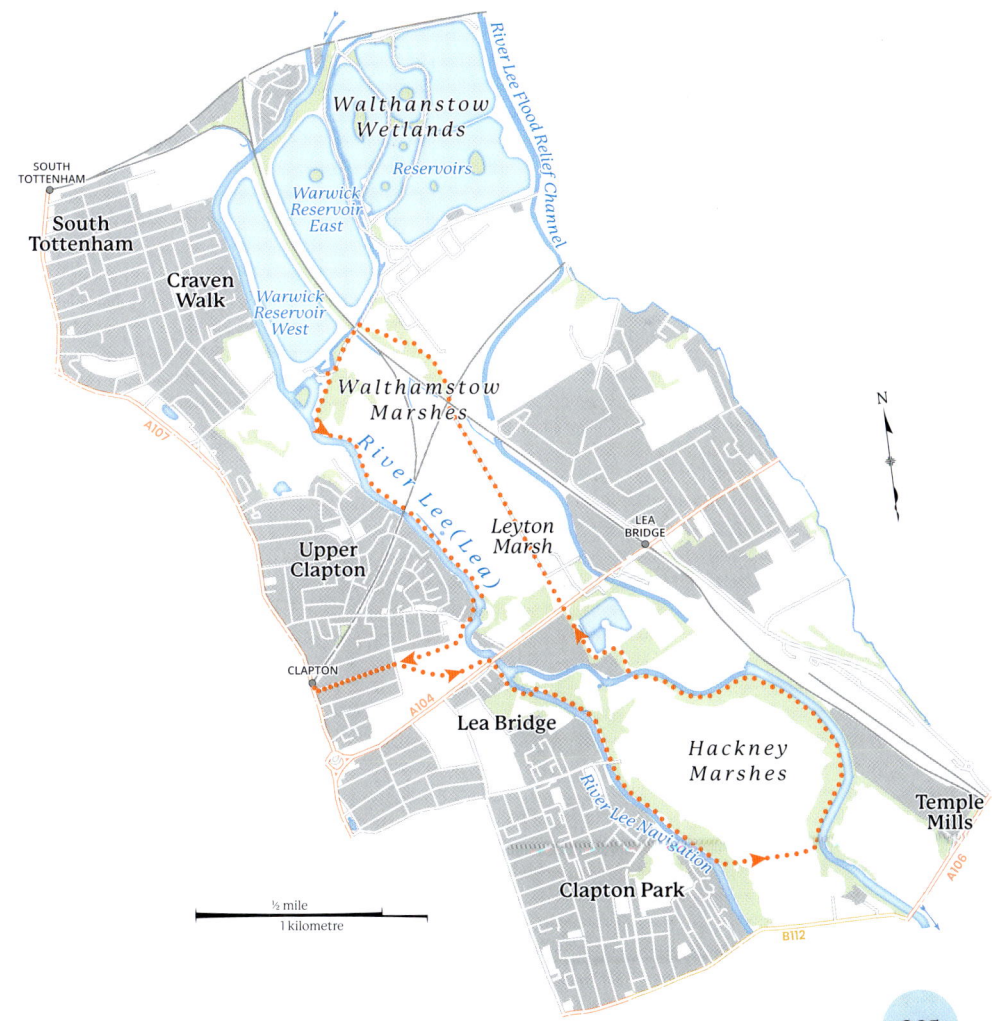

Walk 45

ABOVE *Kingfisher*

BELOW *Little egret*

OPPOSITE *Walthamstow Marshes*

After 1.5 miles (2.4km) from Clapton, there is a path across Hackney Marshes (space for 88 football pitches) to the River Lea. A delightful hard path follows the river upstream in a belt of trees to the bridge over a cross stream between the Navigation and the river. The path to Walthamstow Marshes is shown on waymarker posts, passing the sewage works that has a visitor centre and a small nature reserve. Going north, the combined foot and cycle path runs under Lea Bridge Road, then between the Lea Valley Riding Centre and Leyton Marsh. Further, on the west side is Lammas Meadow and, beyond the railway bridge, Walthamstow Marshes. It is worth looking to see how flooded the marshes are to decide whether to walk through the marsh or go around the edges on the next leg of the walk. The car park in Coppermill Lane is the northerly turning point on the walk. A pop-up café offers a welcome break, 4 miles (6.4km) along the route.

Go under the railway bridge at Coppermill Lane and through the gate into Walthamstow Marshes. If dry, the shortest way is the diagonal path through the marsh heading for the railway bridge over the Navigation. If wet, it is safer to go along the northern edge of the marsh to the towpath at Horse Shoe Bridge. Walking south beside the Navigation under the railway to Leyton Marsh, where the first British-built aeroplane flew in 1909. The workshops of the AVRO aircraft company were in the arches of the railway bridge. A short distance further, the towpath crosses the Navigation to the green near Clapton Station.

Hackney to the Thames Downstream is the Queen Elizabeth Olympic Park (560 acres/226ha) with a fascinating mixture of dramatic buildings, acres of grass, miles of paths, wetland corners and the Lea serenely passing down the middle. It is a very interesting example of conservation of the contemporary, creating a legacy that will stand comparison with ancient buildings and monuments.

At this point, the River Lea and the Lee Navigation unite for the last mile (1.6km) before Bow Locks. There are several side streams, such as the Waterworks River, used for the industries that flourished in East London to serve the City and for trade around the world through the nearby docks. The Three Mills are an example standing majestically above the tidal waters of Bow Creek.

The tidal end of the river becomes Bow Creek. This has an exaggerated S shape, creating a peninsular on which the Bow Creek Ecology Park is used for open-air teaching. There are also several walks from the Lea's confluence with the Thames from Trinity Buoy Wharf, in north-east London, which offers many sights of interest, including London's first moon and tide clock and the beautiful Longplayer singing bowls display. Located in the Lighthouse, this daily musical display is open for public access Here, 39 metal bowls positioned sequentially are part of the 66ft (20m) wide orchestral instrument that has been playing live since its commission in 2012.

28 River Lea

Singing Bowls

GETTING THERE

OS EXPLORER MAPS | 174 Epping Forest & Lea Valley; 194 Hertford & Bishop's Stortford

RESOURCES

AEDA River Stort fact file: *http://www.environmentdata.org/archive/ealit:2983*

Canal & River Trust Lee Navigation: *www.canalrivertrust.org.uk/enjoy-the-waterways/canal-and-river-network/lee-navigation*

Cicerone Guides: these have been divided into sections according to the railway stations along the route with all zones being available from London stations

Lea Valley Walk by Leigh Hatts: *www.leavalleywalk.org.uk*

Lea Valley Walk guide: *www.bertuchi.co.uk/leavalleyindex.php*

Let's Go! Lea Valley Walk at Luton: *www.letsgo.org.uk/OldCMS/2805099_6.htm*

Lee Valley Park: *www.visitleevalley.org.uk*

Lea Valley Walk – TfL: *https://tfl.gov.uk/modes/walking/lea-valley*

Longplayer: *www.longplayer.org*

Upper Lea Valley Walk Guide: *https://www.luton.gov.uk/Transport_and_streets/Lists/LutonDocuments/PDF/Engineering%20and%20Transportation/Cycling/Walking/lea%20valley%20walk.pdf*

Wardown House: *https://www.culturetrust.com/venues/wardown-house-museum-gallery*

River Roding

LENGTH: 31 miles (50km)

SOURCE: Molehill Green near Stansted, Essex

CONFLUENCE: Barking Creek

Ford near Molehill Green

A wet weekend at Stansted Airport may not sound tremendous fun, but it adds variety to the life of a river explorer. The urge to find the source of the Roding required a ramble around the fields at Molehill Green, a village beyond the runway at Stansted. Walk down School Lane to a bridleway through the flat wheat fields, where there is a ford – and here is a river! A look at the map and a search for signposts will find footpaths that lead back to the village, crossing ditches on footbridges made in a style that says Essex. At Chapel End in the village is a stream beside the cricket field, a thatched cottage and a residence called Rodings House, making a very satisfactory source for the Roding.

What's in a name?

The river's name is derived from the villages at its upper end. An earlier name (1062) was Angrices burne, which may be linked to the names of Chipping Ongar and High Ongar.

29 River Roding

Roding in Fyfield

The Roding runs from Essex farmlands, through Epping Forest, the suburbs of Loughton and Woodford, the densely populated Ilford and East Ham to reach the Thames at Barking under a tidal barrier.

The Rodings Moving downstream from the source, the river runs through Little and Great Canfield where the Parish Council have updated the footpaths and published 12 local walks, including one to the source. This area has eight villages that share the river's name from High Roding to Beauchamp Roding, with Aythorpe, White, Leaden, Abbess and Margaret Rodings in between. Arable farming flourishes on the rich Essex clay where the river peacefully meanders. A windmill still stands at Aythorpe Roding and it suggests that the river did not have enough force to power watermills here.

A rural 3 mile (4.8km) riverside walk follows the Essex Way between Fyfield and High Ongar. You can return using the Three Forests Way on the east side of the river, or by bus from Chipping Ongar (no. 46 along the B184). From High Ongar to Loughton there are no enticing riverside paths.

WALK 46 Loughton

4 miles (6.4km)

Borage wildflower

The next place to find good riverside walking is in the Roding Valley Meadows Nature Reserve at Loughton. This is the largest area of flood meadows in Essex and is rich with wildflowers in summer. It is well served by the Central Line (London Underground). There are several ways from Loughton into the meadows. A good one is from Debden Station in Chigwell Lane. From the station, walk down the river to the Three Forests Way, which follows the river downstream for 1 mile (1.6km), winding among reeds, tall grasses and willows. When you reach playing fields, stay on the path beside the river until you reach a footbridge. Cross the river to the next part of the nature reserve. Walk over the meadow to a crossing of paths. Turn right to go past more meadows into woodland until you reach the nature reserve car park beside the David Lloyd Sports Centre. This is another possible starting point. Continue on the tarmac driveway outside the fence around the sports centre until you reach the river again. On the west bank, walk with the lake on your right side and the playing fields on your left. The hard-surfaced path follows the river back to the bridge between the two parts of the reserve. From there, instead of going back along the

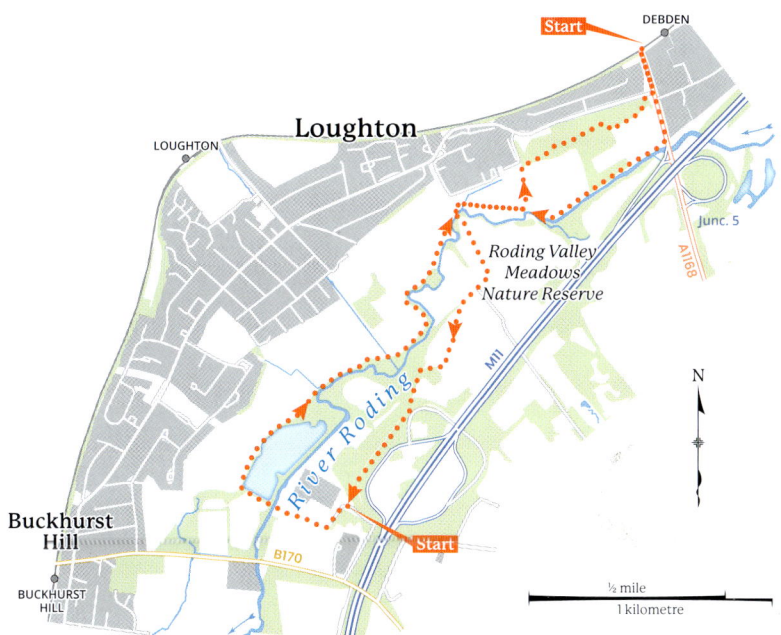

Walk 46

Three Forests Way, there is easier walking along the north edge of the reserve to return to Chigwell Road and Debden station.

As you walk through the meadows, you see many wildflowers, such as the borage which must have inspired William Morris, the textile designer, who grew up nearby in Water House, Walthamstow. Borage is one of the floral patterns produced by his company and its blue colour is a natural dye.

Roding Valley meadows

Woodford to Wanstead The Roding Way is a cycle and pedestrian route from Ray Park in Woodford to Barking. The signage and use of roads suggests that the route is intended more for cycling than walking. There are riverside paths which can be found near the road bridges crossing the Roding. The top entrance to Ray Valley Park is tucked away at the end of Oxford Road, off Prospect Road in Woodford. Walkers can use the Roding Valley Way signs to note where they are, but generally go in the direction that follows the river south, which is rewarded by grassy paths, trees, reeds and safe ways across the main roads. There is an orchard and a splendid Victorian pumping station in Redbridge. Even the industrial sites nearby do not spoil the sense of being fortunate to have a green space in which to explore the river.

After 3 miles (4.8km), the riverside path and the Roding Valley Way enter Wanstead Park. This park is owned by the City of London as part of its Epping Forest estate. Originally this was a deer park attached to Wanstead Manor. It was changed to a landscaped

Grotto ruins in Wanstead Park

29 River Roding

garden around a stately home, Wanstead House, in the 18th century when the lakes and grotto were constructed. In 1822, the owners of Wanstead House were declared bankrupt, the contents of the house auctioned and the house demolished. Eventually, the park was sold to the City of London, which conserved it as a lovely place to stroll and picnic.

Barking Creek It is difficult to follow the river through Ilford, where it is close to the North Circular Road. It is more fun to go directly to Barking Creek, as the tidal portion of the Roding is called. There is a 2 mile (3.2km) walk from Barking Abbey to the Thames at the mouth of Barking Creek. All that remains of the Abbey is the name, one archway and St Margaret's Church. From the church, cross the recreation ground (Abbey Green) to Abbey Road, through the new apartment buildings at Spring Place to cross the river at a lock and weir. The track goes round an inlet to Fleet Road and on to a path that leads under the A13 to reach Beckton Creekside Nature Reserve. The Roding Creekside Trail goes past the Beckton Sewage Treatment Works to the tall flood barrier, where the air is fresh and the view of Gallions Reach extends from the Royal Docks upstream to Halfway Reach downriver.

OPPOSITE *Barking Flood Barrier*

GETTING THERE

OS EXPLORER MAPS | 162 Greenwich & Gravesend; 174 Epping Forest & Lee Valley; 183 Chelmsford & the Rodings

RESOURCES

Great Canfield Village: *www.greatcanfield.org.uk/footpaths--walks.html*
Ray Park: *https://visionrcl.org.uk/wp-content/uploads/2020/10/roding-valley-may-19.pdf*
Roding Valley Meadows Nature Reserve: *www.essexwt.org.uk/nature-reserves/roding-valley*
Wanstead Park, City of London: *www.cityoflondon.gov.uk/things-to-do/green-spaces/epping-forest/where-to-go-in-epping-forest/wanstead-park*

River Rom and Beam

LENGTH: 10 miles (16km)

SOURCE: Stapleford Abbotts, 3 miles (4.8km) north of Romford

CONFLUENCE: Dagenham

The Rom is a short river and starts as a collection of small streams and ditches in the fields of South Essex where there are few paths. More water is gathered as it goes south beside Hainault Forest to become a small river, where it is crossed by the London Loop footpath. It goes underground in Romford. When it emerges in Dagenham, it is called the River Beam.

The Rom can be found by walking along the London Loop Trail in Hainault Forest. Start from Chigwell Row, where there are several car parks. Find the London Loop and follow it in a south-east direction out of the forest and across the Hainault Golf Club course, where we met a tame fox. Walk down a gentle slope to

View of East London from Hainault Forest

What's in a name?

The Rom's name means the place with a 'wide (roomy) ford'. The Beam probably refers to a bridge.

ABOVE *Eastbrookend Park Discovery Centre*

BELOW *The Chase Local Nature Reserve*

cross the Rom, where it flows between banks of nettles and docks. Turn right (south) to Carter Lane, past an equestrian centre. Leave the London Loop to go south on Carter Lane to the houses on the north edge of Romford. At Firbank Road, there is a bridge over the river and a path that runs in a grassy corridor beside the river for 1 mile (1.6km) to Collier Row Park. Soon after this, the Rom goes underground. The easiest way to return from Collier Row to Chigwell Row is by bus (nos. 247 and 362), reducing the walk to 3 miles (4.8km). However, it is an easy walk for a mile along the pavement beside the B174 and A1112 roads to reach Hainault Forest Country Park with its lake and a magnificent view of the towering offices around Canary Wharf. Finish your walk by wandering among the oaks and ponds to reach your starting point.

The last part of the River Beam is in the Ford Motor Works, which made Dagenham a household name. There has been no public right of way down to the Thames for many years. There are apartments being built on former factory land close to the Beam, so we can hope that riverside paths may come in the future.

GETTING THERE

OS EXPLORER MAPS | 162 Greenwich & Gravesend; 175 Southend-on-Sea & Basildon

RESOURCES

Eastbrookend: *https://barkinganddagenhamcountryparks.com/eastbrookend-discovery-centre/*

Walking by the River Rom by John Rogers: *https://thelostbyway.com/2021/05/walking-the-river-rom.html*

WALK 47 Dagenham dog bone-shaped walk

5 miles (8km)

The lower part of the Rom, where it is called the Beam, flows beside three nature reserves in Dagenham. To explore these reserves, start in Eastbrookend Country Park where the Discovery Centre has a cheerful café, toilets and information boards. From the Centre take the hard-surfaced path signed to Beam Valley Country Park that goes on the west side of a lake. At the end of the lake, turn left and then right to a mud path. This passes an entrance to The Chase Local Nature Reserve, which you can visit on the way back. A footbridge over the railway brings you into the Beam Valley Country Park. This has become a nature reserve in recent years with much improvement of its riverside willows and reedbeds. It is a pleasure to walk in both

Reed Beds in Beam Valley Nature Park

directions through it. At the southern end, cross the A1112 to go into what is now called Beam Parklands. This is the last green space beside the Rom and Beam before its final section through the Ford Motor Works. Walk along the main path with the river on the left and the remains of the Romford Canal on the right. Also on the right, you will come to an information board which illustrates the Beam Parklands Heritage Trail. Use this trail to make a loop around Hospital Hill. Start the return journey through Beam Valley Country Park. After the railway, go into the Chase Local Nature Reserve to make a loop beside the ponds and meadows until you see the Discovery Centre again.

Beam Parklands Heritage Trail

River Ingrebourne

31

LENGTH: 27 miles (43.5km)

SOURCE: Noak Hill near Romford, and Weald near Brentwood

CONFLUENCE: Rainham

The Ingrebourne, like the Roding, Rom and Beam, rises in Essex and joins the Thames in a London Borough (Havering). This group of three rivers is in one catchment partnership formed in 2012 to improve the wildlife habitats and recreational space for people. The Ingrebourne has two large tributaries: Paine's Brook (also known as Carter's Brook at its source), which rises at Noak Hill (north-east Romford) and Weald Brook, which springs from an underground well within the property of the 600-year-old Sabine's Farm, Naverstock, to the west of Brentford. The two brooks meet and become the Ingrebourne at the Old Brick Works on the south side of the A12 road at Harold Wood in Romford.

Harold Hill to Hornchurch

Carter's and Paine's Brook can be followed for most of its length using the London Loop section 21 (Havering-atte-Bower to Harold Wood). The London Loop route reaches Carter's Brook at Tees Drive near the Deers Rest pub in the Harold Hill district of Romford. The Brook and the path go through the Central Park, where it becomes Paine's Brook. The green corridor has two children's playgrounds before it reaches the A12. The London Loop leaves the Brook to a pedestrian crossing over the busy A12 and again at the railway line where it goes to Harold Wood train station. Some people think that Harold Hill and Wood are named after King Harold II, who was killed at the Battle of Hastings. However, the area could have been a favourite hunting ground of earlier Saxon royalty including Harold I (Harold Harefoot), who reigned 1035–1040.

Source of the Ingrebourne in a private garden

From Harold Wood to Upminster is section 22 of the London

What's in a name?

The name Ingrebourne was first recorded in 1062 and maybe derived from a reference to a person called 'Inga'.

Ingrebourne flows into the Thames at Rainham

Loop. The route comes back to the river in Harold Wood Park where it has become the Ingrebourne. There is a delightful path in Pages Wood, which features wooden sculptures of forest creatures. The river flows under the A127 Southend Arterial Road. The walking route crosses to the west side of the river to get over railways and main roads. A more direct way to reach Upminster station is to follow the cycle route along Hall Lane on the east side of the river. An attraction near Upminster station is the windmill, built in 1803 and one of the few surviving smock windmills in the country. Given how much we have celebrated watermills, it is a wry thought that the Thames tributaries have three such good windmills near their banks (Beverley Brook, Roding and Ingrebourne).

The London Loop section 23 continues the riverside walking from Upminster to Rainham station. However, Hornchurch Country Park has so many attractions that we recommend it as a circular walk instead of a linear walk between stations.

WALK 48 Hornchurch Country Park

6 miles (9.7km)

Reedbeds by the Ingrebourne at Hornchurch

Hornchurch Country Park and the Ingrebourne Valley Nature Discovery Centre are owned by Havering Council and managed by the Essex Wildlife Trust. The centre has an observation hall, an education room, a café and information about the local wildlife and the history of the airfield in the First and Second World Wars. There are car parks at the centre and at the north (Hacton Bridge) and south (Ingrebourne Hill) ends of the Country Park.

We like to start at Ingrebourne Hill at the southern end. From the car park, take the route signed as Bramble-Conifer-Pyramid-Stillwell paths, which goes past a lake and zigzags up to the top of Ingrebourne Hill. After admiring the view, follow the well-trodden but unsigned path north, gently descending across meadows to Albyns Farm Lake. Here, you pick up the well-signed London Loop and National Cycle Network Route 135, which goes close to the river with a splendid viewing point over the marshes and features one of the largest continuous areas of freshwater reedbeds in London. When you reach the Visitor Centre, follow the sign to Hacton Lane pointing right, towards the river. The riverside walk continues until you reach Hacton Bridge car park.

On the way back, bear right to follow a path through fields and woodland on the western side of the park. Back at the centre, continue on the western side — a more level route — to return to the start.

The diverse habitats attract many species of birds from barn owls to waterfowl, even the occasional osprey on migration. There are plenty of wildflowers and butterflies in the meadows, dragonflies over the water, fungi in the woods and songbirds in the shrubs.

The information boards are excellent, explaining the history of the park as an airfield during both world wars. During the First World War, Suttons Farm Airfield claims to have shot down three Zeppelins in 1916. By 1917, the airfield was at the forefront of defending London against the German bomber aircraft known as Gothas. In 1919, the land was farmed again. Ten years later, a larger aerodrome was opened and named RAF Hornchurch. During the Second World War,

Airfield Defences at RAF Hornchurch

Spitfire squadrons in the Battle of Britain were based here and developed tactics called the Hornchurch Wing. As you walk along the paths, you keep being surprised by the defences of the airfield, including pillboxes, gun emplacements and communication points. The centre features an RAF Hornchurch memorabilia room.

283

31 River Ingrebourne

Hornchurch to the Thames Leaving Hornchurch, you cross Red Bridge and enter Rainham village, with cafés and pubs and the distinctive Rainham Hall. This National Trust house and garden was built in 1729. It has a 7.4 acre (3ha) garden, stable-converted café, small selection of gifts and second-hand books in the brewhouse, and the stunning hayloft, available to rent for meetings and receptions.

The River Ingrebourne ends by becoming Rainham Creek before it joins the Thames. To reach the Thames, you cross the railway beside the station and follow the London Loop along Ferry Lane. You pass under the major roads of the A1306 New Road and the A1 and enter Rainham Marshes. The streams that you see are drainage channels, not the Rainham Creek, which is further west. You reach the Thames where there is a plaque on the sea wall describing the Pilgrim Ferry, which was a crossing point to Kent in the Middle Ages. There is a car park here which is useful if you have a second car. Otherwise, return to Rainham for trains to London. The London Loop section 24 continues down the side of the Thames to Purfleet, making a link to the Mardyke (Chapter 33).

OPPOSITE *Ingrebourne meadow*

GETTING THERE

BUS SERVICES | 165/365, via Havering Country Park, Collier Row, Romford, Elm Park, South Hornchurch and Rainham; 252, via Collier Row, Romford, Elm Park and Hornchurch; 256 (the Hornchurch Hopper) via Harold Hill, Harold Wood and Hornchurch

TUBE | District Line to Hornchurch station

OS EXPLORER MAP | 162 Greenwich & Gravesend

RESOURCES

The Catchment Plan is accessible from Thames Chase: enquiries@thameschase.org.uk or the Essex Rivers Hub www.essexrivershub.org.uk

Hornchurch Country Park: *www.essexwt.org.uk*

Rainham Hall: *www.nationaltrust.org.uk/visit/london/rainham-hall*

River Darent

LENGTH: 20 miles (32km)

SOURCE: Several streams arising between Westerham and Crockham

CONFLUENCE: Between Crayford and Dartford

The Darent is a stunning Thames tributary and its valley is a beautiful natural playground with several walking trails in wonderful Kent countryside scenery. It gives a fascinating view into our Roman and Norman heritage.

The Darent begins as a chalk stream from springs in the woods near the Iron Age fort at Goodley Stock in the North Downs, about a mile (1.6km) south of Westerham. In this Area of Outstanding Natural Beauty, the forest rivulet quickly becomes a flowing stream as other streams join it between Westerham to Sevenoaks.

Summertime beside the upper Darent

What's in a name?

The name Darent is derived from the Old English Diorente. It may be similar to the derivation of the River Dart, which is interpreted as Oak River. Or, it may mean 'clear water'. Either way, it was called 'an earthly paradise' by the Victorian artist Samuel Palmer, who lived on its banks and painted the Darent landscape in the 1800s.

Bridge and ford at Eynsford

To reach the Thames at Dartford, it flows through picturesque villages, past a Roman villa, the ruins of a Norman Castle and under historic bridges.

The most obvious walking trail of 19 miles (30.6km) is the Darent Valley Path (DVP), built by the Kent County Council in the 1980s. It is a well signposted route starting near Sevenoaks and going downstream. Note that some guides describe the route going upstream from Dartford. The path is mostly flat, well looked after and easily accessible for all ages. It is popular with joggers, walkers and cyclists.

The DVP begins in the village of Chipstead close to the junction of the M25 and M26 motorways. A more convenient start, if using public transport, is Sevenoaks Wildlife Reserve at Riverhead, about a mile from the rail station at the centre of Sevenoaks. The two starting routes come together at Otford, which is where we start our favourite Darent walk.

WALK 49 Otford to Shoreham and Eynsford (return by train)

5.5 miles (8.9km)

This walk combines three pretty villages and plenty of history in the Garden of England. From the car park in the Otford High Street, opposite The Bull pub, turn right to walk west towards the river. This street is part of the Pilgrims' Way from Winchester to Canterbury, the ancient road that we met on our walk beside the River Wey near Guildford. Before the bridge over the mill stream, a private road on your right is the DVP past the former mill buildings. The path goes through fields and beside a golf course for 1 mile (1.6km) and then, turns right to climb the hill. Turn left at the crossing of paths to reach Shoreham village. Turn left down the lane, past the Samuel Palmer pub to the bridge beside the river. Samuel Palmer lived

Viaduct over Darent valley at Lullingstone

288

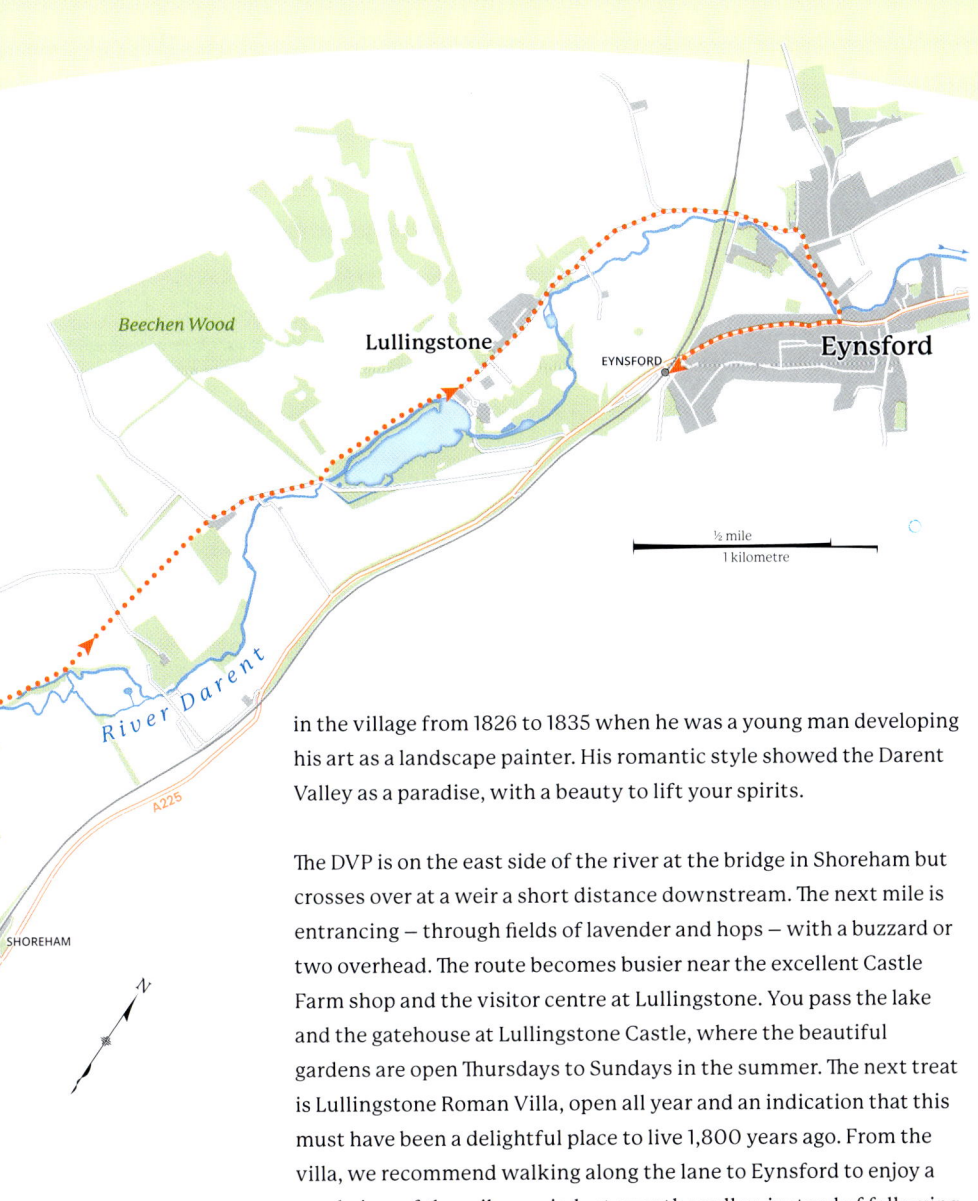

in the village from 1826 to 1835 when he was a young man developing his art as a landscape painter. His romantic style showed the Darent Valley as a paradise, with a beauty to lift your spirits.

The DVP is on the east side of the river at the bridge in Shoreham but crosses over at a weir a short distance downstream. The next mile is entrancing – through fields of lavender and hops – with a buzzard or two overhead. The route becomes busier near the excellent Castle Farm shop and the visitor centre at Lullingstone. You pass the lake and the gatehouse at Lullingstone Castle, where the beautiful gardens are open Thursdays to Sundays in the summer. The next treat is Lullingstone Roman Villa, open all year and an indication that this must have been a delightful place to live 1,800 years ago. From the villa, we recommend walking along the lane to Eynsford to enjoy a good view of the railway viaduct over the valley, instead of following the DVP around the fields.

At Eynsford, if you want to travel to Otford by train, stay on the lane close to the river to cross the bridge to the main street beside the church. Turn right and look for Station Road on the left side. Back in Otford, the path from the station car park goes through the churchyard and across the village green to the High Street. If you have time in Eynsford, it is worth following the DVP a little further wto see the ruins of the medieval castle.

289

Eynsford to Dartford

From Eynsford to South Darenth, the Darent valley continues to be lovely, and the path remains in touch with the river. St John's Jerusalem chapel and garden (National Trust) in Sutton-at-Hone is another corner of the 'earthly paradise'. When the river reaches Dartford, it has picked up debris from major roads and factories and loses its clarity.

Below Dartford town bridge, the river is tidal and known as the Dartford Creek. The ford at Dartford was used in the Roman conquest of England. Paul Talling's *London's Lost Rivers* includes the interesting explanation of how a ferry, operated by a hermit, was established in 1235. 'The post of hermit continued until 1518, long after the first bridge was built (a footbridge, constructed during the reign of Henry IV (1399–1413) and surviving until the mid-18th century).' The Darent is joined by its major tributary, the River Cray, which started in Orpington. Much of the Cray, from Foot's Cray to Crayfordness, can be followed using the Cray Riverway. With a river trail on each bank, Darent Creek passes through open, isolated marshes to meet the Thames. In this barren, windswept, but strangely inviting landscape, the Darent flood barrier is a landmark, protecting the low-lying land in the event of an estuary flood.

Tidal barrier at Dartford Creek

Dartford marshes and confluence

GETTING THERE

TRAIN SERVICES | Southeastern Railway and Thameslink form a complex network serving the Daren and Cray valleys from several London termini: Victoria, Cannon Street, Blackfriars and London Bridge.

OS EXPLORER MAPS | 147 Sevenoaks & Tonbridge; 162 Greenwich & Gravesend

RESOURCES

Cray River Path: *http://www.bexleywildlife.org/wp-content/uploads/2020/06/Cray-river-way-1.pdf*

Darent Valley Path: *https://explorekent.org/activities/darent-valley-path/* and accompanying map: *https://shareweb.kent.gov.uk/Documents/leisure-and-culture/countryside-and-coast/walks/Darent Valley Path.pdf*

Darent Valley Path – LDWA detailed map: *www.ldwa.org.uk/ldp/members/show_publication.php?publication_id=12189*

Darent River Preservation Society (DRiPS): *www.darent-drips.org.uk*

Further conservation activities on the Darent are being conducted by several parties working together with the Environment Agency, including:

Darent Catchment Partnership: *www.darentpartnership.org.uk*
North West Kent Countryside Partnership: *www.nwkcp.org*
South East Rivers Trust: *www.south-eastriverstrust.org*
Sustrans volunteers maintain National Cycle Network Route 1, which follows the Darent Valley Path. To get involved contact them at: *volunteer-uk@sustrans.org.uk*

33 The Mardyke

LENGTH: 11 miles (17.7km)

SOURCE: Great Warley (near junction 29 on M29)

CONFLUENCE: Purfleet

The Mardyke drains the flat clay fields of South Essex and flows through Thurrock to the Thames at Purfleet. Its course has been straightened as part of the drainage of the Bulphan and Orsett Fens to make farmland from the 16th century to 19th century. There are accounts of barges being able to reach the farms at Orsett to collect food for London in the 19th century. Today, this is hard to imagine in summer, but in winter the river channel certainly looks large enough for a small Thames barge. The river was tidal up to Orsett before a sluice gate was built in 1760 at the same time as the Gunpowder Stores at Purfleet. There are no signs of wharves along the river so commercial navigation must have been on a small scale. There is a footpath beside the river from Bulphan to Davy Down, which might have been a towpath. This is now called the Mardyke Way.

RIGHT *The Mardyke Way*

OPPOSITE *Mardyke at Bulphan Fen*

What's in a name?

Its name (variously spelt as one or two words) suggests that it was an important boundary. There is an Anglo-Saxon record of it as a boundary between two hundreds listed in the Domesday Book: Chafford on the west side; and Barstable on the east.

WALK 50 Davy Down and North Stifford

3.5 miles (5.6km)

This is a relatively short circular walk but it encompasses many of the key features of places that we hope you enjoy as much as we do. It starts at the car park of Davy Down in Pilgrims Lane, which is a turning off the A1306. Davy Down was a farm where fruit and vegetables were grown for the markets in London a century ago. The farm became unprofitable in the 1950s and the land lay derelict. Now, it has been conserved as a country park on a modest scale, with waterside meadows, reedbeds and paths on both sides of the river. From the car park, walk down the path beside the mown field and bear right to walk east. The path becomes narrow between banks of shrubs, brambles and nettles – all good for birds and butterflies – until it emerges at a junction of Pilgrims Lane and Stifford Hill. Walk along the pavement up Stifford Hill and continue on the High Road in North Stifford. This village has retained its cricket ground, shop and local pub, the Dog and Partridge.

Beyond the pub, a footpath on the left goes down to the Field of Peace. This riverside meadow was donated to the elderly residents of the village by Lady Mary Milward Clarke (who lived at Coppic Hall in the village) in 1933 to be a place to sit in peace – a lovely thought, which has resulted in a perfect picnic spot halfway along the Mardyke Way. The Field of Peace is a genuine flood meadow with tall

Stifford Viaduct at Davy Down

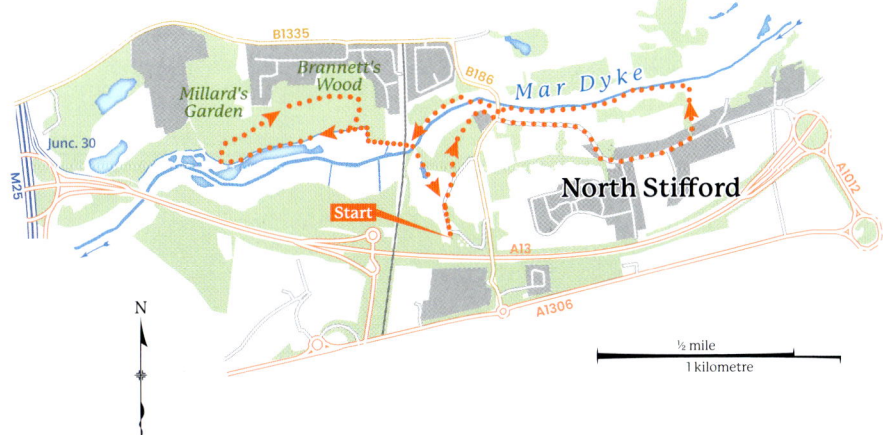

grasses, meadowsweet flowers and hidden side channels that wet the feet of the unwary. Find the Mardyke Way beside the river and follow it down to Stifford Bridge. The path comes out at the road junction where you left Davy Down. Back in Davy Down, when you come to a bridge over the river, cross and turn left along the path on the north side of the river. Go towards the railway viaduct to find the fascinating iron sculptures beside the next bridge. You could go further along the Mardyke Way to explore Brannett's Wood, but you will have to come back the same way. To complete the walk, cross the meadow to the car park.

Fish sculpture on the footbridge at Davy Down

33 The Mardyke

Bulphan to Davy Down To explore the river, it is best to start at Hatch Bridge near Bulphan where a notice board displays the start of the Mardyke Way. This 7 mile (11.3km) route closely follows the river for the first 4 miles (6.4km) to Davy Down near South Ockenden. This first section is peaceful, easy walking on the grassy bank through flat arable fields. Wild geese, swans, moorhens, mallards, skylarks and the occasional buzzard will catch your attention as you follow the gently flowing river. You are unlikely to meet other people until you reach North Stifford village, where lies our final favourite walk.

Davy Down to Purfleet The next mile (1.6km) is noisy amid the concrete pillars supporting the A13 and M25, but the route becomes more pleasant at Ship Lane. The Way crosses the river to wander along the streets of Purfleet, returning to the riverside shortly before it reaches the Thames. Close to the mouth of the Mardyke, the Purfleet Heritage and Military Centre displays the history of the gunpowder stores used for 200 years from 1759 to 1962. On the other side of the river is the Royal Society for the Protection of Birds Rainham Marshes Reserve, where there is always a warm welcome from the volunteers who run the café – a great ending to the walk beside the Mardyke.

OPPOSITE *The Thames and the Queen Elizabeth Bridge at Purfleet*

GETTING THERE

BUS SERVICES | 565 service (First Essex) from Brentwood and West Horndon; 44 Service (Ensignbus) between Lakeside (Thurrock) and Grays stops close to RSPB Rainham Marshes Reserve in New Tank Road. The reserve is a 20 minute walk from Purfleet station Train stations to Bulphan passes over Hatch Bridge

OS EXPLORER MAPS | 162 Greenwich & Gravesend; 175 Southend-on-Sea & Basildon

RESOURCES

Davy Down walk: www.thameschase.org.uk/uploads/TC_WALKS_LEAFLET_No.10_(WITH_30_YEARS_LOGO).pdf
Mardyke Way: www.thurrock-history.org.uk/MardykeWay.htm
Purfleet Heritage & Military Centre: www.purfleet-heritage.com/
RSPB Rainham Marshes Reserve: www.rspb.org.uk/reserves-and-events/reserves-a-z/rainham-marshes/

Acknowledgements

We thank the River Thames Society who encouraged the authors to explore the tributaries of the Thames, publishing their findings, to stimulate other people across southern England to appreciate the wildlife and natural spaces that are free for everyone to enjoy. The natural beauty and diversity of these rivers is due to the hard work of staff and volunteers of the conservation organisations in the Thames catchment area. Looking after and enjoying these green spaces gives us a sense of community and continuity, where the past flows into the present and the present connects with the future.

We are grateful to Jenny Clark and Thomas Storr of Conway, Bloomsbury Publishing for their ongoing support and assistance to publish this second book together, which shares our enthusiasm and love of the Thames natural river environment. We extend our thanks to cartographer John Plumer and book designer Nicola Liddiard at Big Orange Door for their dedication and expertise.

The wildlife of the river is a useful indicator of river health, habitat condition and water quality. We can all work together to respect, protect and enjoy our rivers to keep the natural balance between the needs of people and wildlife, and to maintain a sustainable and vibrant ecosystem so the many species who need the river and its environment can survive.

Index

A
Alton 192–3
Ampney Brook 37–9
Ampney Crucis and Ampney St Peter 37–9
Avebury 130–1
 to Silbury and East Kennet 132
Aylesbury 112, 114
 to Thame 114–16

B
Bagnor to Boxford 137–8
Banbury
 Cropredy to 94
 to Thrupp 94–9
Barking Creek 274
Basingstoke, Basing Trail at 148–9
Battle Lake 34
Baunton, Cirencester to 28–9
Beam Valley Country Park 278–9
Beckenham Place Park 251
Beverley Brook 236
 Richmond Park to Putney 238–9
Bibury to Coln St Aldwyns 61–2
Black Down, Camelsdale to 198
Black Jack's Lock, Rickmansworth to 172–3
Blackwater Valley Path 154–7
Bledington
 to Charlbury 86
 Moreton-in-Marsh to 84–5
Blenheim Palace 92
Bourton-on-the-Water 77
Boxford, Bagnor to 144
Bradfield to Stanford Dingle 124–5
Brent Cross, Mill Hill 230–31
Brent River Park, Horsenden Hill to 232–4
Brentford, Hanwell to 235
Bricket Wood to Rickmansworth 170–1
Brockham Village circular walk 206
Bulphan to Davy Down 296
Burford 76

C
Camelsdale to Black Down 198

Charlbury
 Bledington to 86
 Chilson and Pudlicote 87–8
 to the River Evenlode confluence 88
Charney Bassett, Stanford in the Vale to 106
Charwelton and Hellidon 95–6
Chedworth Roman Villa to Fossebridge 58–9
Chenies, Chess Valley at 180–1
Chertsey Meads Nature Reserve to Weybridge 187–8
Cherwell Valley Walk 99
Chess Valley at Chenies 180–1
Chess Valley Walk 179, 183
Childwickbury and Redbournbury, St Albans to 176–7
Chilson and Pudlicote, Charlbury, 87–8
Chiseldon, Coate Water to 50–2
Cirencester
 to Baunton 28–9
 Seven Springs to 25–7
 to South Cerney 31
Clattinger Farm 20
Coate Water to Chiseldon 50–2
Cobham circular walk 211–12
Coleshill 52
Coln St Aldwyns
 to Bibury 61–2
 Fossebridge to 60
Colnbrook 168
Colne Valley Trail 171–4
Compton 122–3
Cothill and Sandford nature reserves 110–11
Crane Park and Kneller Gardens 226–7
Cranford Park 228
Crawley to Minster Lovell 78–9
Cray River Path 291
Cricklade
 and Down Ampney 40–1
 South Cerney to 31–3
Cropredy to Banbury 96

D
Dagenham dog bone-shaped walk 278–9
Dance Common nature reserve 36
Darent Valley Path 287, 290–1

Davy Down
 Bulphan to 292
 and North Stifford 294–5
 to Purfleet 296
Deptford, Waterlink Way: Lower Sydenham to 251–53
Dinton Pastures to Twyford 152–3
Dollis Brook: Mill Hill to Brent Cross 230
Donnington Castle and Bagnor, Speen to 237–8
Dorchester to Long Wittenham 118
Dorking to Leatherhead 208–9
Down Ampney and Cricklade 40–1

E
East End Roman Villa 89–90
Esher to Molesey 215
Ewell Trail 223

F
Fairford to Lechlade 63
Farnham 192–3
Fetcham, Leatherhead to 210
Fobney Island Nature Reserve and Reading 142–3
Fossebridge
 to Chedworth Roman Villa 58–9
 to Coln St Aldwyns 60
Freeman's Marsh, River Dun to 136
Frensham Little Pond and Pierrepoint Farm, Tilford to 196

G
the Glyme 84, 91–3
Godalming to Guilford 200–1
Grand Union Canal 225, 229, 235
Greystones Farm Nature Reserve 73
Greywell and Odiham Castle, North Warnborough to 158–9
Greywell Moors Nature Reserve 158–9
Guildford
 Godalming to 200–1
 to Weybridge 202–3

H

Hackney Marsh, Walthamstow Marshes to 265–6
Hampnett and Upper End, Northleach 66–9
Hampstead Norreys, woodland and river walk at 123
Heather Farm Nature Reserve 188, 189, 191
Hellidon and Charwelton 95–6
Hertford
    to Rye House 258–60
    to Waltham Abbey 261
High Wycombe 160
Hogsmill Valley Walk 223
Hornchurch Country Park 281–3
Hornchurch to the Thames 284
Horsenden Hill to Brent River Park 232–4
Hungerford to Newbury 136

I

Ickenham to Cranford Park 225
Inglesham to Lechlade 52–3

J

Jurassic Way 94–6, 104

K

Kennet and Avon towpath
    from Hungerford to Newbury 136
    from Newbury to Reading 139
Keston Common 249–50
Kirtlington 102–3

L

Lambourn Valley Way 137–9, 143–4
Lea Valley Walk 256, 268
Leatherhead
    Dorking to 208–9
    Fetcham 210
Lechlade
    Fairford to 63
    Inglesham to 52–3
Letcombe Brook 109–10
Littlecote and Ramsbury 134–5
London Loop Trail 174, 220, 222–3, 225–7, 230, 249–50, 276–7, 280–2, 284
Long Wittenham, Dorchester to 118
Loughton 271–2

M

Mannington Recreation Ground 44–5
Mardyke 292–3
    Bulphan to Davy Down 293
    Davy Down and North Stifford 296–7
    Davy Down to Purfleet 293–4
Marlborough 130–1
Mill Hill to Brent Cross 230
Minster Lovell, Crawley to 78–9
Mole Valley Trail 208–9
Molesey to Esher 215
Monarch's Way 27, 33
Moor Copse and Pangbourne 127–9
Moor Copse Nature Reserve 127
Moor Park, Farnham 193–4
Morden Hall
    to the Thames 242–3
    Waddon Ponds to 244–5
Mouldon Hill Country Park 46–7

N

Newbridge, Witney to 80
Newbury
    Hungerford to 136
    to Reading 130
North Warnborough to Greywell and Odiham Castle 158–9
Northleach to Hampnett and Upper End 66–8

O

Ock Valley Walk 106–7
Odiham Castle 159
Otford to Shoreham and Eynsford 288–9
Otmoor and the River Ray 104
Oxford, Thrupp to 100–1

P

Painshill Park and West End Common 213
Pangbourne and Moor Copse 127–9
Purfleet, Davy Down to 293–4
Purton Wood, Shaw Forest to 46–7
Putney, Richmond Park to 238

Q

Queen Elizabeth Olympic Park 267

R

Ramsbury and Littlecote 134–5
Reading
    Newbury to 130
    to Twyford 151
Reading and Fobney Island Nature Reserve 142–3
Red Lodge Plantation 34–6
Richmond Park to Putney 238–9
Rickmansworth
    to Black Jack's Lock 172–3
    Bricket Wood to 170–1
    to Uxbridge 171
River Blackwater 146, 154–5
River Bourne 184
    Chertsey Meads to Weybridge 187–8
    Heather Farm Nature Reserve 188, 189
    North Bourne 185–6
    South Bourne 189
River Brent 229–30
    Dollis Brook: Mill Hill to Brent Cross 230
    Hanwell to Brentford 235
    Horsenden Hill to Brent River Park 232–4
    Welsh Harp Reservoir 231
River Bulbourne 178–9
River Cherwell 94
    Banbury to Thrupp 97–9
    Charwelton and Hellidon 95–6
    Cropredy to Banbury 97
    Kirtlington 102–3
    Otmoor and the River Ray 104
    Thrupp to Oxford 100–1
River Chess 179
River Churn 24–6
    Cirencester to Baunton 28–9
    Cirencester to South Cerney 31
    Seven Springs to Cirencester 24–6
    South Cerney to Cricklade 31–3
River Cole 48
    Coate Water to Chiseldon 50–3
    Coleshill 52
    Inglesham to Lechlade 52–3
River Coln 56–7
    Bibury to Coln St Aldwyns 61–2

Chedworth Roman Villa to Fossebridge 58–9
Fairford to Lechlade 63
Fossebridge to Coln St Aldwyns 63
River Colne 168–9
  Bricket Wood to Rickmansworth 170–1
  Chess Valley at Chenies 180–1
  Lower Colne: Uxbridge to Staines 174–5
  Rickmansworth to Black Jack's Lock, near Mount Pleasant 172–3
  Rickmansworth to Uxbridge 171
  St Albans to Childwickbury and Redbournbury 176–7
  tributaries 175–83
  Upper Colne 168–9
River Crane 224
  Crane Park and Kneller Gardens 226–7
  downstream to the Thames 228
  Ickenham to Cranford Park 225
River Cray 289
River Darent 286–9
  Otford to Shoreham and Eynsford 288–9
River Dun to Freeman's Marsh 136
River Enborne and Greenham Common, Thatcham 140–
River Evenlode 84
  Bledington to Charlbury 86–7
  Charlbury, Chilson and Pudlicote 87–8
  Charlbury to the confluence 88–9
  East End Roman Villa 89–90
  East End to the Thames 91
  the Glyme 91–3
  Moreton-in-Marsh to Bledington 84–5
River Gade 178–9
River Hogsmill 218–19
  source to the Thames 220–2
River Ingrebourne 280
  Harold Hill to Upminster 280–1
  Hornchurch Country Park 284–5

Hornchurch to the Thames 282–3
Upminster to the Thames 281
River Kennet 130
  Avebury to Silbury and East Kennet 232–3
  Bangor to Boxford 144–5
  Fobney Island and Reading 142–3
  Kennet and Avon towpath from Hungerford to Newbury 136
  Kennet and Avon towpath from Newbury to Reading 139
  Marlborough 134
  Ramsbury and Littlecote 134–5
River Lambourn/Lambourn Valley Way 143–4
  Shaw-cum-Donnington 145
  the source 130–1
  Speen to Donnington Castle and Bagnor 137–8
  Thatcham and River Enborne to Greenham Common 140–1
River Key 34–6
River Lambourn 143–4
River Lea 254–6
  Cheshunt, Fishers Green, Waltham Abbey 262–3
  Hertford to Rye House 258–60
  Hertford to Waltham Abbey 261
  Upper Lea 256–7
  Walthamstow Marshes to Hackney Marsh 265–6
River Leach 64
  Northleach to Hampnett and Upper End 66–9
River Loddon 146
  Basing Trail at Basingstoke 148–9
  Dinton Pastures to Twyford 152–3
  North Warnborough to Greywell and Odiham Castle 158–9
  Reading to Twyford 151
River Blackwater 154–6
River Whitewater 156
  Sherfield on Loddon 150
  Stratfield Saye House 150
  Swallowfield 150–51

River Misbourne 182–3
River Mole 204–5
  Brockham Village 206
  Cobham circular walk 211–12
  Dorking to Leatherhead 208–9
  Esher to Molesey 215
  Leatherhead to Fetcham 210
  Painshill Park and West End Common 213
River Ock 105
  Cothill and Sandford nature reserves 110–11
  Letcombe Brook 109–10
  Ock Valley Walk 106–8
  source and headwaters 105
  Stanford in the Vale to Charney Bassett 106
River Pang 122–3
  Pangbourne and Moor Copse 127
  the source at Compton 122–3
  Stanford Dingle to Bradfield 126–7
  woodland and river walk at Hampstead Norreys 123
River Ravensbourne 244–5
  Beckenham Place Park 250
  Keston Common 249–50
  Waterlink Way: Lower Sydenham to Deptford 251–3
River Ray 42–5
  Mannington Recreation Ground 44–5
  Otmoor 104
  Shaw Forest to Purton Wood and back via Mouldon Park 46–7
  Wroughton to Rushy Platt 42–3
River Roding 269–70
  Barking Creek 274
  Loughton 271–2
  the Roding villages 270
  Woodford to Wanstead 273–4
River Rom and Beam 276–7
  Dagenham dog bone-shaped walk 278–9
River Thame 112
  Aylesbury 115–16
  Dorchester to Long Wittenham 118
  Lower Part 116–17

303

River Ver 175–6
River Wandle 242
   Morden Hall to the Thames 242–3
   Waddon Ponds to Morden Hall 244–5
River Wey 192
   Alton 193
   Camelsdale to Black Down 198
   downstream from Tilford 199–200
   Farnham 193–5
   Godalming to Guildford 200–1
   Guildford to Weybridge 202–3
   South branch 197
   Tilford to Frensham Little Pond and Pierrepoint Farm 196
River Whitewater 156
River Windrush 72–3
   Burford 74, 76
   Minster Lovell to Crawley 82–3
   Sherbourne to Windrush village 74–5
   Upper Windrush 72–3
   Windrush and Sherbourne 73
   Witney to Newbridge 80
River Wye 160–3
   West Wycombe 161–2
   Roding Valley Meadows Nature Reserve 271–2
   Roding Valley Way 273–4
   Rowhill Nature Reserve 141
   Rushy Platt, Wroughton 42–3
   Rye House, Hertford to 258–60

S

Sandford and Cothill nature reserves 110–11
Seven Springs 24–6
   to Cirencester 27
Shaw-cum-Donnington 145

Shaw Forest to Purton Wood 46–7
Sherbourne and Windrush 73–5
Sherfield on Loddon 150
Shoreham and Eynsford, Otford to 288–9
Silbury and East Kennet, Avebury to 132–3
Silbury Hill 132–3
South Bucks Way 182–3
South Cerney
   Cirencester to 31
   to Cricklade 31–2
Speen to Donnington Castle and Bagnor 137–8
Spiceball Country Park 97
St Albans to Childwickbury and Redbournbury 176–7
Staines, Uxbridge to 174–5
Stanford Dingle, Bradfield to 124–5
Stanford in the Vale to Charney Bassett 106
Stratfield Saye House 150
Swallowfield 150–1
Swill Brook 18–20
   Lower Mill Farm and Swillbrook Nature Reserve 21
   Lower Moor and Lower Mill 20
   and Thames junction at Waterhay 23
Swindon & Cricklade Railway 36, 44–5

T

Thame, Aylesbury to 114–16
Thame Valley Walk 114–16
Thames
   East End to the 91
   Hornchurch to the 282–3
   Morden Hall to the 242–3
   Upminster to the 281
Thatcham and River Enborne to Greenham Common 140–1
Thrupp
   Banbury to 97–8
   to Oxford 100–1

Tilford to Frensham Little Pond and Pierrepoint Farm 196
Twyford
   Dinton Pastures 152–3
   Reading to 151

U

Upminster
   Harold Hill to 280–1
   to the Thames 281
Upper Colne 168–9
Upper Windrush 72–3
Uxbridge
   Rickmansworth to 171
   to Staines 174–5

V

Ver-Colne Valley Walk 170–1, 176

W

Waddon Ponds to Morden Hall 244–5
Waltham Abbey
   Hertford to 261
Walthamstow Marshes to Hackney Marsh 265–6
Wandle Trail 242
Wanstead, Woodford to 273–4
Waterlink Way: Lower Sydenham to Deptford 251–3
Watford 170–1
Welsh Harp Reservoir 231
West End Common and Painshill Park 213
West Wycombe 161
   House and Park 163
Weybridge
   Chertsey Mead Nature Reserve to 187–8
   Guildford to 202–3
   Windrush and Sherbourne 73, 74–5
Witney to Newbridge 80
Woodford to Wanstead 273–4
Wroughton to Rushy Platt 42–4
Wychwood Forest 86